MANAGING CRIMINAL JUSTICE ORGANIZATIONS

An Introduction to Theory & Practice

Richard R.E. KANIA

Jacksonville State University

anderson publishing
A member of the LexisNexis Group

Managing Criminal Justice Organizations:
An Introduction to Theory and Practice

Copyright © 2008

　　　Matthew Bender & Company, Inc. a member of the LexisNexis Group
　　　Newark, NJ

　　　ISBN-13: 978-1-59345-523-1

　　　Phone　877-374-2919
　　　Web Site www.lexisnexis.com/anderson/criminaljustice

LexisNexis and the Knowledge Burst logo are trademarks of Reed Elsevier Properties, Inc.
Anderson Publishing is a registered trademark of Anderson Publishing, a member of the LexisNexis Group

Library of Congress Cataloging-in-Publication Data

Kania, Richard.
　　Managing criminal justice organizations / Richard R.E. Kania.
　　　　p. cm.
　　　ISBN 978-1-59345-523-1 (softbound)
　　　1. Criminal justice, Administration of. I. Title.
　　HV7419.K36 2008
　　364.068--dc22   2008031228

Cover design by Tin Box Studio, Inc.

EDITOR　　Ellen S. Boyne
ACQUISITIONS EDITOR　　Michael C. Braswell

Dedication

This book became possible because of the support and encouragement extended to me by Dean J. Earl Wade, my faculty colleagues in Criminal Justice at Jacksonville State University, especially Richards P. Davis, Wade C. Mackey, Vance McLaughlin, and Randal L. Wood, and our department secretary Mrs. Sue Gardner. I also wish to thank Michael C. Braswell for inviting me to submit this manuscript to Lexis-Nexis (Anderson) and to Ms. Ellen Boyne and Ms. Rebecca Scharding for their help in bringing this project to its conclusion.

RREK 2008

Table of Contents

Chapter 3
Historical Antecedents   **41**

1
An Introduction to Criminal Justice Management

A textbook on criminal justice management should begin by answering some basic questions about what management is and why studying it is important. Often the words *administration*, *organization*, and *management* are used as if they were synonymous. Other related key terms important in this discussion are *supervision*, *agency*, *functionaries*, and *bureaucracy*. This imprecision in our language will result in some disagreement and confusion about these terms that we and others are and should be using. Different authors have used them in different ways. So we will begin by discussing these concepts.

Management is the art of overseeing, controlling, and exercising authority over the workforce of an agency and the organizational activities needed to guide it to accomplish a purpose or function. The *management* of an organization is the leadership team of the organization, and is comprised of the chief executive, department or division heads, middle-level managers, and their support staffs. A *manager* is an official who has authority managerial, and supervisory functions.

Administration is the art of attending to an organizational activity or function—being in charge of some aspects supporting the conduct and exercise of that function and of the individuals assigned to achieve it. The *administration* of an organization is the leadership team of the organization, comprised of administrators and their support staffs. An *administrator* is an official who has authority and administrative and supervisory functions.

Organization is the art of planning, arranging, and structuring human activities and agencies, and also the condition of being organized. An *organization* is a work group united for some purpose or function, and includes managers, administrators, first-line supervisors, the support staff, and the functionaries of the organization. **Functionaries** are those who do the actual work of the agency. Organizing is the task of applying systematic structure and order to a human enterprise such as a governmental bureaucracy. Champion discusses "units

1

of analysis," (2003: 10-14) by which he means the individuals of an agency, the small interpersonal work groups (the teams), and the formal organization as a whole (the agency).

A **bureaucracy** is a specific type of organization managed by officials selected and appointed on the basis of their objective preparation, talents, and merits. A **bureaucrat** is an official or functionary within such a bureaucracy.

Generally courses and textbooks in business curricula prefer the term *management* (Drucker, 1954, 1980, 1985, 1990; Fiedler and Chemers, 1974; Hersey and Blanchard, 1982; Massie, 1987; Roethlisberger, 1941; Roethlisberger and Dixon, 1939; Sisk and Williams, 1981; Taylor, 1911), while courses and textbooks in government and political science have preferred to use the term *administration*, as in public administration (Berkley, 1981; Mosher, 1975; Nigro and Nigro, 1973; Stahl, 1971). Many authors in criminal justice follow the preference for *public administration* (Carlson and Garrett, 1999; Champion, 2003; Phillips and Roberts, 2000; Souryal, 1995; Swanson and Territo, 1983; Wilson and McLaren, 1977), but there are numerous exceptions who prefer the term *management* (Buchholz, 1990; Chase and Reveal, 1983; Cohen and Ward, 1980; Greene, 1982; Lynch, 1986: Lynch and Lynch, 2005; McDonald, 2002; Roberg, Kuykendall, and Novak, 2002; Thibault, Lynch, and McBride, 2001; U.S. Bureau of Prisons, 1973; Whisenand, 1981; Whisenand and Ferguson, 1978). There are also criminal justice authors who employ both terms comfortably (Klofas, Stojkovic, and Kalinich, 1990; Peak, 2006).

Because *management* is the term more commonly associated with business, it carries additional connotations of greater initiative, more innovation, and more entrepreneurial efforts. *Administration*, the term in greater favor among political scientists, carries with it an implication of subservience to political institutions, the legislature, courts, and the elected chief executive. This subtly transfers initiative and innovation to those branches of government and leaves administration to the carrying out of the policies those three branches establish. As we will discover in Chapter 3, there is room for innovation, entrepreneurship, and initiative within the senior levels of the bureaucracy. It is for this reason that this book prefers the focus on management. Yet it should be clear that the differences of administration and management are subtle and reflect the approach of the author choosing to write about them.

Dean Champion writes (2003: 5), "For our purposes, the administration of justice, or justice administration," is the description and elaboration of the structural, functional, and managerial processes involved in the coordination of activities related to determining the incidence of criminal conduct, the detection and apprehension of alleged criminals, an assessment of the credibility of evidence against the accused, a formal judgment about that conduct, and how that conduct is punished."

While all that is true, the main focus of this book is on the *managing* of criminal justice organizations. What we will study has less to do with the traditional approaches to the study of criminal justice, crime, or criminological theory than it does with business administration or public administration, but this management aspect is critical to understanding the proper running (both managing and administering) of criminal justice agencies in their efforts to reduce and ameliorate crime. As Kenneth Peak (2006) uses and explains it, the concept of "administration" includes both management and supervision. His view is that it also involves the processes whereby workers are organized to achieve organizational objectives. Peak sees management as part of administration. In this book we will reverse that. Peak and several others place administrators at the top of the organization hierarchy, managers in the middle, and supervisors at the working level. It might be just as well to place managers on top, administrators next, and agree that first-line supervisors are in the third rank of the administration-management team of an organization.

We do agree that all are involved in the organization of the work force, and we also agree that there are basic, sound principles of organization in play that effective supervisors, administrators, and managers will employ in the running of their agencies. So this book is about criminal justice *organization*, *administration*, and *management*, viewed from the perspective of a criminal justice *manager*. Managers use principles of administrative science to manage. Like Peak, this book includes within management the concept of *supervision*, even though it might be better seen as an aspect of leadership, to be discussed in a later chapter devoted to that topic.

As this discussion has suggested, the study of administration, organization, and management is complicated by popular misunderstandings of the key terms. It is not uncommon to find even bright, well-informed students who confuse management with administration and mix both with organization. It is easy to limit the conceptualization of *organization* to only its "corporate-entity" meaning, a synonym for *agency* (e.g., the organization, as in the FBI), thereby ignoring its process meaning (e.g., organization), that is, the process of arranging and structuring cooperative human effort. Indeed, there are scholars who use these words with such indiscrimination that the distinctions are blurred. The study of *organization* is not the study of *organizations*, but the science of how organizations are best organized, i.e., structured and arranged. Champion tells us what a criminal justice organization is (2003: 7): "Any criminal justice organization is a predetermined arrangement of persons whose interrelated tasks and specialties enable the total aggregate to achieve goals." He also warns us that the agencies have diverse goals, implicitly, and sometimes conflicting goals (2003: 6). Part of the task of the manager is sorting all of this out.

Management, as to be used in this book, is not just the study of the management teams of organizations, but is also the study of the art of managing, including both skills in organization and in administration. Administration here is more than just the administrative personnel component of the agency; it is the science and art of the administrative process by which the agency is operated.

Box 1.1 • Five Friends, Five Managers

So, who then is a criminal justice manager? Let me introduce you to five young criminal justice managers who recently came together for their tenth anniversary class reunion. Each had majored in criminal justice at the university, and each has followed a different path in his or her career. Each is working in a different city, and they have not seen much of each other over the past decade. Over dinner they recount their careers for each other and for you. Each has enjoyed the "fast track" in his or her career, and each is now a criminal justice manager. None is yet the chief executive officer of their agency, but each of them has the ambition to be.

Paul was a fair athlete, playing in both team and individual sports at the university. He was hired by the police department in Vollmer City right after graduation, stayed in uniform, and recently was promoted to lieutenant in the patrol division. He still plays golf and tennis when he can find the time. His department sent him to the FBI National Academy in Quantico, Virginia, last year.

Carol Anne always had a talent for writing and was also quite sophisticated in the use of computers. She was hired as a deputy clerk of court after taking some additional paralegal courses and now is the chief clerk of the lower, misdemeanor court for Vanderbilt County. She also is writing a novel based on some of the interesting and unusual cases that have passed thru her court.

Jerry minored in psychology, and went into juvenile justice. After working as an intake counselor for the juvenile court and completing a master's degree in counseling, he now runs one of the residential juvenile shelters for delinquent youths in his city. He was in a rock band while at the university and sponsors a similar group of amateur musicians among the teens assigned to his juvenile home. He feels that encouraging their musical talents will help them turn their lives around, give them career options, and enhance their social skills, and he observes that their playing entertains the other young men in their residence.

Cory went into federal corrections at graduation, leaving the state to work in a federal correctional unit. He completed an MPA part-time, online while working for the "feds." He moved back home four years ago to take a supervisory position in the state correctional system where he now is the deputy warden of a medium-security custodial unit, the Alexander Maconochie Correctional Center. He had enjoyed gourmet cooking while at the university and worked in an upscale restaurant while a student, but an assignment placing him in charge of the prison kitchen at the federal correctional institution spoiled his love for cooking for several years. He

Box 1.1 *(continued)*

reports rediscovering the fun of gourmet cooking only recently, now that running a kitchen is not a major part of his state job.

Diane went to law school right after graduation, passed the bar, took a position as an assistant district attorney, and now is the chief deputy DA in charge of a team of junior deputy DAs dealing with high-priority and career-criminal felony prosecutions for her district. She was politically active at the university, held office in student government, and admits to her dream of becoming the district attorney some years from now when her current boss retires.

As they compare notes about their careers, families, and life experiences to date, they find that each of their positions involves them in many of the same responsibilities: leading, organizing, making decisions, evaluating individual subordinates and entire work teams, taking part in staffing actions, training subordinates, allocating resources, and reporting on their and their units' activities. They remember a criminal justice management class at the university where they learned Luther Gulick's "POSDCORB," the mnemonic acronym standing for planning, organizing, staffing, directing, coordinating, reporting, and budgeting (1937), and they discuss how it applies to their work as middle managers now.

They also see some aspects of their work that POSDCORB does not fit quite as well. For example, while each is involved in budgeting to some degree, their duties involve other allocation functions related to agency budgets, but not directly involving financial transactions. Paul explains that he must assign police patrol officers to various duties, making sure each is provided the appropriate equipment necessary to do their jobs. Jerry agrees, noting that running a juvenile detention facility involves all manner of decisions and resource allocation duties indirectly bearing on agency finances and budgets. Cory observes that it is much the same in his correctional unit, especially so when he was managing the federal prison kitchen. Moreover, each is involved in agencies that operate "24-7" (24 hours a day, seven days a week), so that time also is a major factor in their resource allocation decisions.

All five agree that Gulick's formulation did not really cover training, but that too is a major responsibility each of them has. Diane points out that each new junior assistant DA knows sufficient law right out of law school, but most do not have enough experience with practical procedures to prepare and present a case in court. She explains that she pairs a newly hired assistant with a more experienced litigator. Paul says that's much like the FTOs (field training officers) his police department assigns, and Carol Anne joins their chorus. All agree that they are held responsible for any training shortcoming of their subordinates, and must be attentive to their training needs.

Each of them has seen his or her job change. Initially each of them was "doing" criminal justice, but now each of them manages others who are doing criminal justice. Each now has an executive position in his or her agency, and each hopes someday to become the chief executive of that or a similar agency. Each one is a manager.

Rethinking Luther Gulick's POSDCORB

In 1937 Luther Gulick's contribution to management science, **POSDCORB**, first appeared to help us reflect on the questions he asked: "What is the work of a chief executive? What does he do?"

The mnemonic acronym POSDCORB and what it stands for has become common in managerial terminology. Most public administration and management principles texts make at least a passing reference to it. Many textbooks and managerial guides have been written with chapters to correspond to the content, if not also the precise order of planning, organizing, staffing, directing, coordinating, reporting, and budgeting. Many more cover these same topics in slightly different words, as they attempt to answer the questions posed by Luther Gulick.

These questions remain before us today as we study the role of the criminal justice manager anew, not unanswered, but ever in need of refinements to address the changes in the public service workplace. In the 1937 article in which he answers his own questions with POSDCORB, Gulick was writing for his own times. This mnemonic device has been with us ever since, but the times and environment of the public service workplace have changed greatly. We ought to take the time to reflect upon what his ideas have brought to management in the past six decades, and even question if the same answer would be given today. POSDCORB is used less frequently today, and other answers are now being given to Gulick's questions.

Do almost three-quarters of a century of subsequent management experience confirm his answer to his own questions? Certainly, to some extent we can answer "yes," but some consideration of contemporary public administration and commercial management writings suggests that his topics have not fared quite as well as one might initially suppose. The seven-item list has not proven to be exhaustive, as the contemporary emphasis on evaluation shows.

In Gulick's day the more authoritarian, scientific management-based Theory X managerial style was in vogue but was not yet spoken of as such. Although Gulick was aware of the early human relations studies, his was an approach to management solidly based in the scientific management principles advocated by the likes of Frederick Taylor. Today, a modified Theory Y systems approach is the recommended managerial style in most managerial texts and guidebooks. Theory X presupposes that a worker naturally will avoid work and needs to be closely supervised. Theory Y presupposes that a worker has the capacity to be self-motivated. Thus, the "directing" function Gulick championed has been overtaken by events and the trend toward more democratic management. Theory X and Theory Y approaches to managerial leadership will be explained in more detail in Chapter 4.

We are also aware that the order used by Gulick, placing budgeting as the final item, as if an afterthought, ought to be improved upon. Experience has shown that budgeting should not be viewed as a separate activity following the others, but should be an integral part of resource allocation, planning, and decisionmaking. As a key managerial task, it should come up early and often in the astute manager's actions.

LODESTAR versus POSDCORB

Indeed, were Gulick to address his question to us today, I would not reply with his POSDCORB, but with LODESTAR. **LODESTAR** stands for leading, organizing, deciding, evaluating, staffing, training, allocating, and reporting. Not only is the acronym easier to say and recall, it fits the current social and organizational climate better. Its metaphorical value is also worthy of note. The job of the ideal, more democratic manager today is not "directing," so much as serving as a guide to the organization, to point the way, just as the "Lodestar" or "North Star" served as the guide to ancient mariners and travelers. In this book it is the source of the organization and sequencing of the chapters that follow.

LODESTAR, as a new mnemonic acronym and a metaphor for the task of the manager, represents eight managerial functions, some of which Gulick considered, others that are related to his suggestions, and a few new ones that more recent experiences suggest. Even those that are taken from Gulick's original thoughts are recast somewhat to stress the different perspectives and priorities of the present day.

Leading: This has to come first among the managerial functions. Although the concept is similar to Gulick's fourth and fifth terms, directing and co-ordinating, I argue that it should take clear precedence over Gulick's priorities of planning, organizing, and staffing. The volume of literature on this topic is an impressive testimonial to my belief. Leadership is the intangible attribute that sets the successful manager apart from his or her also-ran competitors. In recent years we are discovering that it is not the particular style of leadership that is the critical factor, but the attribute itself that makes one person a leader and leaves others behind as mere supervisors or office holders. An impressive list of top management scholars have examined leadership. Gulick himself does precisely that in his 1937 essay. Mary Parker Follett (1926; Graham, 1995), Chester Barnard (1938), Peter F. Drucker (1967), Douglas McGregor (1960), Theodore Caplow (1983), Fred Fiedler and Martin Chemers (1974), and Warren Bennis (1966, 1973) are among the many who have stood out in offering answers to the question, "What are the best ways to lead an organization?" What is troubling is the discovery that the answers are not always in agreement.

Organizing: No fault can be placed on the emphasis that Gulick gave to sound organizational skills. However, had this article been written in the heyday of Theory Y (human relations) management, its placement might have fallen farther back. The excesses of the human needs emphasis at the expense of efficiency and occasionally even organizational objectives have been set right, but only recently. We again see the wisdom of organizing the workplace intelligently. From human relations we have learned that such organization must consider human factors and not be the cold, impersonal human engineering originally implied by the founding father of American scientific management, Frederick Taylor (1911). We have been warned by James March and Herbert Simon (1958) that some of the basic principles of organization operate in opposition to one another. This represents a further challenge to the astute manager, for the axioms of organization are sound and need to be applied, as in Gulick's day, with the temperance of leadership.

Deciding: This is not the "D" of Gulick's POSDCORB. His "D" stood for "directing." The modern criminal justice manager is not the authoritarian director that once was the norm. The workplace does not operate as it did in 1937. Managers must be more constrained in making their decisions. The ideal criminal justice manager must be deliberative, combining coordinating, planning, budgeting, and decisionmaking into a single synthetic process. Here we will just call it all "deciding" or "decisionmaking," but we must recognize that much more is involved. What we seek to describe is not a unilateral process in the contemporary workplace. The Theory Y advocates have made a sound case for group input, MBO, the Delphi Method, rapping, workshops, task forces, and other group-input activities rather than unilateral managerial decisionmaking. The modern criminal justice manager "directs" at one's own risk. One rarely even "decides" anything without significant input from coworkers, support staff, and subordinates, especially the planners and budgetary analysts on a work team. Collectively they come to answers via a deliberative process. The wise manager is one who knows when and how to assemble the judgments of others; to weigh the suggestions and opinions of subordinates, peers, and superiors; to factor in budgetary considerations; and to plan ahead, developing tactics and grand strategies within the organizational system. In short, the modern manager employs the processes of deliberation before coming to the work team's decision.

Evaluating: Once people have been organized, they have to be converted into an effective team to get the agency's mission accomplished. The criminal justice manager who can put one's people to work on a good idea and can convert it into the successful project remains as rare today as in Gulick's time. This was what he meant by including "coordinating" in POSDCORB, but there is much more to it than just coordinating. With so much of criminal justice work done out of sight of the manager, the modern criminal justice executive needs to develop the means to see how the work is going, who is effective, and who is having problems. This is the role of evaluation, both of individuals and of the entire work team. Having a positive effect on an organization requires the leadership and organizational skills already cited, but evaluation is needed to see that the desired effect is being achieved.

There has been a great deal written in recent years about evaluation. Evaluation conveys the meaning of attaching a value to something and should be viewed as a positive aspect of management. However, evaluation has taken on a somewhat negative connotation in the context of the personnel evaluation, the periodic review that often is associated with unfavorable personnel actions. Evaluation should be understood to contain the concept of "appraising," which retains some of the positive tone of its root, "praising." The modern criminal justice manager has to know how to evaluate and appraise in an upbeat manner. The evaluative responsibility cannot be ignored, but even negative evaluations can be given in a positive, rewarding manner. Even when they contain negative assessments and call for correction of present behavior or performance, appraisals can be positive instructional tools. The effective appraisal should be given in the "I'm O.K., you're O.K." approach that Thomas Harris (1967) advocated in his book of the same name. The manager needs to present himself or herself as being helpful and advisory, and the evaluation itself needs to be positive in tone, even when identifying areas of weakness where improvement is needed. The evaluated worker should emerge from the appraisal process with a sense of self-worth still intact, aware that specific improvements are needed and guided in how to make these improvements.

The modern manager must develop the evaluative techniques that permit him or her to criticize the defects of the work without undermining the self-confidence of the individual or group undertaking the work. Once the flaws, failures, and malfunctions of the organization are recognized, then there must be planned change. Thus, out of the evaluation function will arise organizational development efforts, as the manager seeks to implement a deliberate change strategy to improve organization effectiveness.

Staffing: As one of Gulick's original seven concepts, staffing has remained as important as ever, and may even be more important in this era of affirmative action, equal opportunity, equality of and for women, comparable pay for comparable work, veterans' preference, and so on. When Gulick wrote of staffing, he was thinking of it in the original, limited sense of matching the right person to the right job, arranging for the perfect fit of a prospective employee's skills to job requirements. This is no longer adequate today; staffing involves far more that that. Especially in the public service sector, the manager has been obliged to accept social responsibilities toward the whole community and cannot just consider what will be best for the organization. Programs initiated in the 1970s, such as CETA (Comprehensive Employment and Training Act) and the Job Corps, have given rise to demands that the contemporary manager actively seek employees who do not conform to the ideal type of employment prospect. Also gone are the artificial restrictions that closed the doors to the employment and assignment of women and minorities to responsible positions within organizations. The manager can do, in these areas, what no manager could do in Gulick's day: place a qualified woman or minority member in a key staff position. The available talent pool has more than doubled by the lifting of these old, restrictive social encumbrances.

Training: The greater the demands of the modern workplace, the less likely it will be that the manager will find new staff fully qualified to assume the responsibilities of the workplace at the time they are hired. In-service training programs are more of a management responsibility and concern than they were in the early days of scientific management when Frederick Taylor (1911) spoke of training the workman in the unique requirement of a particular workplace. Increasing levels of education as a precondition to entry into public service careers have not been enough to overcome the demands of the new, high-tech public service workplace. Moreover, training is not simply an entry-level activity in public service careers. Mid-level and executive-level training programs are part of the contemporary career pathways a public service manager must follow for one's self and for one's subordinates.

Allocating: Assigning people to tasks and budgeting funds, time, and resources to support those tasks are part of the allocation functions of the public service manager. Gulick's "budgeting" is expanded, because more than funds are allocated by a manager. Time, space, facilities, labor, resources, and funds are all involved in the allocation processes. Implementation planning or "action planning" as advocated in MBO (management by objectives) manuals is important to this allocation process. Such methods as PERT (program, evaluation, and review technique) and critical path network analysis come into play as the modern manager integrates these resources into the work product.

Reporting: Reporting is one of the original seven responsibilities carried over from POSDCORB. But like some of the other answers retained from Gulick's original response to his own question, this one has been modified and expanded. Reporting now involves far superior data storage and transmission means. There was no photocopier, computer, microfiche file, word processor, or any of the other superior aids to reporting that we now have available to us. CompStat and other computer-aided tools have improved upon reporting functions (Kania, 2004; Magers, 2004; Walsh and Vito, 2004).

Written reports and records are only a small part of the communications process. There is far more to reporting than what Gulick understood in his day. We often are told that this is the age of communication, the era of the Internet and the World Wide Web. Thus, we must see that reporting is an aspect of both communicating and of public accountability. The manager who can communicate effectively both within the organization and between the organization and the general public will be more likely to succeed than the less effective communicator, even if one's work is no better in quality.

Reporting also involves the whole range of public relations activities, conveying one's message to the general public. The anguish some government officials and political figures have felt in giving news interviews is a self-fulfilling prophesy. By showing their discomfort, they convey the negative messages they seek to avoid. Those who have mastered communication skills are able to promote their organizations and themselves. Think of the success of Ronald Reagan's "Teflon coating" or the "aw shucks" appeal of Bill Clinton when they made and admitted mistakes, and the inability of negative press and opposing party smears to stick and hurt their popular appeal. Why did such attacks cripple Johnson and Nixon and yet leave Reagan and Clinton unmarred? Reagan and Clinton certainly were superior presidential communicators, always able to convey their points of view, even in the face of criticism.

Reporting is also the essence of accountability, another key concept and responsibility in the work of the public service manager. How should the political elites, who control the scarce resources a public service manager will employ, function if their subordinate managers are ineffective in passing along their requirements? How is the public to know if a public service organization is successful if the management withholds that news or is evasive in keeping the public informed of its activities?

The LODESTAR functions need to be collectively employed within the general concepts of American public service. These are the abstract values that our criminal justice agencies were created to serve. They are the principles of public management that should guide the criminal justice manager in the conduct of his or her duties and responsibilities. They underlie the ethics of criminal justice professions. As others have before him, Peak makes a good point that the criminal justice system is more of a "nonsystem" than a system because of its internal divisions that often are in competition with one another (Peak, 2006): police try to convict criminals; the courts try to acquit some while agreeing to send some to corrections; and the corrections system tries to process out its referrals. The bureaucratic ideal of uniform and consistent treatment is defeated by both intentional and unintentional biases in the system. Alternatives to the formal process are actually institutionalized, again in violation of bureaucratic simplicity. Some suspects are tried; others are diverted out of the system. Some convicted people are probated; others

Box 1.2 • Principles of Public Management

> 1. In the "Jeffersonian Ideal," a manager is a "public servant" who works for the people as a whole; as such, a manager in criminal justice serves, rather than rules the people.

> 2. Managers in criminal justice are selected to represent the people collectively, rather than satisfy individual, private interests.

> 3. Criminal justice managers must balance competing mandates: for abstract justice, due process of law, professionalism, competence, fairness, equality, consistency, and crime control.

> 4. Managers in the public service seek to make their agencies productive, efficient, and effective within the lawful limits of their constitutional authority.

> 5. The actual tasks of management and labor (the routine administration of a criminal justice agency) are substantially different. Criminal justice managers make agency policy and oversee its implementation. Public administration implements and administers the policies of criminal justice management.

> 6. In a democratic society, senior criminal justice policymakers are held accountable to the public, usually through the elective process, and therefore they should either be elected or politically appointed by elected officials.

> 7. Political loyalty should be one of the essential criteria for selecting people for senior management positions (the policymakers) in criminal justice.

> 8. Objective merit should be the essential criterion for selecting people for appointive criminal justice middle-level management positions.

are incarcerated. Some incarcerated people are paroled; others are held for the full term. On top of it all, the system is horribly backlogged and understaffed. So it is not the efficient "system" that it aspired to be.

The system operates under competing and conflicting mandates. Herbert Packer once explained this tension as the competition of the *due process* and *crime control* models (1968: 153). There are widely differing perspectives governing policy, ranging from consensus views to conflict views. Due process is not very efficient and requires that wrongdoers whom we cannot prove are guilty beyond a reasonable doubt must go free. Paying some people to convict offenders and others to help them beat conviction (public defenders and appointed counsel) seems internally conflicted, and certainly does not suggest efficiency. Yet criminal justice managers (or administrators) are expected to make intelligent public policy amid all of these conflicting expectations, values, and standards.

Private versus Public Management

By choosing management over administration as the preferred focus of this book, it is important to recognize that there are differences in the managerial principles of private, commercial management. Peak makes the point that the "rewards" of work in the private sector are mostly extrinsic (external), and further, mostly are material. For employees of the public-service sector, the "rewards" are more intrinsic and internal. People entering public service careers are told, "you'll never get rich in public service," and my own life experiences confirm that. Yet a public service career can be very rewarding in the satisfaction that doing a good job can provide. Criminal justice practitioners and managers make this a better world by making it safer for us all, and by identifying and punishing the guilty and helping the weak, victimized, and injured.

Just what constitutes doing a good job is hard to determine, however. In the commercial private sector, it is measured by the financial bottom line, income, sales, profits, and so on. There are no comparable measures available to those in the public-service sector. Moreover, it is important to note that people in public service also seek material rewards for their efforts, just as people in commercial private enterprise also enjoy intrinsic rewards. A task of the supervisor, administrator, and manager in public service is facilitating the receipt of these intrinsic rewards.

Characteristics of individuals include personal demographic features (sex, age, race, nationality, education, experience, marital status, etc.) as well as less precise evaluations of motivations, talents, and "professionalism." Champion identifies five aspects of **professionalism**: (1) a defined body of knowledge, (2) a code of ethics, (3) ongoing education, (4) uniform standards in selection, education, training, and performance, and (5) a service or career orientation.

The **agency** is the formal structure of the work group and often is too large to be an interpersonal association. The chief of police of a major city, the DA of a large urban prosecutorial office, the chief judge in a big city, the warden of a large state prison, and other leaders of large units do not know and do not interact at a personal level with their subordinates. In many cases, they will not even know all of their employees' names or jobs. Indeed, it was this attribute of the large organization that gave rise to the principles of administration, organization, and management that will be taught in this class.

One of the points to stress is the role of policymaking in the work of criminal justice management (Champion, 2003: 16-17). Much of criminal justice policy is made by the legislature, but laws often are vague or general guidelines. Executives in police, court, and corrections agencies apply those guidelines in practical ways. They are making secondary policy, that is, "implementation policy." They also advise and counsel legislators on what policies to make. At that point they are involved in formulating primary policy.

Summary

When Luther Gulick asked ""What is the work of a chief executive? What does he do?" and answered his own question with POSDCORB, he expressed the classical views of the role of the manager in the public sector, from thinking derived from the scientific management school. The last half century has shown us some of the inadequacies of this approach to management and has given rise to newer perspectives. LODESTAR is just one possible expression of these newer ideas. It is not a radical departure from the wisdom of Gulick, but a statement of the gradual refinement, adaptation, and evolution of those ideas through decades of public management. It places more emphasis on the "people" aspects of management, (for example, their selection, training, and appraisals), reflecting the human relations emphasis that arose in management theory at about the time POSDCORB was being proposed. It is time to retire POSDCORB to the role of a historical footnote, perhaps to be replaced by LODESTAR, or some other mnemonic device that better sums up the views of this time in the history of ideas.

Learning Objectives

Upon finishing this chapter you should be able to do the following:

▶ 1. Discuss the meanings of the key terms "management," "administration," and "organization" as used in criminal justice.

▶ 2. Distinguish between each of these term-pairs:
- administration versus the administration
- management versus the management
- organization versus the organization

▶ 3. Identify the eight principles of public management, and explain the values each of these principles reflects.

▶ 4. Contrast public versus private management.

▶ 5. Explain how both LODESTAR and POSDCORB answer Luther Gulick's question, "What is the work of the chief executive?"

IMPORTANT TERMS AND NAMES

- agency
- administration
- functionaries

- bureaucracy
- bureaucrat
- LODESTAR

- management
- POSDCORB
- professionalism

References and Supplemental Sources

Barnard, Chester (1938) [1968]. *The Functions of the Executive*. Cambridge, MA: Harvard University Press.

Bennis, Warren (1966). *Changing Organizations*. New York: McGraw-Hill.

Bennis, Warren (1973). *Beyond Bureaucracy*. New York: McGraw-Hill.

Berkley, George E. (1981). *The Craft of Public Administration*, 3rd ed. Boston: Allyn & Bacon.

Buchholz, Rogene A. (1990). *Essentials of Public Policy for Management*, 2nd ed. Englewood Cliffs, NJ: Prentice Hall.

Caplow, Theodore (1983). *Managing an Organization*, 2nd ed. New York: Holt, Rinehart and Winston.

Carlson, Peter M., and Judith Simon Garrett (1999). *Prison and Jail Administration*. Gaithersburg, MD: Aspen.

Chase, Gordon, and Elizabeth C. Reveal (1983). *How to Manage in the Public Sector*. Reading, MA: Addison-Wesley.

Champion, Dean John (2003). *Administration of Criminal Justice*. Upper Saddle River, NJ: Prentice Hall.

Cohn, Alvin W., and Benjamin Ward (1980). *Improving Management in Criminal Justice*. Beverly Hills, CA: Sage.

Drucker, Peter F. (1954) [1984]. *The Practice of Management*. New York: HarperCollins, HarperBusiness.

Drucker, Peter F. (1964) [1993]. *Managing for Results*. New York: HarperCollins, HarperBusiness.

Drucker, Peter F. (1967). *The Effective Executive*. New York: Harper and Row.

Drucker, Peter F. (1980). *Managing in Turbulent Times*. New York: Harper and Row.

Drucker, Peter F. (1985). *Management: Tasks, Responsibilities, Practices, Abridged and Revised Edition*. New York: Harper Colophon Books.

Drucker, Peter F. (1990). *Managing the Non-Profit Organization*. New York: HarperCollins, HarperBusiness.

Gulick, Luther (1937). "Notes on the Theory of Organization." In *Papers on the Science of Administration*, edited by Luther Gulick and Lyndall Urwick. New York: Institute of Public Administration.

Feldman, Martha S., and Anne M. Khademian (2001). "Principles for Public Management Practice: From Dichotomies to Interdependence," *Governance*, 14(3): 339–361.

Fiedler, Fred Edward, and Martin M. Chemers (1974). *Leadership and Effective Management*. Glenview, IL: Scott, Foresman.

Follett, Mary Parker (1926). *Scientific Foundations of Business Administration*. Baltimore: Williams and Wilkins.

Forsyth, Richard (2004). "M-A-N-A-G-E-M-E-N-T Defined - Subordinates' Expectations," *FBI Law Enforcement Bulletin*, 73(3): 23-27.

Graham, Pauline (ed.) (1995). *Mary Parker Follett: Prophet of Management*. Cambridge, MA: Harvard Business School Press.

Greene, Jack R. (1982). *Managing Police Work: Issues and Analysis*. Beverly Hills, CA: Sage.

Harris, Thomas A. (1967). *I'm OK, You're OK: A Practical Guide to Transactional Analysis*. New York: Harper and Row.

Hersey, Paul, and Ken Blanchard (1982). *Management of Organization Behavior: Utilizing Human Resources*, 4th ed. Englewood Cliffs, NJ: Prentice Hall.

Hoover, Larry T. (1975). *Police Educational Characteristics and Curricula*. Washington, DC: National Institute of Law Enforcement and Criminal Justice, L.E.A.A.

Kania, Richard R.E. (2004). "A Brief History of a Venerable Paradigm in Policing," *Journal of Contemporary Criminal Justice*, 20(1): 80-83.

Klofas, John, Stan Stojkovic, and David Kalinich (1990). *Criminal Justice Organizations: Administration and Management*. Pacific Grove, CA: Brooks/Cole.

Lynch, Ronald G. (1986). *The Police Manager: Professional Leadership Skills*, 3rd ed. New York: Random House.

Lynch, Ronald. G., and Scott Lynch (2005). *The Police Manager*, 6th ed. Newark, NJ: LexisNexis Matthew Bender.

Magers, Jeffrey S. (2004). "Compstat: A New Paradigm for Policing or a Repudiation of Community Policing," *Journal of Contemporary Criminal Justice*, 20(1): 70-79.

March, James G., and Herbert A. Simon (1958). *Organizations*. New York: John Wiley and Sons.

Massie, Joseph L. (1987). *Essentials of Management*, 4th ed. Englewood Cliffs, NJ: Prentice Hall.

McDonald, Phyllis Parshall (2002). *Managing Police Operations: Implementing the New York Control Model — CompStat*. Belmont, CA: Wadsworth.

McGregor, Douglas (1960). *The Human Side of Enterprise*. New York: McGraw-Hill.

Mosher, Frederick C. (ed.) (1975). *American Public Administration: Past, Present, Future*. Tuscaloosa, AL: University of Alabama Press.

Roberg, Roy R., Jack Kuykendall, and Kenneth Novak (2002). *Police Management*, 3rd ed. Los Angeles: Roxbury.

Roethlisberger, F.J. (1941). *Management and Morale*. Cambridge, MA: Harvard University Press.

Roethlisberger, F.J., and William J. Dixon (1939). *Management and the Worker*. Cambridge, MA: Harvard University Press.

Senna, Joseph J., and Larry J. Siegel (1990). *Introduction to Criminal Justice*, 5th ed. St. Paul, MN: West.

Sisk, Henry L., and J. Clifton Williams (1981). *Management and Organization*, 4th ed. Cincinnati: South-Western.

Souryal, Sam S. (1995). *Police Organization and Administration*, 2nd ed. Cincinnati: Anderson.

Stahl, O. Glenn (1971). *Public Personnel Administration*, 6th ed. New York: Harper and Row.

Swanson, Charles R., and Leonard Territo (1983). *Police Administration*. New York: Macmillan.

Taylor, Frederick Winslow (1911; 1967). *The Principles of Scientific Management*. New York: Norton Library, Harper and Row.

Travis, Lawrence F., III (2007). *Introduction to Criminal Justice*, 6th ed. Newark, NJ: LexisNexis Matthew Bender.

Thibault, Edward A., Lawrence M. Lynch, and R. Bruce McBride (2001). *Proactive Police Management*, 5th ed. Upper Saddle River, NJ: Prentice Hall.

Trojanowicz, Robert, and Samuel Dixon (1974). *Criminal Justice and the Community*. Englewood Cliffs, NJ: Prentice Hall.

U. S. Bureau of Prisons (1973). *Jail Management: Administration of Jail Operations*. Washington, DC: U.S. Government Printing Office.

Waldron, Ronald J. (1989). *The Criminal Justice System*, 4th ed. New York: Harper & Row.

Walsh, William F., and Gennaro F. Vito (2004). "The Meaning of Compstat: Analysis and Response," *Journal of Contemporary Criminal Justice*, 20(1): 51-69.

Westley, William (1970). *Violence and the Police*. Cambridge, MA: M.I.T. Press.

Whisenand, Paul M. (1981). *The Effective Police Manager*. Englewood Cliffs, NJ: Prentice Hall.

Whisenand, Paul M., and R. Fred Ferguson (1978) . *The Managing of Police Organizations*, 2nd ed. Englewood Cliffs, NJ: Prentice Hall.

Wilson, Orlando W., and Roy C. McLaren (1977). *Police Administration*, 4th ed. New York: McGraw Hill.

Wrobleski, Henry, and Karen M. Hess (1986). *Introduction to Law Enforcement and Criminal Justice*, 2nd ed. St. Paul, MN: West.

2
Management Positions in Criminal Justice

Criminal justice includes the fields of police, prosecutorial court, and judicial administration; adult probation, parole, and custodial correctional administration; juvenile justice administration; and various public services to assist victims, witnesses, and criminal defendants. Most agencies and organizations involved in American criminal justice are governmental, but private commercial and nonprofit, **nongovernmental organizations (NGOs)** also are involved in American criminal justice. The growth of nongovernmental justice-related services, agencies, and alternative programs to support the traditional government justice organizations has expanded the field considerably in recent years. These new agencies and services have introduced new administrative and managerial challenges within the field of justice administration. The traditional justice system also has undergone much internal change in the past two decades, spurred on by the now-defunct **Law Enforcement Assistance Administration (LEAA)** in the mid-1960s and the 1970s, and continuing under its own momentum ever since.

In spite of great change in the justice system, classical managerial strategies and priorities continue to be followed within most of the subfields of justice administration and management, especially in law enforcement (Wilson and McLaren, 1977) and corrections (U.S. Bureau of Prisons, 1973). These general administrative and managerial principles were set out first in the 1930s (Gulick, 1937). They have persisted because they have served justice administrators well in the past, but these managerial principles have needed updating to match the times.

Since the early 1930s our justice system has been subjected to much well-deserved criticism. The **Wickersham Commission** began the trend, identifying numerous problems in the administration of justice during the Prohibition Era (National Commission on Law Observance and Enforcement, 1931). Much was done in the following two decades to professionalize the administration of justice, applying managerial principles taken from the field of public administration. In the 1960s and 1970s the criticism began anew. The police encountered considerable negative attention from the communications media and the public for police brutality allegations, mishandled riots, and civil disturbances; resisting the civil rights movement; tragic applications of deadly force; and corruption scandals. All tarnished the image of policing in the United States and forced police departments all over the country to take action to correct their problems and improve their public images. In the same period, bloody prison riots and the attention paid to prison conditions put the correctional establishment in the spotlight, forcing much-needed reforms. The image of justice improved somewhat in the 1970s, as community relations efforts began to bear fruit (especially for police departments). In the 1980s the judicial process came under much criticism and adverse attention as the insanity defense, seemingly incredible acquittals, and inappropriately light or heavy sentences were heavily publicized and criticized. Civil cases over rather inconsequential issues and the scandalous behavior of some personal injury lawyers brought discredit to the courts and the legal profession. The death penalty continues to be a sore spot in the relationship of the justice system and many community elements.

It is the duty of criminal justice managers to devise and recommend remedies to the problems of the criminal justice system. Indeed, criminal justice managers over the last four centuries have risen as leaders and reformers who have done exactly that. That promise and opportunity remains possible today, as new problems and issues arise for criminal justice agencies. So who are the managers of criminal justice agencies who need to deal with such matters?

The Police and Law Enforcement Management

The best known and most visible officials of our justice system are the police. They serve the law enforcement function by aiding in crime prevention, traffic regulation, criminal investigation, criminal apprehension (arrest), and many additional public safety, service, and order maintenance responsibilities. Managerial ranks in law enforcement often parallel the ranks and titles of the military, with such terms as sergeant, lieutenant, captain, and commander. The chief executive officer of many local police agencies is spoken of as "the **chief**," but in a sheriff's department, the managers are the sheriff and the chief deputy sheriff. In many state and federal investigative agencies the senior manager is designated a **director**. The number of middle managers and the rank titles used will reflect the size of the agency. When in uniform, these managers often wear chevrons, metal bars, oak leaves, eagles, and stars copied from military ranks.

The police function in the United States is divided among many entities at five different jurisdictional levels. Police services are authorized under the jurisdiction and authority of (1) private entities, (2) localities, (3) the state, (4) the federal government, and (5) international organizations. The police also are given power over law enforcement matters of special, limited jurisdiction. There are both general and specialized law enforcement agencies. The general law enforcement agencies are obliged to enforce a wide range of laws, while special-

Military-style rank insignia used in American police and corrections organizations, various styles of sergeants' chevrons ("stripes") and samples of lieutenant, captain, major, colonel, and general rank insignia (samples from author's collection).

Richard R.E. Kania

ized agencies focus on one category of laws, such as wildlife and environmental protection laws, occupational safety laws, liquor and drug control laws, banking regulations, or postal laws.

Private Police and Law Enforcement: The **private investigator** (the PI), so well known from television and the movies, and the highly visible uniformed private security firms doing business in our communities are the most conspicuous representations of private law enforcement. In detective fiction they are often loners like Sam Spade or Philip Marlowe, maybe having a partner or two and a secretary. Such small offices may have office managers, but managerial functions are often handled by the PIs themselves.

The lone-eagle private investigators are not alone in the private security industry, though. Private law enforcement includes the investigative offices of commercial utilities companies, the railroad police, a variety of corporate police, large security corporations, the security offices of private colleges and universities, as well as numerous other entities.

The key feature of private law enforcement is that their policies and services are designed to fulfill the needs of the private persons or corporations employing them. This is the most rapidly growing sector of law enforcement employment. Because the laws of each state differ, some have powers equal to those of public law enforcement officers, while others have very limited law enforcement powers. Management of most of these private law enforcement organizations will follow business models because the organizations exist to achieve a profit as well as to provide public service.

Most of the larger private security services are modeled on public police agencies. Many issue their officers uniforms and use the rank insignia and titles of public law enforcement. Their mid-level and top management positions typically are filled by merit hiring and promotion from within.

Local Police: The first echelon of publicly controlled police operate at the local level, in our towns, cities, and counties. These are the police we think of most often when the word "police" is spoken. Local law enforcement includes the **sheriffs** and their deputies who provide law enforcement services to our counties, the town and city police who serve our urban communities, and specialized local law enforcement officials who are not as often thought of as police, but perform local policing functions (e.g., building inspectors, dog catchers, health inspectors, and other local regulatory officer). In most American cities and towns, police chiefs usually are chosen by their city governments, and mid-level police managers are chosen by some variety of civil service or merit selection process. Sheriffs, however, are elected within their counties, and their deputies often are personal, patronage appointees of those elected sheriffs.

State Law Enforcement: Many but not all of our state governments have general law enforcement police agencies. Others have state highway patrols that are specialized traffic law enforcement agencies, while still others have state investigative agencies modeled on the Federal Bureau of Investigation. There are many additional specialized law enforcement agencies at the state level of jurisdiction. Most states have some form of motor vehicle or drivers licensing law enforcement agencies, wildlife or game protection officers, tax investigation units, and liquor licensing agencies with law enforcement powers. Their top managers often are political appointees, but usually are chosen from a pool of experienced professionals. Mid-level managers are chosen, usually from within, by a civil service or merit selection process. Most employ paramilitary ranks and titles. Some refer to managers using the title **inspector**, indicating one of the managerial functions of that office: the inspection of the subordinates they supervise.

Federal Law Enforcement: The U.S. Marshal's Service is the oldest federal law enforcement agency, formed in 1789. Other federal law enforcement agencies followed: the Internal Revenue Service (IRS) in 1862, the U.S. Secret Service (formed within the Treasury Department) in 1865, and the Immigration and Naturalization Service (INS) in 1891. INS is now called Immigration and Customs Enforcement (ICE), and falls within the **Department of Homeland Security (DHS)**. The most publicized federal law enforcement agency is probably the Federal Bureau of Investigation (FBI), founded in 1908 within the Department of Justice (Wrobleski and Hess, 1986: 20, 23). Other specialized agencies involved in federal law enforcement include the Drug Enforcement Agency (DEA), the U.S. Postal Inspectors, the Occupational Safety and Health Administration (OSHA), the Coast Guard (USCG), the Transportation Security Administration (TSA), and many more. The growth in federal regulations and legislation since the 1930s has produced the requirements for an ever-increasing number of specialized law enforcement officers and agencies within the federal government. The senior managers of these federal agencies are political appointees of the president, with senatorial advice and consent. Mid-level federal managers are promoted internally based on merit and civil service procedures. Several federal agencies use the term **"special agent-in-charge"** to identify managerial officers.

International Law Enforcement: U.S. representatives serving with **INTERPOL** and the CIA and officials of the U.S. State Department are involved in law enforcement and policing on an international basis. These international police are officers of our federal government or other national governments cooperating with ours who function extraterritorially, beyond our own national political borders, and typically are appointed within the executive ranks of their organizations. Some federal agencies have international jurisdiction, such as the Drug Enforcement Agency, which can operate both within and outside our national borders. The police units of our military services also operate both at home and internationally, but usually only in dealing with U.S. service people and in accordance with "status of forces" agreements with the host countries wherein they are deployed.

Managing the Prosecution of Criminal Suspects

The **prosecution** function includes submission of criminal charges and supporting evidence to grand juries and preparation of cases for trial. Also known by such titles as district, state, or commonwealth "solicitor" or "attorney," in most states prosecutors are elected. In the federal system they are political appointees of the Justice Department. Whether an appointee or an elected official, a prosecutor often is a highly visible public figure, especially when involved with a celebrated criminal case. The prosecutor manages the office district attorney and in larger offices will appoint managerial deputy DAs to help with supervision and case management.

The prosecutor has several functional roles to play in the American justice system, some reflecting the personalities of the office holders. Abraham S. Blumberg has identified five (1979: 133-139). The "collection agent" facilitates the payment of civil judgments, threatening to file criminal charges if the debts are not paid. For merchants holding bad checks or those entitled to child support, this help in recovering overdue payments is an important but unglamorous aspect of the prosecutorial role. The "dispenser of justice" works closely with law enforcement agencies, bringing criminal cases to trial or disposition by plea bargaining. The "power-broker/fixer" enjoys the exercise of power in bringing highly visible cases, often involving prominent individuals or important social issues, to quick solutions. The "political enforcer" uses the office to attack political opponents, to "get" someone by public embarrassment and legal harassment, even if no criminal conviction will result. The mass media are much more important to these unethical prosecutors than juries. The "overseer of police" role involves monitoring police cases and activities closely. By screening police cases, these prosecutors are reviewing the quality of the police work, often requiring more investigation, dismissing weak cases, and bringing to trial only those that are well prepared.

The relationship of the prosecutor to the grand jury is one worthy of special attention. A grand jury is comprised of private citizens, often having little or no experience or training in criminal procedures or law. The investigative grand jury operates in secret, and the actions of the prosecutor are not subject to the normal review. Prosecutors have been known to present hearsay, illegally acquired evidence, and other categories of evidence not admissible in a court case. Suspects may not be given the opportunity to hear the charges made against them. Witnesses who might be able to speak in the defense of suspects might be excluded. Testimony given before a grand jury is not subject to cross-examination. These factors give an unscrupulous prosecutor license to use the grand jury to damage the reputations of personal or political opponents by bringing charges and inspiring indictments against persons whose rights and protections in a courtroom would preclude conviction.

The high visibility of the prosecutor in a major criminal case, and occasionally in major government-initiated civil litigation, can make the incumbent of the office an instant celebrity. Highly successful prosecutors have used this fact to garner free publicity in their quest for higher political office. Among those who have used the prosecutor's office to seek still higher civic offices were Thomas E. Dewey, a DA who became governor of New York and was the Republican presidential candidate in 1948; Robert Kennedy, from the U.S. Attorney General to U.S. Senator and a leading candidate for the Democrat presidential nomination in 1968; and, more recently, former U.S. Attorney of New York Rudolph W. Giuliani as the Republican mayor of New York City and a candidate for the Republican presidential nomination in 2008.

Defense Attorneys: Public Defenders and Private Counsel

The right to legal counsel in a criminal case is guaranteed under the provisions of the Sixth Amendment to the U.S. Constitution. The *Gideon v. Wainwright* and *Miranda v. Arizona* rulings of the U.S. Supreme

Court extended this right to persons charged under state laws and to those too poor to afford counsel. Previously, private lawyers hired by those accused provided this counsel. The expanded rights meant that the states and the federal government had to provide legal **defense counsel** to people who could not pay for these services (indigents). Some of this indigent defense is provided by appointed counsel, lawyers in private practice who are assigned criminal cases by the court and are paid by the state. In other jurisdictions, full-time defense attorneys are employed by public defender offices.

The defense attorney performs several roles before, during, and after trials. In addition, attorneys develop personal styles. Abraham Blumberg has observed and named several of these. The lawyer who undertakes "social causes" is the "pro bono ideologue." Usually financially independent and often personally quite colorful, this defender of causes rather than cases often achieves major reforms within the system (Blumberg, 1979: 237). Years ago Clarence Darrow and William Jennings Bryan met in a small town in Tennessee to contest the legal aspects of the creationism-vs.-evolutionism debate in the celebrated "monkey trial." In the 1960s Abe Fortas achieved fame in his defense of Clarence Gideon in the *Gideon v. Wainwright* case, widely publicized by Anthony Lewis's book, *Gideon's Trumpet*. Another such figure is William Kunstler, who has been involved in numerous high-visibility civil rights cases since the 1960s. A second type, the "star," is similar to the ideologue, being equally visible and colorful (Blumberg, 1979: 239). He or she too seeks out high-visibility cases, but not necessarily for the issues they represent. The star is often likely to be representing famous people or bringing suit against celebrities. Another of Blumberg's types is the "hired gun," the talented attorney without an ideology, prepared to argue whatever side of an issue in whatever case comes his or her way (1979: 239). The "patrician" or "courtly gentleman" lawyers are among the best and brightest in the legal profession (Blumberg, 1979: 239). Their stellar reputations often result in their being asked to head investigative commissions or serve as special prosecutors in highly sensitive cases. Although few attorneys in local practice will ever rise to the national recognition levels of Blumberg's characterizations, many attorneys pattern their careers and approaches to similar styles. Every major city has its own stars, ideologues, hired guns, and patricians in daily practice.

Managing Bail, Bond, and Pretrial Detention Services

The U.S. Constitution provides the guarantee of reasonable bail for those held for trial. Bails and bonds are securities that are pledged or paid to insure the appearance of a criminal suspect, and sometimes a civil litigant, at the trial. The security pledged against the promise of appearance is returned if the person appears as promised and is forfeited if the person does not appear. The amount is set by a judicial official, usually either a magistrate or a lower court judge, but can be appealed in higher courts if the defendant feels the amount is excessive and unreasonable. Usually there is a chief magistrate for each district, but in some states this function is managed in the courts.

The **magistrate** or court is called upon to make decisions about the appropriate bail or conditions of bond. If the bail or bond cannot be met, the defendant must remain in pretrial detention until the trial date. In some busy court jurisdictions, this can mean serving many months of jail time without having been convicted. If there is a subsequent conviction later, this pretrial jail time usually will be counted against the punishment, but there is no compensation if the defendant is later acquitted or the charges are dropped.

Managing Victim and Witness Services

In the 1980s victims and witnesses in our system were given considerably more attention than in decades past. Without the active support of these parties, the criminal justice system would be ineffective. Although the importance of witnesses and victims in the workings of the criminal justice system is significant, critics of the justice system have decried their apparent neglect and have identified many legitimate complaints. Agencies have therefore been established (both NGOs and governmental services) to provide services to victims and witnesses (Yeldell and Brown, 2002).

Community organizers and reform activists have taken up the causes of victims of rape, homicide, child and spouse abuse, and drunk driving, among others, to call attention to the patterns of neglect and abuse that they have encountered. The critics often charge that the civil rights of accused criminals have been assigned such high priority that their victims are all but forgotten. Two powerful films on rape, *A Case of Rape* in 1974 and *The Accused* in 1988, make this point very clearly. The rape victim in each story is victimized a second time by her treatment by justice officials, defense attorneys, and the media.

The families of homicide victims are also victims of those crimes. They have endured the losses of loved ones in murders and in drunk driving–caused fatal accidents. Their personal losses are too great for compensation, but they can expect some support and comfort from the justice system and the information media. Because so many homicides are committed by people who know their victims well, the survivors often are treated as the prime suspects. Bodies are held by police pathologists and coroners for what may seem like indeterminable or unreasonable lengths of time. Body parts and personal effects remain in police labs and evidence vaults for years as the case proceeds through investigation, trial, and appeals. Status reports on investigations often reach the press before they reach the survivors. Grisly photographs of their loved ones often appear on television and in newspapers and magazines, sometimes weeks, months, or years after the crime.

The witness in the justice system often has fared no better. Without receiving the sympathy that victims and victims' families often do, they too are victimized by the process of justice. Time is lost from work or other pursuits while witnesses wait for their time to testify. When a plea bargain terminates a case without a trial, occasionally witnesses are not notified and show up to testify unnecessarily, or are left sitting in witness chambers forgotten, as the other principals to the case go home or to their offices or to jail. They are rarely thanked and even less often compensated for their time and effort.

Some abuse of witnesses is deliberate. The common defense attorney strategy of recurring postponements is aimed specifically at witnesses. If a witness becomes discouraged, he or she may fail to appear, leading to a motion to dismiss the charges against the accused. If a witness endures the delays, the duration between the events they witnessed and the date of testimony will be cited as his or her ability to recall is questioned. Defense attorneys are not alone in abusing witnesses. The prosecutor often will employ similar tactics against opposing witnesses. If witnesses are offered any financial compensation for their time and effort, the opposing attorney will attempt to make it appear that their testimony has been purchased and is tainted. If the opposing attorney is especially aggressive in cross-examination, he or she will attack the reputation, integrity, intelligence, motives, and character of the witnesses.

There have been some improvements. The appearance of witness assistance programs has been a major boon to helping overcome these problems. Changes in trial dates are announced, times for testimony are more carefully scheduled, and various services are provided to witnesses while they are waiting. Judges have also been helpful by discouraging postponements and in thwarting the efforts of opposing attorneys attempting to attack witnesses without just grounds.

Managing the Judicial System

The image of the black-robed judge presiding over a trial from his or her elevated bench in the courtroom is a powerful one. It is an impression that actually runs counter to many of our national democratic ideals. There is no question about the basic inequality of people in the courtroom. The **judge** is almost an imperial presence. Even more than the police officer, the judge personifies the power of the state over our lives. Judicial rulings are non-negotiable orders backed by the power of government. They may be appealed, but they cannot be ignored. Only other judges have the power to correct fellow judges. Their formal role as interpreters, arbiters, and defenders of the law and the state and federal constitutions places them above all other civil servants and public service managers, legislators, mayors, governors, and even presidents on occasion.

A judge on the bench is not, however, a manager, but there are chief judges in judicial units and chief justices in the state and federal supreme courts whose off-bench duties are managerial. Many states and the federal courts provide assistance to these judges by operating offices for courts administration. Their directors are managers.

Some judges have been known to become overawed by their own power. Those who flaunt their powers are soon widely known and much disliked, but they are hard to deal with, discipline, or dispose of in a justice system that has sought to provide them with great protections from outside pressures. In states with elective judiciaries, the polling place provides one avenue of relief, but federal judges serve for life unless removed by impeachment in the U.S. Congress (a rare event even when obviously warranted).

Even those judges who do not become despots often acquire other unappealing personal traits—or bring these traits with them—to the displeasure of attorneys, victims, witnesses, media representatives, and/ or defendants who must deal with them. Abraham S. Blumberg (1979: 264-266) identified six role patterns in the judges he observed. The roles of "intellectual" and "hack" carry the burdens of court work with little attention or public visibility. The "political adventurer" is using one's current judicial post to rise higher in public life. This type of judge will cultivate good media and public relations. The "benchwarmer" has been given a judgeship as the final step in a political career, becoming a "judicial pensioner," as if the post were a retirement reward. The "hatchet man" is a close ally of the prosecutor's office who functions to expedite high-visibility cases. The final role described by Blumberg has three aspects: "tyrant-showboat-benevolent despot." This type of judge is egocentric, and uses the judicial bench as a stage for one's personal advantage, especially enjoying media attention.

The judge is only one of a collection of key personalities in the judiciary. In each courtroom are other justice officials who are also important functionaries. The court reporters, bailiffs, clerks of court, and magistrates all play important roles in the operation of the court and in the shaping of the image of the judicial system in the eyes of the public.

The **clerks of court** are among the most influential of these other officials. They schedule the trials, manage the paper flow, keep the records, and have the most frequent dealings with persons outside the judiciary. Clerk's offices are managed by a chief clerk, often an elected official. When efficient, helpful, and courteous, clerks are effective entities, but unfortunately this is not always the case. Because most clerks work for judges, or perceive themselves as doing so, some are uninterested in serving their other clients. It is common for a visitor to the clerk's office to find stuffy formality, indifference, and a lack of cooperation among the clerical staff.

The courts have not escaped criticism for these faults. Judges, clerks, and other judiciary officials have been called to task for their more serious shortcomings. The awe and esteem given the courts and judges requires them to pay great attention to their responsibilities to the public they are there to serve.

Managing Adult Corrections

Adult offenders convicted of crimes can experience a wide range of punishments, ranging from simple admonishments not to violate the law again to the death penalty. The potential penalty usually is set in law, but the penalty is the product of judicial decisionmaking. Severity of the offense, circumstances associated with the offense, the victim's role in the crime and relationship to the offender, prior criminal record, degree of cooperation with the authorities leading up to trial, efforts taken to make restitution, prospects for rehabilitation, and numerous other factors are taken into consideration in rendering sentences; often under legal guidelines. Other, extralegal factors also come into play in sentencing: sex; race; ethnicity; unorthodox political, sexual, religious, or ideological views; social standing of the victims; and economic status of the offenders and victims among them.

There exists a wide range of formal correctional options and penalties that a judge can employ. The laws set limits, but judges are given varying degrees of autonomy in selecting sentences within these limits. Some of these are explained in Box 2.1, but the list is neither exhaustive nor in absolute rank order of severity. Other punishments exist. Some corrections options can be combined and often are. Furthermore, once a person is under sentence to prison, there are additional correctional options available.

Custodial Corrections – The Jails: Jails are used for pretrial detention and for short terms of punishment under the supervision of the county. The sheriff is the manager of the county jail, but many sheriffs will appoint a jail manager to run day-to-day jail operations.

Custodial Corrections – The Prisons: Prison often is the first option that most people outside of the justice system think of when they consider possible criminal penalties. However, it is not the most common penalty assessed. Fines, probations, and short jail terms are used more frequently, if only because most criminal offenses are relatively minor and do not justify prison terms. Most states use their limited prison resources to house only the most serious and dangerous criminals, using other correctional alternatives for less risky offenders. Prisons are managed by wardens, and larger prisons have large numbers of middle-level managers, usually using officer ranks borrowed from the military. Because prisons operate 24/7, there are shift managers so there are representatives of the managerial team on duty, whatever the hour.

Prison Sentences: Prison sentences can be either determinate or indeterminate. A determinate sentence is fixed at the time of trial and cannot be increased. It may be decreased only in accordance with formal rules and guidelines of the correctional or parole system of the state. An indeterminate sentence is given as a range of time, within which the sentence is to be served (e.g., "three to five years," or as a maximum limit, "for a term not to exceed five years"). The actual sentence is computed by the parole or correctional officials of the state, who review each case for evidence of rehabilitation. Whichever system of sentencing is used, it is rare for an offender to serve the maximum length of the sentence given. States using determinate sentencing, though, tend to operate more consistently, leaving their correctional and parole officials less discretion in reducing sentences.

Discharge from Prison: Once offenders are in prison, they can exit legally via several means. One is discharge of sentence. They serve their full time or are granted clemencies or pardons and are discharged, with no more time left to serve. There are few prisoners who exit under these terms. Most are released conditionally. The institution of parole is the means most commonly used to discharge prisoners before the end of their full sentence terms. Various other programs, such as furloughs, also readmit sentenced criminals into the general population.

As prisoners near the end of their active prison sentences (even before parole in many cases), they need, argue correctional theorists, an opportunity to be reintegrated into the society that has excluded them by exiling them to prisons. This can be achieved by a number of means. Three of the most popularly used are furloughs, work release, and halfway house placements.

Furloughs: A furlough is a temporary period of release from custody, a brief vacation from confinement. It may be either supervised or unsupervised, according to the rules of each state. When supervision is provided, a correctional officer can be assigned to be the constant companion of the convict, but this is rare. More often, there is little actual supervision, and the offender merely has to check in at pre-appointed times to meet the conditions of the furlough.

Work Release and Study Release: Related to the furlough programs are work release and study release programs that allow recurring furloughs to allow inmates to attend schools or engage in regular jobs outside prison walls. These programs have been especially attractive because the work or classroom environment provides some supervision for the convicts while they are outside the walls and because they are either acquiring work skills or an education that can serve the cause of their rehabilitation.

Halfway House Placement: A halfway house is a facility in a community in which prisoners must stay overnight but can go out to workplaces or educational institutions during the normal hours for these activities. The residence is supervised by a special group of correctional officers who function much like probation officers, ensuring that the conditions of conditional release from prison are met. Violations can result in immediate return to secure custodial institutions and even lengthening of sentences.

Parole: Parole is conditional release from prison. As long as the conditions are met, the former prisoner can remain in society without having to return to prison. Those conditions and their supervision operate much like probation. Parole supervision is managed from community offices. Violations are a matter for parole or correctional authorities to deal with administratively. A parole revocation hearing does not require reinvolvement of the sentencing judge. The parole officials can order the reincarceration of a parole violator if the hearing concludes that the conditions were violated.

Community Organizations

The role of private citizens in the justice system has grown in recent years. Far more community organizations have taken over functions that were once exclusively the preserve of the government. This has been most obvious in juvenile and adult corrections, victim assistance, and judicial oversight activities.

Most correctional activities are under the control of either states or localities. However, in recent years a number of private institutions have become active in rehabilitation efforts and have offered some communities sentencing options not previously available. Most of these private efforts have been in the area of counseling and therapy, but some are even semi-custodial, providing housing for clients directed to them as conditions of probations or paroles.

Among the more successful and well known of these private semi-custodial efforts is the Delancey Street Foundation, a program that began in California, and has branched out to other parts of the country. A typical Delancey Street Foundation program will provide a group residence, like a halfway house, under strict discipline of the staff, many of whom are reformed offenders themselves. The client population will be employed in industries and enterprises run by the Delancey Street Foundation. Profits from these enterprises are used to sustain the houses. The clients are given wages for their work from which they are expected to contribute to the operating expenses of the residence. Like every correctional effort, these programs have their failures, but they have had a good success rate with referral clients and have costs the public far less than either prisons or close supervision parole.

Victim assistance programs were not given much attention until the feminist movement selected rape victimization as one of its causes (Kania and Mackey, 1983). The attention given to women as victims helped direct public attention to victims more generally. From these rape victim assistance programs have come many similar services designed to help all types of victims. In addition to counseling victims and helping them cope with the psychological, financial, and physical consequences of their victimizations, these programs have been quite successful in mounting lobbying efforts in state legislatures on behalf of victim compensation legislation and improved standards for the treatment of victims by the police, prosecutors, and the courts.

Other private community groups are attempting to bring about additional improvements in the judiciary. Several groups have targeted the courts for special attention. Because judges are relatively immune from public criticism and critique from within the legal profession, these groups have undertaken to provide this service. Court accountability projects, such as Court Watch of North Carolina, have undertaken the evaluation of judges of the civil family courts, using trained volunteer observers in the courtrooms. The judges are critiqued with regard to their demeanor on the bench, their treatment of litigants, and their efforts to facilitate justice and help litigants (usually women seeking help in collecting court-ordered child support payments). Several state and local chapters of Mothers Against Drunk Driving (MADD), a nonprofit organization opposed to the criminal act of drunk driving, have undertaken the evaluation of criminal court judges and their handling of drunk driving cases. The records of judges in bringing convictions are contrasted, and the imposed sentences are compared. Judges who are characteristically prone to acquit or to render light sentences are publicly identified. This attention to their activities has put judges on notice that they are not a privileged elite immune from critical evaluation. It also has helped them reform their profession and correct their mistakes without resort to more radical remedies.

Juvenile Justice

The place of juveniles in our justice system differs somewhat from that of adults. Beginning late in the nineteenth century, the courts began to treat younger offenders differently, establishing the notion of *parens patriae*, the idea that the state stands in place of the parents when a juvenile comes into conflict with the law. Under this doctrine, in theory, the courts act in the best interest of the juvenile, not to punish but to guide and reform the youthful offender. As a result, separate reform and training schools replaced jails and prisons as the places where juveniles were held in custody.

The courts set up a separate **juvenile justice system** of intake officers to review cases involving juveniles and probation officers and counselors to work with those found in violation of the laws. These officials are responsible for determining what is in the best interests of the child. Punishment of the guilty is not the objective of the court's judgment. Instead the objective is the correction, rehabilitation, and reintegration of the juvenile offender into society. Although penalties are assessed in some juvenile court cases, the findings and judgments are not usually severe. Court findings of what is best for the juvenile offender can include loss of freedom by assignment to training schools and reformatories, which can be viewed very much like being sentenced to prison.

After the U.S. Supreme Court ruling in the case *In re Gault*, the courts were obliged to provide juvenile defendants with the same legal rights that adults possess: the right to counsel, the right to confront their accusers, the right to trial, and so forth. The federal courts had come to view some state juvenile courts as predominantly punitive entities that did not afford juveniles "due process of law" and occasionally denied juveniles the full opportunity to defend themselves against complaints. The Supreme Court has taken the position that juvenile suspects have all the same rights as adults, plus some additional protections because of their status as minors. For example, a juvenile cannot be called upon to waive his or her legal rights to legal representation or the protection against self-incrimination without parental consultation; juveniles in police custody or in correctional institutions must be kept separate from adult offenders; and educational opportunities for juveniles cannot be denied as a consequence of correctional custody.

There exists a shadow system of juvenile justice that parallels the adult criminal justice system. In police departments there are juvenile officers specializing in juvenile law enforcement. Intake officers serve a role similar to that of magistrates in reviewing charges against juveniles and deciding whether to release them or hold them in custody while pending trial on the charges. If held, offenders are placed in juvenile detention centers, rather than local jails, to await trial. Cases are heard by juvenile courts and judges specializing in juvenile law. Juvenile probation officers and counselors work with those found in violation of the laws but not ordered into state custody. Some offenders are assigned to foster care for intensive probation within a family environment. Those ordered to be held in secure custody go to reform or training schools to serve their time. Halfway houses are used to reintegrate them into society, and aftercare programs function like supervised parole.

Summary: The American Justice System

Some years ago there was a running debate about whether the American approach to criminal justice constituted a system. In the final analysis of that debate, everything depended on how an author defined or meant to use the concept of a "system." The debate served us well, though, because it allowed scholars to make the point that the American approach to justice is very disjointed and decentralized. It is not an efficient system by any measure of efficiency. Its actors are in conflict or in competition as often as they work in cooperation.

The criminal justice system in the United States is uniquely American. Although many of its institutions are derived from English models, the American criminal justice system ceased being like the English one long ago. The **decentralization**—that is, the lack of formal integration of agencies into cooperating entities—that characterizes the American criminal justice system is unparalleled in the rest of the world. The division of responsibilities defies logic or easy explanation. It is organizationally "ugly." Nevertheless, it seems to work—although not always well—in achieving its competing objectives of protecting society and protecting the civil rights of our citizens, even the criminally inclined of them; identifying and punishing the guilty; and preventing crime and reintegrating criminal offenders into the general population. The American justice system exists to respond to the demands of a diverse nation. Because Americans are not of one mind about what the justice system should be doing for whom, the laws and the parties who are called upon to enforce (or not enforce) them are given conflicting requirements to fulfill.

These conflicting requirements introduce upsetting contradictions and give rise to much of the criticism that is attached to American justice. The system hires the lawyers who try to exonerate the offenders whom we hire police and prosecutors to put away. The legal system employs lawyers for the convicts who are suing our correctional officials. When public officials crack down on crime, their critics decry the encroachments on the civil liberties of us all. When they faithfully protect the rights of criminal suspects, they are criticized for being soft on crime. One segment of America objects to the inhumane conditions

Box 2.1 • A General View of the Criminal Justice System (LEAA)

What is the sequence of events in the criminal justice system?

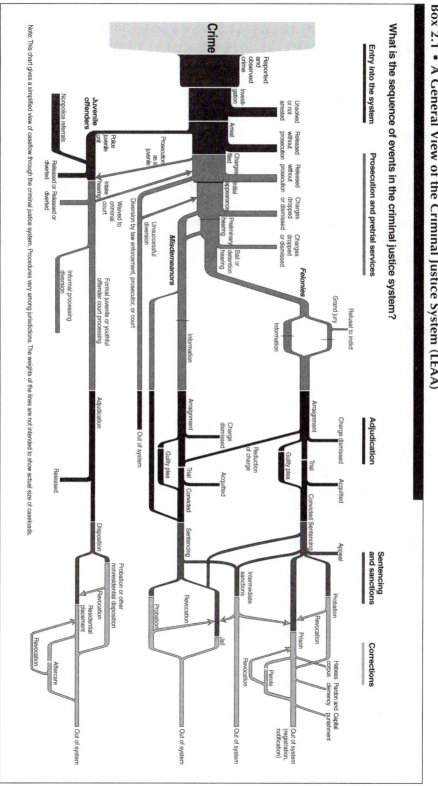

Note: This chart gives a simplified view of caseflow through the criminal justice system. Procedures vary among jurisdictions. The weights of the lines are not intended to show actual size of caseloads.

produced by prison overcrowding, while another segment (including some of those in the first segment) resists prison construction. Moreover, a third segment (including some of those in the second segment) demands that we keep our criminals locked up. All of these contradictions are part of the price of representative democracy. In a totalitarian state we would be free of these conflicts. Only one role would be assigned to our justice system, and it would respond to that singular obligation. Only where there is very broad consensus is the system relatively immune from criticism.

While it may be a system that does not always function smoothly and efficiently, it is a system that has at least the potential to function as it should. A criminal case can come to the attention of the system, be solved, arrests made, and a trial set. Suspects are defended, tried fairly, given the opportunity to confront their accusers as well as the evidence against them, and acquitted if found not guilty. If found guilty, they will be sentenced, given ample opportunity to appeal, and will serve sentences that are at least humanely executed in relatively good conditions by world standards. Not all cases follow this ideal sequence, but enough do in a timely enough fashion to give some critics at least hope that the whole system can be made to work better.

Similarly, the civil justice system appears to have the potential to function well. Justice too often is slow and costly, but important personal and social issues do get resolved in the civil courts. Both rich and poor get heard. Influential and invisible people alike have their days in court. Both socially significant and inconsequential cases eventually get resolved. Like the American criminal justice system, civil justice has the potential to be improved.

Knowing how the justice system should work is a first step toward making it work. Whether the interested person reading this book is a justice administration student, a justice system volunteer, a professional practitioner, a journalist, or a private citizen simply interested in the connection between American justice administration and information media relations, a basic understanding of the fundamental organization and functions of the major justice system components is essential. This chapter leaves far too much unsaid and should be seen only as an introduction to the subject matter. In the bibliography that follows are numerous titles that can be consulted for further information. Especially useful as reference materials are the reports of the two national commissions studying American criminal justice institutions in the 1960s and 1970s: the **President's Commission on Law Enforcement and Administration of Justice** and the **National Advisory Commission on Criminal Justice Standards and Goals.** Knowing the system well is a duty for those whose careers include serving in it, managing it, and reporting upon it, and is prudent for those whose lives will be touched by it.

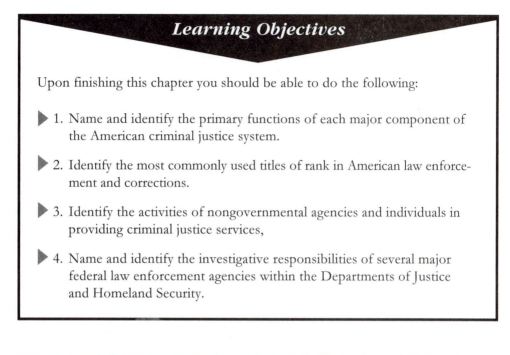

Learning Objectives

Upon finishing this chapter you should be able to do the following:

▶ 1. Name and identify the primary functions of each major component of the American criminal justice system.

▶ 2. Identify the most commonly used titles of rank in American law enforcement and corrections.

▶ 3. Identify the activities of nongovernmental agencies and individuals in providing criminal justice services,

▶ 4. Name and identify the investigative responsibilities of several major federal law enforcement agencies within the Departments of Justice and Homeland Security.

IMPORTANT TERMS AND NAMES

- chief
- clerks of court
- decentralization
- defense counsel
- Department of Homeland Security (DHS)
- director
- In re Gault
- Gideon v. Wainwright
- inspector
- INTERPOL (International Police Organization)
- private investigator
- jails
- judge
- juvenile justice system
- Law Enforcement Assistance Administration (LEAA)

- magistrate
- Miranda v. Arizona
- Mothers Against Drunk Driving (MADD)
- National Advisory Commission on Criminal Justice Standards and Goals
- nongovernmental organizations (NGOs)
- parole
- President's Commission on Law Enforcement and Administration of Justice
- prison
- prosecution
- sheriffs
- special agent-in-charge
- Wickersham Commission (National Commission on Law Observance and Enforcement)

References and Supplemental Sources

Blumberg, Abraham (1979). *Criminal Justice: Issues and Ironies*, 2nd ed. New York: New Viewpoints, Franklin Watts.

Champion, Dean J. (2003). *Administration of Criminal Justice*. Upper Saddle River, NJ: Prentice Hall.

In re Gault, 387 U.S. 1 (1967).

Gideon v. Wainwright, 372 U.S. 335 (1963).

Gulick, Luther (1937). "Notes on the Theory of Organization." In *Papers on the Science of Administration*, edited by Luther Gulick and Lyndall Urwick. New York: Institute of Public Administration.

Feldman, Martha S., and Anne M. Khademian (2001). "Principles for Public Management Practice: From Dichotomies to Interdependence," *Governance*, 14(3): 339–361.

Hoover, Larry T. (1975). *Police Educational Characteristics and Curricula*. Washington, DC: National Institute of Law Enforcement and Criminal Justice, L.E.A.A.

Kania, Richard R.E. , and Wade C. Mackey (1983). "A Preliminary Analysis of Feminist Views on the Crime of Rape," *Southern Journal of Criminal Justice*, 8(1): 88-104.

Lewis, Anthony (1964). *Gideon's Trumpet*. New York: Random House.

Miranda v. Arizona, 384 U.S. 436 (1966).

National Advisory Commission on Criminal Justice Standards and Goals (1973). *Corrections*. Washington, DC: U.S. Government Printing Office.

National Advisory Commission on Criminal Justice Standards and Goals (1973). *The Courts*. Washington, DC: U.S. Government Printing Office.

National Advisory Commission on Criminal Justice Standards and Goals (1973). *The Criminal Justice System*. Washington, DC: U.S. Government Printing Office.

National Advisory Commission on Criminal Justice Standards and Goals (1973). *The Police*. Washington, DC: U.S. Government Printing Office.

National Advisory Commission on Criminal Justice Standards and Goals (1976). *Juvenile Justice and Delinquency Prevention*. Washington, DC: U.S. Government Printing Office.

National Advisory Commission on Criminal Justice Standards and Goals (1976). *Private Security*. Washington, DC: U.S. Government Printing Office.

National Commission on Law Observance and Enforcement (Wickersham Commission) (1931). *Wickersham Commission Reports*. Washington, DC: U.S. Government Printing Office.

Peak, Kenneth J. (2008). *Justice Administration: Police, Courts, and Corrections Management*, 6th ed., Chapter 1. Upper Saddle River, NJ: Pearson, 2008.

President's Commission on Law Enforcement and Administration of Justice (1965). *Task Force Report: Juvenile Delinquency and Youth Crime*. Washington, DC: U.S. Government Printing Office.

President's Commission on Law Enforcement and Administration of Justice (1967). *Task Force Report: The Courts*. Washington, DC: U.S. Government Printing Office.

President's Commission on Law Enforcement and Administration of Justice (1967). *Task Force Report: The Police*. Washington, DC: U.S. Government Printing Office.

Radelet, Louis A. (1980). *The Police and the Community*, 3rd ed. New York: Macmillan.

Senna, Joseph J., and Larry J. Siegel (1990). *Introduction to Criminal Justice*, 5th ed. St. Paul, MN: West.

Travis, Lawrence F., III (2008). *Introduction to Criminal Justice*, 6th ed. Newark, NJ: LexisNexis Matthew Bender.

Trojanowicz, Robert, and Samuel Dixon (1974). *Criminal Justice and the Community*. Englewood Cliffs, NJ: Prentice Hall.

U. S. Bureau of Prisons (1973). *Jail Management: Administration of Jail Operations*. Washington, DC: U.S. Government Printing Office.

Waldron, Ronald J. (1989). *The Criminal Justice System*, 4th ed. New York: Harper & Row.

Westley, William (1970). *Violence and the Police*. Cambridge, MA: MIT Press.

Wilson, Orlando W., and Roy C. McLaren (1977). *Police Administration*, 4th ed. New York: McGraw-Hill.

Wrobleski, Henry, and Karen M. Hess (1986). *Introduction to Law Enforcement and Criminal Justice*, 2nd ed. St. Paul, MN: West.

Yeldell, Stanley, and Margaret Brown (2002). *Victim Assistance Handbook*. Dubuque, IA: Kendall Hunt.

3
Historical Antecedents

People have been seeking better ways to manage large-scale human activities and provide good governance from the earliest times. In ancient Greece, both Socrates and Plato considered questions anticipating the development of the managerial sciences some 2,400 years ago. **Socrates** noted that the basic concepts of organizing an army and staging a chorus for a play required similar managerial talents. **Plato** asked rhetorical questions about the training and selection of the ideal "guardians" for society, and offered answers he attributed to Socrates. About 2,000 years ago Romans created a standing army and established outposts across Europe where the soldiers were based and imperial governors managed the Roman colonies for another 400 years. The Byzantines carried on their practices for another thousand years. Concurrently, the Roman Catholic Church established a system of church self-governance parallel to the Roman and Byzantine civil authorities. A thousand years ago the Chinese were developing a professional civil service and the institution we now call a **bureaucracy**. Yet these developments also faced setbacks as these empires fell and the church underwent schism. As a result, both governance and criminal justice suffered in Europe until the Enlightenment.

A new form of the state was emerging in Europe in the seventeenth century. In France, Cardinal Richelieu (1585-1642) was calculating ways to reduce the feudal privileges of the hereditary nobles and begin the modern political state with early notions of bureaucracy and merit selection of **civil servants** (i.e., civilian public-sector employees working for a government department or agency). **Merit selection** is a way of choosing employees that uses a nonpartisan commission to locate, recruit, investigate, and evaluate applicants. What he created developed into Europe's most advanced public bureaucracy. Under his leadership, new judicial institutions were created in France that employed an educated, merit-selected judiciary under the authority of the King to supplement

Richard R.E. Kania

Armand-Jean du Plessis, the Cardinal de Richelieu, from the painting by Phillippe de Champaigne of the Cardinal now displayed in the Louvre, Paris. Cardinal Richelieu introduced a merit-based criminal justice bureaucracy to Europe while reforming the French judiciary.

and replace older, more corrupt, and less effective practices (Richelieu, 1947: 230-249; 1961: 75-89; Carey, 1981: 14-21).

At about the same time, the English were undergoing the final stage of their "Great Rebellion" (1648-1649), which established the practice of holding even the King accountable to the law, at the expense of the head of King Charles I (Durant and Durant, 1961: 219-221). Thereafter, the British monarchy learned the necessity of sharing power with its legislature, the Parliament. Although they seemed to have forgotten it by 1776, it was a lesson that the colonial Americans heeded in creating a three-branch government in 1789.

In Chapter 1 you were introduced to eight principles of public management: leading, organizing, deciding, evaluating, staffing, training, allocating, and reporting. These were recent creations among the ideas of humankind. Three intellectual threads have been crossing since 1776 to bring us to where we are in American criminal justice. They are ideas taken from political philosophy, merged with ideas from managerial science and reform ideas within criminal justice.

Pioneers and Predecessors of Modern Public Service Management Theory

In the seventeenth and eighteenth centuries, several important pioneers in the social, managerial, and organizational sciences developed concepts applicable to criminal justice. Cesare Beccaria and Jeremy Bentham offered rational, utilitarian ideas on justice and crime control, and Bentham also contributed novel ideas in sentencing and penology. In the new American republic, new ideas about a democratic civil service were proposed and implemented by Thomas Jefferson. In the nineteenth century, the United States was an established entity. Prominent American figures such as Andrew Jackson, Dorothea Dix, Zebulon Brockway, and Woodrow Wilson made significant new contributions to public service and criminal justice.

Europeans continued to make contributions, especially in the areas of management science. Robert Owen, Charles Babbage, Augusta Ada Byron,

Henri Fayol, and Max Weber all contributed. John Stuart Mill expanded upon the libertarian concepts found in the public philosophy of Thomas Jefferson, while conservative "Tory" political leader Sir Robert Peel created an original synthesis of organizational and managerial concepts to give Britain and then the United States a new model for municipal policing. At the same time Alexander Maconochie pursued reforms in corrections.

The pioneers of the early twentieth century—including Frederick W. Taylor, Luther Gulick, August Vollmer, O.W. Wilson, Bruce Smith, Raymond Fosdick, and Roscoe Pound—built upon these ideas to expand social, managerial, and classical organizational theory and added ideas that were applicable to criminal justice:

As mentioned, interest in management and organizational principles dates back to the earliest large-scale human enterprises. Indeed, most of the basic principles of organization and management arose from military applications, and as such, they were heavily influenced by the coercive, order-giving style of militaristic leadership. However, in the eighteenth and nineteenth centuries, new factors came into play that created the non-coercive approach to management and organization that is now more in favor. It is in this new, more democratic, performance-based model that American public service management concepts are founded. As we will learn, though, not everyone was of one mind on how to manage public service, and the roots of current disagreements rest deep in our history.

The American public service ideal was forged from three elements: managerial concepts borrowed from commercial enterprise; political concepts about representative, democratic institutions; and scholastic social science theories about what does and does not work. Thus, we must be prepared to study management, political science, and the social sciences to grasp fully what is expected of a person entering a career in the public service.

en.wikipedia.org

Cesare Beccaria: Cesare Beccaria (1738-1794) was an Italian political philosopher and social reformer who was deeply troubled by the practices in the administration of justice in the eighteenth century. He wrote *On Crimes and Punishments* in 1764 [in the original Italian, *Dei Delitti e Delle Pene*]. French (1766) and English (1767) translations soon followed. In this book he clearly established his view that crime was a rational choice, influenced by three deterrent factors: the swiftness, surety, and sufficient severity of punishment. He felt that it was important to forego torture to extract confessions, and generally believed that the death penalty was an excessive punishment. He

Cesare Beccaria wrote his booklet, *Dei Delitti Delle Pene*, in Italian in 1764 as a critique of the administration of justice in Europe in the middle of the eighteenth century. Soon translated into French and English, it became a major influence on legal reforms in Europe and America, read by the likes of Thomas Jefferson and John Adams.

also felt that the laws needed to be publicized, the public needed to be educated on the law, and the laws needed to be consistently enforced.

The small book was highly influential in his lifetime, and among its many readers were Voltaire, Thomas Jefferson, and John Adams. Beccaria became a prominent criminal justice reformer in Europe. He was selected to serve on a board revising the judicial code for the region around Milan in 1791.

en.wikipedia.org

Adam Smith was both a civil servant and a moral philosopher who, in 1776, introduced Europeans and Americans to the productive and economic virtues of the division of labor, a key element in organizational theory to this day.

Adam Smith: Adam Smith (1723-1790) is best known for *The Wealth of Nations* (1776). In Chapter 1 of that work, titled "Of the Division of Labor," he illustrated how an industrious individual pin-maker, a master craftsman, could make fewer than 20 pins a day, but 10 men dividing the tasks into 18 distinct operations could make 48,000—240 times as many per worker as could be made by one highly skilled craftsman. Three basic principles were involved in the **division of labor**: increased dexterity in doing a few simple operations per worker, time savings by not shifting from one task to another, and the application of labor-saving machines. This reduced costs, while improving the quality of life for everyone. Common people could afford inexpensive pins, hence demand would rise to create more work (now known as supply-side economics).

Smith also explained how social and economic trends occurred, as if brought about by some "invisible hand." These "caused" events were brought about not by deterministic forces but by the cumulative effect of many thousands of individual decisions, each reflecting individual reasoning and free will. Smith's work influenced Benjamin Franklin, Alexander Hamilton, Thomas Jefferson, James Madison, and John Adams among our "founding fathers" (Moriarty, 1986).

This point of view on trends is particularly valid for the analysis of change. Instead of seeking some single causal force to explain what we now speak of as a "megatrend," the researcher should examine the event as each individual does, looking for the common elements that all the decisionmakers consider. Hence, per this view, the abstraction of "poverty" does not cause the behaviors known collectively as "crime." Certain particular conditions, which taken collectively are known as "poverty," are critical factors in the individual decisionmaking of all rational individuals, some of whom will decide to act criminally.

Smith himself was a bureaucrat, a customs inspector for Scotland. He wrote one other influential book, *The Theory of Moral Sentiments* (1759), reflecting his interest in moral philosophy. As an economist he made major contributions to the promotion of free markets and capitalism. In management theory his major contribution is his explanation and defense of the concept of the division of labor.

Thomas Jefferson: Thomas Jefferson (1743-1826) was the principle author of the Declaration of Independence (1776), third president of the United States (1801-1809), founder of the University of Virginia, and a lifelong champion of the ideal of a limited government designed to serve the people rather than rule them. He felt that there were social elites who were responsible for serving the public—an undemocratic *noblisse oblige* concept—but he also believed in the native dignity of all men (other than Indians, African Americans, and those "men" who were born

en.wikipedia.org

The Jefferson Memorial in Washington, DC, has a statue of Thomas Jefferson set in front of the inscribed Preamble of the Declaration of Independence. Thomas Jefferson was the principle author of the Declaration of Independence and third president of the United States. As a political philosopher he called for limited government and wanted public officials to function as servants of the people, rather than overseers of them.

female), which allowed for the rise of those not hereditarily ennobled based upon their individual merits and accomplishments.

> Free government is founded in jealousy, and not in confidence; it is jealousy, and not confidence, which prescribes limited constitutions, to bind down those whom we are obliged to trust with power ... [Jefferson, cited in The Kentucky Resolutions of 1798, by E.D. Warfield (1887: 157-158); also quoted in Philip Selznick in Law, Society and Industrial Justice (1969: 18)]. Still one more thing, fellow citizens—a wise and frugal government, which shall restrain men from injuring one another, which shall leave them otherwise free to regulate their own pursuits of industry and improvement, and shall not take from the mouth of labor the bread it has earned. This is the sum of good government, and this is necessary to close the circle of our felicities [Jefferson, First Inaugural Address, 1801].

Jefferson and those who followed his vision for more than a century saw the role of government enterprise as very limited, and the role of the public service manager as that of noble servant, not overseer. His ideas on public service are seminal in the development of the ethical principles of governance in the United States.

Similar views were held by later philosophers, most notably John Stuart Mill, who believed that governments were obliged to act in some situations and ought be constrained in others. The art of political science was sorting one from the other.

John Howard: John Howard (1726-1790) became involved in correctional reforms when he became a sheriff in Britain. In the eighteenth century, the British experimented with more humane approaches: the hulks (old warships used as floating prisons), work houses, and jails for short-term offenders. These were not humane places in practice, however. The government did not care for its prisoners, and prisoners or their families had to provide food and other necessities. So awful were the conditions that John Howard wrote *The State*

John Howard was a sheriff in Britain who was touched by the appalling conditions of the jails [gaols] of his time. This special English halfpenny is inscribed on the reverse, "Remember the Debtors in Gaol" and "Go Forth." Such halfpennies were given to the poor in Howard's name to help spread the message of his penal reforms.

of the Prisons in 1777 as an exposé of the terrible conditions he found in British prisons, hulks, and jails. This embarrassed the British government into making minimal improvements. Originally employed as a more

human device for controlling lesser offenders, the hulks sank occasionally, taking all their inmates with them (Campbell, 1993). Even so, they were retained in use into the 1850s.

Howard is remembered to this day by the existence of John Howard societies and associations in several English-speaking countries, including Great Britain, Canada, New Zealand, and the United States.

Jeremy Bentham was a penal reformer and quite an eccentric figure. In his will he gave his fortune and his mummified body (called an "auto-icon") to University College of London, where it remains on display. The head today is a wax replica. Among his many reforms was the "panopticon" prison. His penal reforms applied the philosophy of rational choice and utilitarianism to sentencing.

Jeremy Bentham: As a leader in the cause of **utilitarianism** (i.e., the balance of pain and pleasure in making rational decisions), Jeremy Bentham (1748-1832) also was a pioneer in social, judicial, and penal reform. He saw humankind as potentially rational, and thus subject to influence by rational policies. For him and his followers, utility and efficiency were higher-order values. Trained in the practice of law, and influenced by Cesare Beccaria, he in turn influenced both British and American social policy on many matters, including penology. Jeremy Bentham was a wellspring of utilitarian ideas. Under the influence of Bentham, the British built the "panopticon" prison, in which a central guard station and cells in tiers around this central "hub" allowed the guards to look into all the cells, and thus fewer guards could monitor the behavior of the prisoners.

Bentham also recommended sentences calculated to fit the crime, and established six rules for punishment:

1. Punishment should be designed to outweigh the advantages of crime.

2. The more severe the offense, the more a scaled, increasingly severe is justified.

3. Punishment should move people to choose lesser criminal options, if it cannot discourage them from crime altogether (to steal to meet one's needs rather than to murder or rob).

4. Each offense should have its own, unique punishment, appropriate to the character and the gain of the offense (a punishment to fit the crime).

5. Punishment should be no more than that minimally necessary to achieve deterrence; excessive punishment is needless cruelty.

6. The usual penalty designed with general deterrence in mind, but sentences calculated with circumstances added in.

Andrew Jackson: Andrew Jackson (1767-1845) was the seventh president of the United States (serving 1829-1837) and first modern "democrat." The United States had not seen a populist of his like again in national office until the election of Jimmy Carter in 1980. He was a back-woods man, Indian fighter, war hero, and rabble-rouser of a politician. He won the popular vote but not the majority of the electoral college, losing the presidency in 1824. He won it in 1828 and again in 1832.

Jackson's greatest contribution to public affairs was the institutionalization of the spoils system in American government. The patronage appointment was not just the norm for this age, it was viewed as the expression of a political ideal. At the national level Andrew Jackson had announced that the spoils system was to be official government policy when he came to office in 1829, but he certainly was not the first politician to see it this way. In New York City in 1816, the city watchmen who preceded the police were political appointees of the prior Federalist administration and went out with the party that named them (Richardson, 1970: 21).

en.wikipedia.org

Andrew Jackson was the seventh president of the United States and an advocate of the common man. He brought ordinary citizens into public service, expanding participation in government, but he also justified partisan selection of political loyalists as a key criterion for public service appointment.

What Jackson did with his announcements on the spoils system was provide it with an ideological rationalization. As an advocate of egalitarianism, Jackson operated from the assumption that a common man of normal intellect could perform a government job as well as any aristocratic Federalist holdover. If the new, politically loyal appointee could perform as well as the outgoing incumbent, then no harm could come to government by the exchange. In this period, which Frederick C. Mosher (1968: 61-63) has described as "government by the common man," the spoils system was viewed as an integral part of the democratic process. President Jackson was careful to select educated and capable men for his appointments, aware in practice that not just anyone could do the work of government. However, not all those who followed his words also followed his example (Mosher, 1968: 62-63):

> Jackson's view of public office as a central tenet of an egalitarian philosophy nevertheless became a symbol and guide for his colleagues and successors, not only at the national level of government but in the states and local units as well. Among the consequences of the spoils system, run rampant, were: the periodic chaos which attended changes in administration during most of the nineteenth century; the popular association of public administration with politics and incompetence; the growing conflicts between executive and legislature over appointments [. . .]; the development of political machines in states, counties, and cities (where most government actually was); and the rise to pre-eminence of lawyer-politicians in every branch of government and at every level.

The patronage system of appointments introduced dramatic personnel changes to the civil service. Experienced appointees of one administration were discharged en masse to make room for the untrained followers of the new administration (Richardson, 1974: 35-41). An extreme example of this flux was Cincinnati Police Department, which saw 239 of its 295 officers depart in 1880 and 246 of its 305 police discharged in 1886 as the political fortunes rotated the parties in and out of power (Walker, 1977: 9).

Some of the patronage-induced changes were not as negative. Ethnic and racial minorities secured some government positions through political alliances, making those government administrations more representative of the communities they served (Walker, 1980: 61). The numerous advantages prolonged the patronage system well into the twentieth century, but its problems already were well known and led to numerous calls for its reform. Among those seeing both the pluses and minuses of patronage appointments was Woodrow Wilson. To this day we retain some patronage appointments in government, although usually only at the upper-managerial levels.

Robert Owen: Robert Owen (1771-1858) was a Welsh industrialist who sought to create a utopian workers' community around his textile mills. A social reformer, he hoped to create an ideal employment climate. Thus, he previewed what was to become, a century later, the Human Relations School of industrial relations. He saw his workers as "vital machines" who had to be cared for with the same attention given other machines (Ott, 1989: 11). The mill town of New Lanark, Scotland, was his experimental utopian town. In cooperation with fellow investors, Quaker William Allen and social theorist Jeremy Bentham, he provided his workers with a wide range of employment benefits and services and a fair wage. He used productivity data to show that these extra expenses paid dividends in employee stability and high productivity.

en.wikipedia.org

Robert Owen was a nineteenth-century British industrialist and advocate for the "vital engines" of commerce, his workforce. By the criteria of the times, he paid well and provided many benefits to workers and their families.

Owen's book, *A New View of Society* (1813), presented his ideas to the American public in 1825, and his concepts were copied in the building of many mill towns, including New Harmony, Indiana.

Alexander Maconochie: Alexander Maconochie (1787-1860), a naval officer and well-respected geographer, became a penal reformer later in his life. Maconochie served in the Royal Navy, attaining the rank of captain. In 1833 he was named the Professor of Geography at the University of London. His interest and knowledge of the Pacific took him to Australia in 1836.

In 1840 he was named to be the superintendent of the penal colony on Norfolk Island. Conditions there were brutal, and he initiated humane reforms. Maconochie established a system of sentence reduction earned by good behavior. He was replaced in 1844, and many of his reforms were ended (*Gazetteer for Scotland*, 2005).

Sir Robert Peel: Sir Robert Peel (1788-1859) was a British politician who put together the political compromise that became the model for modern policing: the London Metropolitan Police of 1829. Municipal policing is a relatively new concept when viewed against the total expanse of human history. It was a social reform as much as it was a practical response to the serious crime problems of that city. It offered all of the advantages of the traditional decentralized English social control system, while matching the efficiency of the military-model state police forces of the continent in combating crime and disorder. Peel was the Tory Home Secretary who implemented this social innovation. The Tories, the English conservatives,

Sir Robert Peel was Home Secretary and later Prime Minister of Great Britain. He led the reform of law enforcement in 1829 that resulted in the "new model" London Metropolitan Police.

felt threatened by the unrest and expectations of the proletarian, proto-Chartist lower class (Dawson, 1930: 352-354), but they also had to deal with suspicion of government inherent in the Utilitarian doctrines of the rising English middle class. The leading Utilitarians, Jeremy Bentham, Edwin Chadwick, and Patrick Colquhoun, provided the compromise solution that a Tory government could accept: a degree of local control over law enforcement was maintained, under Home Office regulation, and a strong military-style law enforcement organization was formed. The English ideals of liberty were unthreatened, while the Tories acquired a police force strong enough to bring order to London (Critchley, 1972: 49-50). It was a compromise in the best English political tradition.

Like any new idea, the police force experienced problems from its inception, some of which continue to this day. The first police constables were recruited from the ranks of the existing parish night watches and various foot and horse patrols. Although considerable effort was directed toward the selection of suitable men, many of the first recruits were not fit to be police. In the early years there were charges of drunkenness, brutality, spying, and other forms of political tyranny (Critchley, 1972: 52-55). The Home Secretary anticipated many of the problems and drafted instructions and regulations for his new police force (Peel, 1829, quoted in Critchley, 1972: 52-52):

> It should be understood at the onset, that the object to be attained is the prevention of crime.
>
> To this great end every effort of the police is to be directed. The security of person and property and the preservation of a police establishment will thus be better effected than the detection and punishment of the offender after he has succeeded in committing crime...
>
> He [the constable] will be civil and obliging to all people of every rank and class.
>
> He must be particularly cautious not to interfere idly or unnecessarily in order to make a display of his authority; when required to act, he will do so with decision and boldness; ...

He must remember that there is no qualification so indispensable to a police-officer as a perfect command of temper, never suffering himself to be moved in the slightest degree by any language or threats that may be used; ...

In the novelty of the present establishment, particular care is to be taken that the constables of the police do not form false notions of their duties and powers.

Thus, the new model police had features that were unknown, when brought together in one agency, to previous law enforcement arrangements. These police were:

1. Selected for merit, being moral, able to read and write.

2. Paid fixed salaries in a time when most still earned fees.

3. Tax-supported, with both municipal and national funds.

4. Municipal in orientation and obligations; but quasi-municipal in their control, the Home Office having a regulatory role.

5. Patrolled in geographic beats, out among the citizens.

6. Uniformed, but not in the Army style.

7. Without firearms, carrying only wooden batons.

8. Responsible to every citizen equally.

9. Recruited from working classes, rather than elites.

10. Apolitical, unable even to vote initially.

Charles Babbage: Charles Babbage (1792-1871) was the inventor of a precursor of the computer. He called it his "difference engine," but never completed a successful prototype. He attempted to apply new technologies to reduce the labor intensity of early industrial work. He argued that industrialists should evaluate the utility of machines and the division of labor, using criteria of the quality of output and the costs of production (Swade, 2001). He wrote his views into *On the Economy of Machinery and Manufactures* (1832), which previewed most of the ideas now associated with "scientific management," for his essay "On the Division of Labour" Babbage's computer design was built in 1991 and worked as Babbage supposed it would (Swade, 1993: 86-91).

en.wikipedia.org

Charles Babbage was a nineteenth-century British industrialist and inventor who advocated using labor-saving machines to improve both the efficiency of organizations and to reduce the physical demands on his laborers. He also designed a precursor to the calculator, which he called the "difference engine."

Augusta Ada Byron King was a nineteenth-century British associate of Charles Babbage who helped him develop the algorithms for his "difference engine"—in essence, the first person to develop computer software. She also helped finance his research.

Augusta Ada Byron King: Widely known in modern times as Ada Lovelace, King (1815-1852), the Countess of Lovelace and daughter of the famous poet, Lord Byron, is recognized as one of the earliest computer programmers. Lovelace applied her wealth and influence to support early work into calculating machines. Her sponsorship of the work of Charles Babbage's "difference engines" went far beyond financial investment, for she was well known for her mathematical skills and mastery of symbolic logic, which she directed to computer applications, translating and annotating works on the subject (Crawford, 1983: 241-242). She acquired her interest in mathematics from her mother, Anne Isabella Mil'Banke, Baroness Wentworth (1792-1860), who was a recognized mathematician in her own right. The computer language "Ada," formerly used by the U.S. Department of Defense, is so named in her honor (Uglow, 1982: 288-289).

John Augustus: John Augustus (1785-1859) is credited with introducing probation to American courts. In 1841, he posted a bail bond for a criminal suspect and took responsibility for that person. He used his legal control over that man to guide him toward reform and keep him out of prison. In the next two decades he similarly bailed out and tried to reform about 2,000 people. Prior to John Augustus it was common for sheriffs to discharge offenders into the custody of citizens for involuntary servitude, selling convict labor. In the South it was a discredited way of reconstituting slavery. In 1878, the Commonwealth of Massachusetts passed a probation statute making official what Augustus and his successor, Rufus Cook, had been doing for decades. By 1920 every state had a similar system.

Elam Lynds: Elam Lynds (1784-1855) was the first warden of the Auburn, New York, prison, and creator of the "Auburn system" of correctional practice (named after the 1816 Auburn, New York, prison) (Pettigrove, 1910: 31-34). The Auburn system was characterized by the "tier" or "congregate" arrangement. Its rows and tiers of cells were used for solitary and silent confinement, mixed with periods of closely supervised labor and supervised interaction among inmates (congregation).

Today Lynds is criticized as a harsh warden, but for his times he was a progressive reformer. Only troublesome inmates were kept in total silence and isolation all day. Hard work, controlled interaction, and silence were its key features, and as a result it is often referred to as the **"silent system"** (Reid, 1999: 243). Violations were met with severe physical punishment, usually whippings. At Auburn in 1821 prisoners were "classified" by the character of their crimes and segregated within the penal institution. Dangerous offenders were in perpetual isolation, while less dangerous offenders were given some limited social time. Others were to attend workshops where they labored in total silence (Reid, 1999: 244).

Dorothea Lynde Dix: Dorothea Dix (1802-1887) was an American social reformer deeply concerned with the welfare of the insane (Tiffany 1890). She toured the country and lobbied for the establishment of humane mental institutions in the states. As a result, a number of states opened such institutions, and those existing institutions improved the treatment of inmates. During the American Civil War, Dix was the Superintendent of Army Nurses. She used that post to extend care to Confederate prisoners in Union prison camps. She directed some of her efforts to improving prison conditions for conventional offenders, and also worked to improve the treatment of people with various handicaps, such as the blind, the deaf, and the mute.

en.wikipedia.org

Dorothea Dix was a nineteenth-century American social reformer and advocate for the mentally ill and the imprisoned. She used her social standing and position to bring about major reforms in the way inmates were treated and cared for.

Dix's efforts at prison reform were in part inspired by Elizabeth Frye, a noted prison reformer of the early nineteenth century. Because of the connections between insanity and criminality, many of the people she helped were identified as criminally insane. On a visit to a local jail in Boston in 1841, she was teaching a Sunday School class for a group of incarcerated women. She then visited other parts of the jail, including the areas where insane in inmates were chained to the walls. What she saw there led her to begin her reform campaigns on behalf of inmates and the mentally ill.

Zebulon Reed: Zebulon Reed (1827-1920) was another reform-oriented warden. Located at the prison in Elmira, New York, he instituted the Elmira model, which offered inmates the hope of parole for good behavior and cooperation and provided training and educational opportunities to inmates. The Elmira institution was an industrial facility that used slave labor, but it did provide job skills and minimal education to its inmates. As such, it was a major reform in its time (the 1870s through the 1920s). It may be that Reed got the idea from Maconochie and his publicist and supporter, Sir Walter Crofton (Reid, 1999: 245-246): they had recommended rewards, population size control, progressive restriction reduction, and parole eligibility for well-behaving inmates, and implemented such ideas at Elmira both to control the inmate population and to achieve moral rehabilitation of inmates.

en.wikipedia.org

John Stuart Mill was a nineteenth-century British political philosopher who, like Thomas Jefferson, believed in limited government and minimal governmental regulation of human activity, except when that activity was harmful to others.

John Stuart Mill: As Jacksonian Democracy began to supplant Jeffersonian idealism, the government was playing an ever-larger role in people's lives. In Britain, as in the United States, there were individuals who found this objectionable and called for the restoration of the earlier values. As the author of the essay "On Liberty" (1859), John Stuart Mill (1806-1873) expressed many of the views of the Benthamites (Utilitarians) and the nineteenth-century liberals and radicals of Great Britain. His advocacy of limited government was not unlike that favored by Jefferson. He was not an anarchist, as some imply, but believed that governments were obliged to act in some situations and ought be constrained in others. The art of political science was sorting one from the other:

The object of this essay is to assert one very simple principle, as entitled to govern absolutely the dealings of society with the individual in the way of compulsion and control . . . That principle is that the sole end for which mankind are warranted, individually or collectively, in interfering with the liberty of action of any of their number is self-protection. That the only purpose for which power can be rightfully exercised over any member of a civilized community, against his will, is to prevent harm to others. His own good, either physical or moral, is not a sufficient warrant (Mill, 1859: 13).

Human liberty was not without some reasonable restriction. There was justification for requiring people to act in the best interests of others when such actions were not to their own disinterest. "A person may cause evil to others not only by his actions but by his inaction, and in either case he is justly accountable to them for the injury" (Mill, 1859: 15). He wrote, "The only freedom which deserves the name is that of pursuing our own good in our own way, so long as we do not attempt to deprive others of theirs or impede their efforts to obtain it. Each is the proper guardian of his own health, whether bodily or mental and spiritual. Mankind are greater gainers by suffering each other to live as seems good to themselves than by compelling each to live as seems good to the rest" (Mill, 1859: 17). Mill was a true nineteenth-century liberal, and a Jeffersonian idealist. As Mill aged, he became more socialistic in his viewpoints. He did not quite abandon his earlier advocacy of classical liberalism, but became more interested in helping the disadvantaged, especially women, and began to argue in favor of governmental interventions to reverse discriminatory patterns in law and custom.

Woodrow Wilson: Best known as the president of the United States from 1913 through 1921, Woodrow Wilson (1856-1924) also was governor of New Jersey, and before that, a college professor at Princeton. He was the United States' only Ph.D. president (other than honorary doctorates). As a professor of government, he helped carve out the field of public administration within political science and political philosophy.

His major scholarly work was an article, "The Study of Administration," printed in 1887 in *Political Science Quarterly*. In it he wrote: "It is the object of administrative study to discover, first, what government can properly and successfully do, and, secondly, how it can do these proper things with the utmost efficiency..." He argued for the separation of routine administrative functions of government, which he felt should be assigned to career, merit-selected, civil service employ-

en.wikipedia.org

Woodrow Wilson was the twenty-eighth president of the United States and an advocate of civil service reform. He believed that patronage appointments should be limited to policymaking positions only, with all other public servants selected primarily for merit.

ees, from the political and policymaking positions of elective and appointed government officials (the politically loyal leadership).

Roscoe Pound: Educated at Harvard Law School, Nathan Roscoe Pound (1870-1964) practiced law in Nebraska, then returned to Harvard Law to teach (1910–1916) and then serve as its dean (1916–1936). He wrote several books, including *Introduction to the Philosophy of Law* (1922), *Criminal Justice in America* (1930), *Contemporary Juristic Theory* (1940), *Social Control through Law* (1942), and *The Lawyer from Antiquity to Modern Times* (1953). He is credited with bringing social sciences and law together as "sociological jurisprudence." He and future Supreme Court Justice Felix Frankfurter applied content analysis to measure newspaper coverage of crime, and discovered that crime waves were more hype than substance (Pound and Frankfurter, 1922).

Luther Halsey Gulick III: As discussed in Chapter 1, Luther Gulick (1892-1992) was an American author on public administration. He earned his doctorate at Columbia University in 1920 and upon completion of his studies joined the New York Bureau of Municipal Research (renamed in 1921 as the Institute of Public Administration). He taught at Columbia for several years and then returned to the Institute of Public Administration to be its director. He was a prolific author. He wrote *The Metropolitan Problem and American Ideas* (1962) soon after he retired, but his most famous contribution to managerial sciences was the 1937 article that contributed the term POSDCORB to the managerial vocabulary.

Summary

The brilliant minds and carefully considered ideas of a great many men and women in the distant past have been applied to the question of how best to manage a public service or criminal justice organization or how to best provide criminal justice services to the public. Our modern approaches to these issues are rooted in their contributions: merit selection of public servants; the very notion of government officials as public servants and not rulers; the humane treatment of both workers and the people in custody; the intelligent application of labor-saving technologies and principles, such as the division of labor; and new and better ways of providing public services, such as the London police model or the panopticon prison, are all early innovations still with is today. Contemporary criminal justice managers have the capacity and the duty to propose new approaches and bring innovations into the modern criminal justice workplace, just as these past reformers and leaders did.

Learning Objectives

Upon finishing this chapter you should be able to do the following:

▶ 1. Identify the three intellectual sources of the ideas upon which the American public service stands.

▶ 2. Identify three American presidents whose ideas contributed significantly to the development of the American civil service.

▶ 3. Identify leading reformers in policing, corrections, and jurisprudence in Europe and the United States and know their specific contributions.

▶ 4. Identify leading managerial theorists whose ideas have been incorporated into the American criminal justice system.

IMPORTANT TERMS AND NAMES

- John Augustus
- Charles Babbage
- Cesare Beccaria
- Jeremy Bentham
- bureaucracy
- civil servants
- division of labor
- Dorothea Dix
- Luther Gulick
- John Howard
- Andrew Jackson
- Thomas Jefferson
- Augusta Ada Byron King
- Elam Lynds

- Alexander Maconochie
- merit selection
- John Stuart Mill
- Robert Owen
- Sir Robert Peel
- Plato
- Roscoe Pound
- Zebulon Reed
- Cardinal Richelieu
- silent system
- Adam Smith
- Socrates
- utilitarianism
- Woodrow Wilson

References and Supplemental Sources

Babbage, Charles (1835). *On the Economy of Machinery and Manufactures*, 4th ed. London: C. Knight.

Beccaria, Cesare (1764). *On Crimes and Punishments* (original title in Italian, Dei Delitti e Delle Pene).

Zebulon Reed (1912). *Fifty Years of Prison Service*. New York: Charities Publications Committee.

Carey, John A. (1981). *Judicial Reform in France before the Revolution of 1789*. Boston: Harvard University Press.

Crawford, Anne (ed.) (1983). *The Europa Biographical Dictionary of British Women*. London: Europa.

Critchley, T.A. (1972). *A History of Police in England and Wales*. Montclair, NJ: Patterson Smith.

Durant, Will, and Ariel Durant (1961). *The Story of Civilization, Part VII: The Age of Reason Begins*. New York: Simon and Schuster.

Gazetteer for Scotland (2005). The Gazetteer for Scotland ©1995-2005, the Robertson Trust, Royal Scottish Geographical Society, Institute of Geography, University of Edinburgh. See http://www.geo.ed.ac.uk/scotgaz/people/famousfirst733.html

Howard, John (1777). *The State of the Prisons*.

Kim, Eugene Eric, and Betty Alexandra Toole (1999). "Ada and the First Computer," *Scientific American*, 280(5): 76-81.

Mill, John Stuart (1859) [1956]. *On Liberty*. Indianapolis: Bobbs-Merrill.

Moriarty, Don (1986). "Adam Smith: America's 'Adopted' Founding Father," *The Constitution* (November 1986).

Mosher, Frederick C. (1968). *Democracy and the Public Service*. New York: Oxford University Press.

Michael Nelson (1982). "A Short, Ironic History of American National Bureaucracy," *The Journal of Politics*, 44(3): 747-778.

Owen, Robert (1813). *A New View of Society*.

Owen, Robert (1825). *A New View of Society* [first American edition].

Pettigrove, Frederick G. (1910). "State Prisons of the United States under Separate and Congregate Systems," pp. 27-67 in *Penal and Reformatory Institutions, Volume 2: Corrections and Prevention*, edited by Charles Richmond Henderson. Philadelphia: Press of William F. Fell, Inc.

Plato (1961). *The Republic*, translated by Paul Shorey, in *The Collected Dialogues of Plato*, edited by Edith Hamilton and Huntington Cairns. Princeton, NJ: Princeton University Press.

Pound, Roscoe, and Felix Frankfurter (1922). *Criminal Justice in Cleveland*. Cleveland: The Cleveland Foundation.

Reid, Sue Titus (1999). *Crime and Criminology*, 9th ed. Boston: McGraw-Hill.

Richardson, James F. (1970). *The New York Police*. New York: Oxford University Press.

Richardson, James F. (1974). *Urban Police in the United States*. Port Washington, NY: Kennikat Press, National University Publications.

Richelieu, Armand Jean du Plessis, Duke and Cardinal (1947). *Testament Politique, edition critique*, edited and annotated by Louis Andre. Paris: Robert Laffont.

Richelieu, Armand Jean du Plessis, Duke and Cardinal (1961). *The Political Testament of Cardinal Richelieu*, translated by Henry Bertram Hill. Madison, WI: University of Wisconsin Press.

Smith, Adam (1776) [1937]. *The Wealth of Nations*. New York: Random House.

Socrates (1992). Article #1, "Socrates Discovers Generic Management" [an extract from Xenophon], Article 1 in Shafritz and Ott, *Classics of Organization Theory*, 3rd ed., 1992. Pacific Grove, CA: Brooks/Cole.

Swade, Doron D. (1993). "Redeeming Charles Babbage's Mechanical Computer," *Scientific American*, 268(2): 86-91.

Swade, Doron D. (2001). *The Difference Engine: Charles Babbage and the Quest to Build the First Computer*. New York: Viking.

Tiffany, Francis (1890). *The Life of Dorothea Lynde Dix*. Boston: The Riverside Press.

Uglow, Jennifer S., editor (1982). "Augusta Ada Byron King," pp. 288-289 in *International Dictionary of Women's Biography*, New York: Continuum.

Walker, Samuel (1977). *A Critical History of Police Reform*. Lexington, MA: Lexington Books.

Walker, Samuel (1980). *Popular Justice: A History of American Criminal Justice*. New York: Oxford University Press.

Weber, Max (1922). *Economy and Society*, 2 volumes, edited by Guenther Roth and Claus Wittich. Berkeley, CA: University of California Press.

Wilson, Woodrow (1887). "The Study of Administration," *Political Science Quarterly*, 2(2): 197-222.

4
Leading in Criminal Justice

"Leading" is the first of the "LODESTAR" functions of every public service manager. Leadership is a fine art, not a science. Everyone who studies it can ascertain its key ingredients and components, but knowing the right mix of these ingredients is an art. Just as knowing the materials and techniques of painting does not assure the production of great art, knowing the methods and techniques of leadership does not guarantee one will be a great leader, or even a good one. Leading involves giving direction and supervision. It requires authority, and in criminal justice organizations, an office from which to exercise it.

Leadership Selection

Selecting a criminal justice manager in our democratic system of public service can be done in several ways. Each has its appropriate place, sometimes selected by custom and sometimes by sophisticated thought and reasoning. However derived, the decision to appoint a criminal justice manager to lead a criminal justice organization will occur via one of two basic approaches: (1) direct election, or (2) appointment

Elections are conducted in accordance with the laws of the political entity or the by-laws of the public service agency using elective selection. Decision by election can require:

- unanimity, total agreement of all entitled to vote;

- a weighted majority, some percentage greater than half;

- a simple majority, any number more than half of the total; or

- a plurality, the greatest number of votes, but not necessarily the majority cast.

Popular election, usually by plurality or simple majority, is used to select some of the key managers in the criminal justice system: sheriffs, many clerks of court, some judges, district attorneys, police commissioners, and directors of public safety. In most cases these are the chief executive positions within the organization.

Most managers in public service are not elected, however. They are appointed. **Appointments** can occur through several criteria:

- **Performance-based merit selection** of the best qualified, or of one fully qualified, using rational, performance-based criteria.

- **Nonmerit selection,** employing noncompetitive criteria that are not directly performance-based, such as political affiliation, kinship, friendship, contributions and donations (and even bribes), settlement of debts and outstanding obligations, racial or sexual preference, etc.

- **Combined merit/nonmerit criteria;** i.e., selection of one of those fully qualified by additional non-merit criteria (the ideal of affirmative action programs).

Managers in criminal justice are expected to be both leaders and policymakers. Those who are elected to office or serve as political appointees can expect to stay in or lose their positions in direct consequence to the quality and effectiveness of their policy-making abilities.

This was one of the key points made by Woodrow Wilson (1887) in his advocacy of the division between politics and administration: the people who do politics (elected officials and their personal appointees) are subject to the approval or disapproval of the people via the ballot box. However, administrators, in Woodrow Wilson's ideal, are to be generally immune from the harsh realities of elective politics, safe within the civil service system.

Yet these civil servants often also make policy. Ought they not also be held accountable to the public via elective political processes? The answer he gave is "no," and the reason is that these civil service administrators are making "second-order policy," designed only to carry out the "first-order policy" of those elected and the patronage officials who are subject to the ballot.

Chester Barnard discussed the concept of "executive work" (1938): those tasks the leader performs that are not the functional work of the organization. In criminal justice contexts, a police chief does not usually investigate crimes, direct traffic, or write motor vehicle violation tickets. He or she has duties that are quite different from "the rank and file" of the organization, Barnard's "organization work." Barnard observes that executives do a fair measure of "nonexecutive" work, but it is not their *raison d'etre* (the justification for their employment). In his essay he is offering yet another answer to Luther Gulick's question, slightly modified, to "What is the work of the executive?" His answer: maintaining a system of cooperative effort (coordinating), organizational communication (reporting), defining the scheme of organization (organizing), recruiting and dealing with personnel matters (staffing), including acquiring their loyalty and influencing them (leading), and formulating purposes and objectives for the organization (deciding, including planning).

First-order policymaking includes those policies that set the major goals and objectives of the organization, also called primary policymaking. **Second-order policymaking**, also called **secondary policymaking**, includes those policies that are made to implement the major goals and objectives of the organization. For example, the Congress or the state legislature will pass legislation that creates a new program and outlines in general terms what the goals and objectives of that program are. The president or governor and the top cabinet officials then task and organize their agencies to create implementation mechanisms to carry out these mandates, clarifying these goals and objectives. Setting and refining these goals and objectives are political first-order policy matters.

The manager of the federal or state agency assigned to carry out the program mandated by the Congress or state legislature will establish specific policies and procedures to implement the program. These will be in compliance with the legislated goals and objectives; hence, this is second-order policymaking.

Attributes of Successful Leaders

The Traits of a Leader: Several authorities have developed trait lists of attributes that they feel are needed to be an effective leader. This is the *laundry-list approach* that offers a compilation of worthwhile traits. Many such lists have been proposed. For example, Joseph Massie (1987: 102) offered the following traits:

- age
- maturity
- extroversion
- intelligence
- verbal skills
- physical bearing
- attractiveness
- height
- charisma
- education
- popularity
- decisiveness
- aggressiveness

General Mark Clark was a distinguished army commander in World War II, with a long record of public service after the war. Sam Souryal (1995: 106-107) presented General Clark's list and has offered some other thoughts on the list Clark proposed:

- confidence
- energy
- timing
- clarity
- tenacity
- boldness
- concern
- morality
- faith

Rensis Likert is a social psychologist, researcher, and management theorist who has given leadership serious study and consideration. Likert's list takes the approach of a social psychologist with a strong interest in management research (Souryal, 1995: 107):

- unselfishness
- sympathy
- cooperation
- enthusiasm
- intellect
- interest in workers
- friendliness
- morality
- planning ability

The **Leader Behavior Descriptive Questionnaire (LBQD)** was developed at Ohio State University as a project undertaken by the Ohio State Leadership Studies Office, then directed by Carroll L. Shartle. The LBDQ provides a work group the opportunity to describe the behavior of their leader in any kind of organization. The primary condition is that the subordinates routinely have observed their leader in action (Fisher College of Business, 2008). The LBQD allows a researcher to examine the leadership traits workers use to evaluate their leaders. The questionnaire is available for nonprofit use by any organization that can make use of such information. Two dimensions emerge:

> **Considerations:** These include such traits as trust, respect, support, rapport, and communication.

> **Initiating Structures:** The factors defining and structuring the leadership role, including active or passive approaches to planning, directing, and scheduling work activities.

When employees are asked what they like, admire, or appreciate in their managers, they cite certain important qualities:

- patience
- kindness
- wisdom
- trust
- virtue
- knowledge
- empathy
- self-control

Task Analysis: Another approach to determining what makes a good leader involves "task analysis." What skills must the leader master to be effective? Robert Katz (1974) places emphasis on three areas of the **skills of a leader**:

- technical skills
- human relations skills, including empathy, tolerance of ambiguity, and the ability to work within a team
- conceptual skills

Four ideas about leadership in public service organizations have emerged from this skill-focused approach to leadership (Klofas, Stojkovic, and Kalinich 1990: 124-125):

- It is a process for accomplishing organizational goals;
- It can be learned;
- It is a group process, to include:
    - (1) legitimate request,
    - (2) instrumental compliance,
    - (3) coercion,
    - (4) rational persuasion,
    - (5) rational faith,
    - (6) inspirational appeal,
    - (7) indoctrination,
    - (8) information distortion,
    - (9) situational engineering,
    - (10) personal identification,
    - (11) decision identification.

Within the criminal justice system, it is inherently political.

Leadership and Managerial Styles: A third approach deals with **managerial style**, the manner in which a manager operates. Much of the past literature on managerial styles recognizes three major variants

(Souryal, 1985: 71; 1995: 104-106), authoritarian, democratic, and laissez-faire. These are defined or explained first in terms of the level of control the manager seeks to impose over the manager's subordinates, and the degree of concern for the subordinates that the manager reveals, with two major variables we can express as *involvement* and *control*. In this discussion we will introduce a fourth type to supersede the inappropriate "authoritarian" classification.

Authoritarian leadership reduces discretion and reduces the input of the workers, thus maximizing control. Some authors refer to this style as *autocratic*, and some do not view it as negatively as do others. Indeed, it is best to divide the original authoritarian style into two variants, *autocratic* and *despotic*, so that the negative aspects of the style can be distinguished from the positives.

Democratic leadership gives up some control by giving the workers significant say in the decisionmaking of the agency. Input is welcome, and subordinates are encouraged to contribute ideas. This democratic approach seeks to build a team and provide for the collective interests of the members of the work team by giving them genuine input into agency policies and practices. To acquire input, this type of manager is skilled at consensus measuring and valuing the inputs of others. Being both involved in and concerned with the lives of others, the democratic manager can become a "busybody" with a kindly disposition.

The *laissez-faire* manager also relinquishes much control over his or her subordinates, but differs in subtle ways from the democratic manager. The laissez-faire model allows the workers much autonomy, but without team building. In it the concern for the needs and welfare of the workers is not an important issue for the manager, as each worker is expected to attend to his or her individual needs. Either the laissez-faire manager has no concern for these group interests or feels he or she simply has no business becoming involved in them. This style of manager will provide guidance by passive example, the manager being neither directly involved in nor showing concern with the lives of others. This manager will stress autonomy, liberty, and freedom of action.

Autocratic managers will maintain firm control and be comfortable with the exercise of their authority and powers, but they also reveal a genuine concern for the well-being of those they supervise. An excellent example of the autocratic manager is the traditional drill sergeant at the police academy. An order-giving, controlling leader, he or she is very much interested in the welfare and the progress of the trainees under his or her control. The autocratic manager is a "bossy busybody." Frequently—and often erroneously—associated with the Army and Marines, this order-giving, demanding, close-supervision style requires a great deal of commitment and involvement in the work output of others, thus showing concern for the lives and needs of those workers, though less than for the mission or outcome.

The *despotic* manager is the fourth type of manager who may be encountered in the workplace. This is the self-serving, controlling leader who shows no interest or concern in the well-being of the workers and rejects any input from them. This manager is quite different from the autocratic manager who does demonstrate concern for the needs of his or her subordinates (Carey, 2004). The stereotype of the cruel and corrupt prison warden so often seen in prison films is a version of the despotic manager. Control takes precedence over the interests of both prisoners and the prison staff in this stereotype. Ruling by decrees, and never showing an interest in the personal consequences of those decrees, the despotic tyrant seeks total compliance with his or her directions, but has little concern with the workers or their problems in complying.

Authority versus Power versus Influence

Around the time Luther Gulick introduced us to POSDCORB (1937), *leadership* in public service in general and criminal justice in particular was one and the same with *command*, simply the exercise of power. For this reason the "D" in POSDCORB is *directing*. Telling people what to do and expecting them to obey is out of place in most public service work settings. Instead, the leader is expected to motivate the workers to achieve common aims. Thus, the modern leader selects among leadership styles based on factors such as subordinate characteristics, preferences for or distaste for authoritarianism, locus of control, abilities of the leader and the workers, the formal authority and disciplinary system, and work-group dynamics.

In reality, there is a *continuum of leadership behaviors*, ranging from boss-centered to subordinate centered leadership. General George S. Patton once said, "Never tell people how to do things. Tell them what to do and they will surprise you with their ingenuity." Robert Tannenbaum and Warren Schmidt, in a frequently cited and reprinted *Harvard Business Review* article (1958; 1973), described this continuum as follows:

- Manager makes decisions and announces them.

- Manager "sells" decisions to subordinates.

- Manager presents ideas and invites questions.

- Manager presents tentative decisions and accepts ideas from subordinates.

- Manager presents problems, seeks suggestions, and makes decisions based on all inputs.

- Manager defines limits, supplies key data, and asks subordinates to make the decision.

- Manager permits subordinates to operate on their own, within broad, general limits defined by the manager or their position descriptions.

Which Represents What Style? Tannenbaum and Schmidt conducted interviews with a group of highly effective and successful managers working in closely related fields. Each was asked about his or her managerial and decision-making styles. These are some of the statements they collected (1958; 1973):

> "I put most problems into my group's hands and leave it to them to carry the ball from there. I serve merely as a catalyst, mirroring back people's thoughts and feelings so that they can better understand them."

> "Its foolish to make decisions oneself on matters that affect people. I always talk things over with my subordinates, but make it clear to them that I'm the one who has to have the final say."

> "Once I have decided on a course of action, I do my best to sell my ideas to my employees."

> "I'm being paid to lead. If I let a lot of other people make the decisions I should be making, then I'm not worth my salt."

> "I can't waste time calling meetings. Someone has to call the shots around here, and I think it should be me."

True leadership requires the willingness of subordinates to accept authority and to follow the example of or decisions of the nominal leader. So why do people obey a leader? Max Weber undertook to answer that question.

Authority or Coercion: All people will obey if sufficiently coerced. This is one expression of "power." In some cases, that must suffice as a basis for compliance, but it is not cooperation. People will follow willingly and rationally under some circumstances, especially when they accept the "authority" and "legitimacy" of the leader. According to Max Weber, authority has three ideal types:

Charismatic: The "natural leader," emotion-inspiring, confidence-inspiring. Weber, a German, once described American municipal administration as "Caesarist" (1919: 84). A Caesar comes to power by wide popular support, and then rules absolutely.

Traditional: By custom, a king because he is a king's son, the occupant of a status because that status is a leadership status regardless of the incumbent. Ascription!

Rational-Legal: A person selected because of his or her technical competence, or other merit principles—as enforced by "legal" procedural selection, relying on credentials.

In actuality every leader shows aspects of all these types of authority. A police chief, warden, or parks director is chosen by rational-legal civil service or merit selection criteria. The job title of "police chief," "warden," or "director" is a traditional office of leadership, but the person ideally selected has "something extra," a charismatic appeal that makes him or her stand out from other qualified applicants.

In *Complex Organizations* (1961), Amitai Etzioni offered another approach to understanding power in organizations:

1. coercion: the threatening aspect of leadership

2. remuneration: the rewards that the leader can bestow

3. normative: the commitment that both the leader and the subordinate have toward complying with the rules of organization, society, or the law

Applying Managerial Styles: Early in the twentieth century, leaders were expected to be controlling, autocratic managers, giving orders, supervising closely, and using coercive measures to ensure discipline. By the latter part of the century, other approaches were in favor. Among the leading voices in the first approach were Henri Fayol, Frederick Taylor, Luther Gulick, and Max Weber.

Henri Fayol: Henri Fayol (1841-1925) was a French engineer and industrialist who was the leading proponent in Europe of the ideas now known as "principles of scientific management." His ideas arrived late to the United States. The English translation of his major work, *General and Industrial Management*, was released in the United States in 1949 (translation by Constance Storrs). Fayol's ideas preceded the translation, though, and he was an influence—even if only indirectly—on the rise of American scientific management concepts at the start of the twentieth century.

Fayol's principles included the division of work, authority, discipline, unity of command, unity of direction, subordination of interests to the general interest, remuneration, centralization, "scalar chain" (established lines of authority), order, equity, personnel stability, initiative, and esprit de corps (morale). All were to reappear in the works of American advocates of scientific management, including both Frederick W. Taylor and Luther Gulick (1937), who cites Fayol directly.

en.wikipedia.org

Henri Fayol was a French engineer and advocate of "scientific management" in the workplace. His ideas were widely applied in Europe at the end of the nineteenth century, and later were carried to the United States.

Frederick W. Taylor: Known in the United States as the founder of "scientific management," Frederick Taylor (1856-1915) is best known for his *Principles of Scientific Management* (1911). He was emphatic about the use of the scientific method to observe, categorize, and quantify work as a preliminary step to better job design. His ideas led to time and motion studies, better workplace layouts, and even some engineering improvements to tools and machines.

Frederick W. Taylor was an American advocate of "scientific management" and efficiency studies applied in the industrial workplace, and later in government. His ideas influenced public service management decisively for the first half of the twentieth century.

en.wikipedia.org

Taylor offered four principles about matching workers to the workplace: (1) use empirical observations to reduce each job to its component parts, formulating discrete rules for the most efficient performance of each; (2) scientifically select workmen who are capable of doing the work for which they were hired, giving them additional training on the specifics of their employment once hired; (3) bring the employee, the technology, and the manager into cooperative harmony; but (4) divide the responsibilities of management from labor. He had observed how the workplace had become too complex for the average novice worker to know his or her job. Therefore, training was necessary. He also was aware that being a good laborer did not make one suited to being a good manager or foreman. He felt that managerial skills had to be sought out in prospective managers, just as mechanical skills had to be possessed by prospective mechanics. His approach became quite popular and his adherents called the approach "Taylorism." Essentially Taylor was treating workers as if they were interchangeable replacement parts in the machinery of commerce, industry, and government. The scientific management leader establishes and enforces performance criteria and is goal-oriented. Luther Gulick was influenced by Taylorism and approached public service leadership in much the same way (1937). August Vollmer and Orlando W. Wilson were influenced by both Taylor and Gulick as they brought scientific management ideas into policing.

Human Relations School Theorists and the Hawthorne Studies

At about the same time that Gulick was penning his mnemonic POS-DCORB and Wilson was applying the ideas of scientific management to American police management, a new approach was being developed in

American workplaces. Led by several professors of management at the Harvard Business School (among them Elton Mayo, Frederick Roethlisberger, and William J. Dixon), the "human relations school" emerged. In this approach a leader seeks to fulfill needs of employees in order to make the work satisfactory. Workers and managers were expected to communicate with one another. Order-giving was not considered good practice. As Mary Parker Follett (1868-1933) advocated, "not the face-to-face suggestion... so much as the joint study of the problem." Follett, an intellectual predecessor to the human relations school, also favored circular or reciprocal communications and advised against order-giving (1926). (See Chapter 11.) The school took shape in the lessons learned in what have become know as the Hawthorne Studies in the 1930s.

The **Hawthorne Studies** were a series of management experiments done for the Western Electric corporation. They began in the structure of the "scientific management school," but their unexpected findings gave rise to a new way of approaching management theory: the "human relations school." The key figures in this transition were Elton Mayo and Frederick J. Roethlisberger.

Elton Mayo: An Australian-born Harvard professor, Elton Mayo (1880-1949) is often credited with bringing about the shift from scientific management to human relations. He helped organize the Hawthorne Studies. His major works are *The Human Problems of an Industrial Civilization* (1933) and *The Social Problems of an Industrial Civilization* (1945). In earlier research he was able to demonstrate with scientific precision that requiring less in terms of actual time worked would result in more productivity. Workers were protected from exhaustion and thus could complete their work day as productively as they had begun it. He and Roethlisberger and Dixon, his Harvard associates in the Hawthorne Studies, later discovered the role of the workplace social environment in productivity.

F.J. Roethlisberger: F.J. Roethlisberger (1898-1974) provided the research details of the Hawthorne Studies in his 1941 book, written with William Dickson, *Management and Morale* and in *Management and the Worker* (1939). The studies were done in the 1930s, during the Depression. Workforce reductions were in progress. Other cost-cutting schemes were being considered. Western Electric commissioned a study of the impact of illumination on productivity. It was a controlled experiment. A test group whose lighting was varied upward in intensity was compared to a control group whose lighting was kept at a constant level. Productivity records were compared for both groups and contrasted with prior production records for the plant. Then lighting was reduced in the test group. In both sets of experiments production improved for both groups. Further experiments were designed. Teams were organized, and tests were made with variations in several factors, including temperature, illumination, humidity, the physical condition of workers, and workers' eating, sleeping, and rest periods. When "better" working conditions were introduced, productivity went up above the old base levels. When the experiments ended after a year and a half, and the old "bad" conditions were restored, productivity remained at the new level rather than return to the pre-experiment level.

What Was Going On? The Four Sentiments

Social—not mechanical—engineering was the key to what was discovered in the Hawthorne Studies. Four basic "sentiments" were identified from the study findings (Roethlisburger and Dickson, 1939: 522):

1. Don't bust rate

2. Don't chisel

3. Don't squeal

4. Don't be officious

The first pair set the "normative" work pace for each work group. The next two defined relationships among workers and between workers and management. If these sentiments are satisfied, a worker becomes a part of the social group of the workplace, and this keeps up morale in the workplace. "Workers are not isolated, unrelated individuals; they are social animals and should be treated as such...A human problem to be brought to a human solution requires human data and human tools" (Roethlisburger, 1941).

Abraham Maslow: Hierarchy of Human Needs

Abraham Maslow (1908-1970) was the next major contributor to the human relations school. He wrote "A Theory of Human Motivation" (1943) in *Psychological Review*, and expanded upon it in a subsequent book, *Motivation and Personality* (1954). In it he introduced a *hierarchy of human needs (basic goals)* that can be satisfied by work:

- physiological (homeostasis and appetites; food and shelter)

- safety (compulsive-obsessive neurotics lock in here)

- affiliation (close social relationships); "love"

- achievement and esteem (self-respect)

- self-actualization (need to develop one's skills and responsibilities to the maximum).

To motivate an individual the manager must find the means to associate the organizational goals with the laborers' level of needs. In the nature of human needs, we are often unaware of our own requirements and only vaguely sense that something is bothering us. The manager has to be quite perceptive to discover what it is that the worker is lacking in order to find a way to bring the worker fulfillment.

Frederick Herzberg: Motivation and Hygiene

Frederick Herzberg (1923-2000) was very much influenced by Maslow and the Hawthorne Studies. He wrote *The Motivation to Work* with Mausner and Snyderman (1959) and expanded upon "Motivation-Hygiene Theory" in *Work and the Nature of Man* (1966) wherein he discussed motivational and hygienic factors in work. He followed up on this with an often-cited article, "One More Time: How Do You Motivate Employees?" in the *Harvard Business Review* (1968).

Hygiene versus Motivators: His explanation of the differences between true motivation and more subtle forms of coercion focused on what he called **hygiene factors** involved in the latter. Those are the factors generating potential dissatisfaction. People are unhappy if hygiene factors are insufficient. However, people are not automatically happy if those hygiene factors are satisfied. In contrast, **motivational factors** are those factors generating potential satisfaction.

Hygiene (cited as sources of workplace problems):
- Company policy
- Supervisor/supervisor relations
- Working conditions
- Salary
- Peer relations

Motivation (cited as bringing workplace satisfaction):
- Achievement
- Recognition/rewards
- Work content/challenges
- Responsibility
- Advancement/growth

Douglas McGregor and Theory X versus Theory Y: Douglas McGregor (1906-1964) wrote *The Human Side of Enterprise* (1960), in which he struck a contrast between what he described as *Theory X*, associated with scientific management and what he called the **Type A Manager**, and *Theory Y*, associated with human relations and what he called the **Type B manager**. McGregor clearly was advocating Theory Y.

Theory X Assumptions (1960: 33-44):

1. Management is responsible for the key productive elements (Taylor, separate the functions of labor and management).

2. Workers are there to be directed, motivated, controlled.

3. Workers are passive or resistant to organizational needs.

4. The average worker does as little as possible.

5. The average worker lacks ambition.

6. The average worker is self-centered and indifferent.

7. The average worker will resist change.

8. The average worker is easily duped by charlatans.

Theory X is associated with the military model (structured, hierarchal, and command control–oriented). It relies upon coercive practices, negative reinforcement, and punishment. It is preferred by both autocratic and despotic managers. It is useful among novices, the unskilled, and those clearly not motivated.

Theory Y Assumptions (1960: 45-57):

1. Management retains responsibility for the key productive elements, but can count on support from the work force.

2. People are not passive or resistant to organizational needs.

3. Self-motivation, potential, capacity for responsibility, and the ability to be a team player are in all workers.

4. The essential role of the manager is to arrange working conditions and resources so that the work force can best achieve their personal goals while serving the organizational goals.

Theory Y is associated with the cooperative work model and team work. It relies upon true motivation via self-actualization. It is employed by both democratic and laissez-faire managers. It relies upon positive reinforcement and offers workers positive feedback and rewards. It is most useful among the talented, competent, and motivated.

Not everyone agrees with McGregor that Theory Y is preferable. Indeed, several studies, including that noted in the famous Tannenbaum and Schmidt article, demonstrated that there are highly successful managers who employ Theory X approaches. As a result, several subsequent authors have argued that the style employed should vary to match the leadership situation. Ideas like *contingency management*, *reality leadership*, and *situational leadership* are the result. Deciding which factors should determine which style to employ is a leadership decision.

Fiedler, Luthans, and Contingency Management

Fred Fiedler: Fred Fiedler (born in 1922) wrote *A Theory of Leadership Effectiveness* (1967), in which he advocated "The Contingency Model: A Theory of Leadership Effectiveness." He saw leadership constrained by three situational dimensions:

1. leader-member relationships (trust, affection, respect, fear)

2. task structure within the organization (organizational mission and objectives)

3. leader's ability to exercise genuine power (e.g., the power to hire and fire)

Fiedler held that once these are determined, a management style could be selected that best fit these contingencies.

Fred Luthans: Fred Luthans (born in 1939) expanded these ideas in *Introduction to Management: A Contingency Approach* (1976), which was essentially a textbook. In it he identified problems with both Theory X (scientific management) and Theory Y (human relations) approaches. Solutions to these problems gave rise to alternatives, including what some call a "systems approach," others call "situational management," and what Luthans called a "contingency approach." All three concepts saw the flaws in trying to apply rigid principles to the workplace, and all saw that excessive interest in human relations concepts made the workplace employee centered at the expense of productivity. Moreover, Mary Parker Follett's idea of "taking orders from the situation" was rediscovered, most conspicuously in the contingency approach of Fred Luthans. He advocated that the contingency leader, who projects likely situations, with "if-then" plans for each, rather than follow rigid principles governing management decisions. Such a leader considers "environmental" factors, "resource variables," and "management variables" in making decisions.

Environmental factors, resource variables, and management variables include:

- organization size
- interaction possibilities
- personalities of workers
- goal congruence
- decision-making echelons
- technology
- organizational performance record

Proper management requires determination of the impact of such variables on each organization and fitting a managerial strategy to the situation and circumstances of a particular workplace.

The *management leadership grid* is an illustrative model developed by R.R. Blake and J.S. Mouton in *The Managerial Grid* (1964) to identify and measure managerial styles. A psychological questionnaire was administered to score each manager on two scales:

1. Vertical Scale for Concern for People (rated from one to nine).

2. Horizontal Scale for Concern for Production (also rated from one to nine).

For Blake and Mouton there emerged five styles of management:

1. **The Country Club Style** (1,9): This style has a high concern for people and a low concern for production. Managers using this style will pay a great deal of attention to the needs, security, and comfort of their subordinates in hopes that this will increase their performance. The resulting atmosphere is usually cohesive and friendly but not necessarily highly productive.

2. **The Produce-or-Perish Style** (9,1): With a high concern for production, and a low concern for people, managers using this style will provide their subordinates with adequate wages and benefits and expect high levels of performance in exchange. Managers using this style also pressure their employees through rules and punishments to achieve the organizational goals. This style is associated with McGregor's Type A manager of Theory X, and will merge in crisis situations.

3. **The Middle-of-the-Road Style** (5,5): Managers using this style try to strike a balance between organizational goals and the needs of their subordinates. By showing concern for both people and production, managers who use this style hope to maintain a balance to achieve acceptable performance.

4. **The Team Style** (9,9): In this style, high levels of concern are given to both people and production. Managers choosing to use this style encourage team work and com-

mitment among their subordinates. This method seeks to help them feel themselves to be integral, contributing parts of the organization. The Team Style closely approximates McGregor's Theory Y.

5. **The Impoverished Style** (1,1): This style reflects the absence of leadership. The manager ranks low on both concerns. Such a manager is a "seat holder," one who occupies the position and collects the salary, but does little to justify having either.

Figure 4.1 • Blake and Mouton's Styles of Management

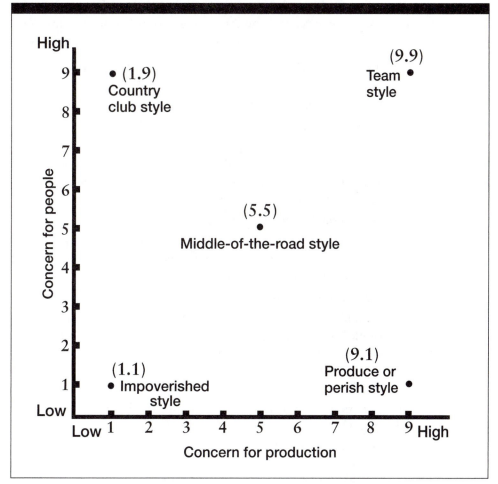

Leading by Negotiation: Modern leaders have learned to motivate people by applying incentives. Implicit in Maslow's hierarchy and Herzberg's motivators is the idea that the manager will manipulate inducements to encourage and reward desirable behavior among subordinates. Clearly the modern manager cannot hope to succeed by raw intimidation and coercion, at least not for long. As Mary Parker Follett's discussion about taking orders from the situation and joint study of the problem pointed out, a leader does better to negotiate solutions than demand them. The old order-giving directional style is not viable in most cases. Give-and-take strategies will work better.

The 1938 essay by Chester Barnard, "Economy of Incentives," was an early statement of this awareness. He observed that incentives could be specific or general, the former suited to working with an individual to meet his or her needs, and the latter open to all to meet commonly shared needs. Barnard identified several classes of such inducements:

1. material inducements (not just money, not even "perks" alone)

2. personal nonmaterial opportunities (prestige, power, titles)

3. desirable physical conditions (the "perks" of the job)

4. ideal "benefactions," the opportunities to achieve personal objectives or fulfill personal values via the job, including satisfying feelings of loyalty, aesthetic, or spiritual feelings; pride in performance or workmanship; etc.

5. associational attractiveness

6. adaptive strategies, recognizing the weight of customary practices and shared attitudes and values, implicitly avoiding too much or radical change

7. expanded participation

8. "condition of communion," those highly "intangible and subtle" incentives, involving social relationships that are comfortable and rewarding (very close to the aspects of "associational attractiveness," but for Barnard, importantly different)

In an important 1959 article, "A Behavioral Theory of Organizational Objectives," Richard Cyert and James March view the organization as a coalition. They acknowledge that there are individual differences in what participants want from a decision, and that bringing people "on board" requires some "side-bargaining" to meet those wants and needs, but once these negotiations have been successfully concluded, the coalition can be considered a unit with a common purpose organizationally (implement Policy X) and many personal aims will be fulfilled at the same time. These "side-bargains" could include money, personal treatment, and policy advantages.

Cyert and March conclude that five basic mechanisms are needed:

1. "a mechanism that changes the quantitative value of demands over time" has an ability to evolve situationally

2. an attention-focusing mechanism that can move among the three states (active-set, inactive-set, and non-considered-set) implicitly promising that everyone's needs will be met at some point, although not all right now

3. a mechanism to direct attention to problems and demands that are, or should be, organizational priorities

4. a mechanism that recognizes the potential weaknesses of participants and assures performance consistency in spite of them—knowing now to use a weakness to an advantage

5. a mechanism for choosing which coalition among competing coalitions will serve best—applying "game theory" to group decisionmaking

March, in collaboration with Michael Cohen (1974: 195-229; 1992), went further in expressing this image of the organization as a coalition, suggesting several rules to help the manager make order out of organizational anarchy:

1. spend time
2. persist
3. exchange status for substance
4. facilitate opposition participation
5. overload the system
6. "provide garbage cans" (raise diversions)
7. manage unobtrusively
8. interpret history

Some of Cohen and March's ideas may seem subversive, but they are rules that keep most of the players in the game and keep the game being played while the leader guides the game toward his or her objectives. A manager must be prepared to manage one's own schedule and those of others. A manager needs to be satisfied with abstract (indirect) job satisfaction—satisfied with the achievements of one's subordinates rather than one's own successes (like parental pride). A manager must be comfortable being an evaluator, judging others, and listening to the judgments of others. A manager must have the capacity to deal with long-term and unusual problems and must be able to leave routines to subordinates. A good manager is always aware that an agency's key resources are its people.

Direct Supervision: A leader is expected to be a supervisor over subordinates. In the days of the authoritarian scientific manager, this meant direction; indeed the "D" in Luther Gulick's POSDCORB stood for "directing." With the focus shifted to less authoritarian styles, leadership is now expected to be less directional and more cooperative and consultative, but what does that do to the issue of supervision? The manager still has supervisory responsibilities that must be fulfilled. Theodore Caplow has suggested a list of 12 supervision principles for the modern workplace that fit the criteria, and also identifies major managerial mistakes (1983: 81-88):

Supervision Principles:

1. Set unmistakable goals (objectives).
2. Supervise the work, not the worker.
3. Distinguish essential or nonessential rules.
4. Reward sparingly; punish more sparingly.
5. Give credit where credit is due.
6. Listen to complaints; don't bitch back.
7. Defend the faith.
8. Form an inner circle.
9. Protect status of subordinates.
10. Retain final control.
11. Innovate democratically.
12. Take infinite pains to see things go right.

Major Managerial Errors:

1. overcontrolling (authoritarian managers' problem)
2. undercontrolling (laissez-faire and democratic)
3. one-way communicators:
   — order givers
   — silent listeners (giving no guidance)
   — appeasers (yielding to subordinates too often)
   — nondelegators (never giving subordinates independence)
   — halfway delegators (assigning responsibilities but not sharing authority).

Summary

The art of leadership is vital to the criminal justice manager. Scholars continue to study what styles and approaches work for the successful leader, but the shift from scientific management to a human relations approach has had a considerable impact on the practice of management in the twentieth century and beyond.

Learning Objectives

Upon finishing this chapter you should be able to do the following:

▶ 1. Identify which criminal justices in your locality and state are elected.

▶ 2. Distinguish between first-order and second-order policymaking.

▶ 3. Discuss some of the traits that you consider to be very important in a criminal justice leader.

▶ 4. Discuss the skills you feel that a criminal justice leader should possess.

▶ 5. Identify four distinct managerial styles and compare them in terms of concern for subordinates and concern for maintaining control.

▶ 6. Compare and contrast scientific management and human relations approaches to leadership and management.

▶ 7. Discuss various models of contingency or situational leadership.

▶ 8. Identify incentives that can be used in criminal justice management.

IMPORTANT TERMS AND NAMES

- *appointments*
- *considerations*
- *elections*
- *Henri Fayol*
- *Fred Fiedler*
- *Hawthorne Studies*
- *Fred Herzberg*
- *hygiene factors*
- *influence*
- *initiating structures*
- *Leader Behavior Descriptive Questionnaire (LBQD)*
- *Fred Luthans*
- *managerial style*
- *Abraham Maslow*
- *Elton Mayo*
- *Douglas McGregor*

- *motivational factors*
- *nonmerit selection*
- *performance-based merit selection*
- *primary/first-order policymaking*
- *F.J. Roethlisberger*
- *secondary/second-order policymaking*
- *supervision principles*
- *task analysis*
- *traits of a leader*
- *skills of a leader*
- *Frederick Taylor*
- *Theory X assumptions*
- *Theory Y assumptions*
- *Type A manager*
- *Type B manager*

References and Supplemental Sources

Barnard, Chester (1938) [1989]. "Economy of Incentives" in *Classic Readings in Organizational Behavior*, edited by J. Steven Ott (1989). Pacific Grove, CA: Brooks/Cole.

Blake, R.R., and J.S. Mouton (1964). *The Managerial Grid: The Key to Leadership Excellence*. Houston: Gulf.

Burns, James MacGregor (1978). *Leadership*. New York: Harper Torchbooks.

Caplow, Theodore (1983). *Managing an Organization*, 2nd ed. New York: Holt, Rinehart, and Winston.

Carey, Benedict (2004). "Fear in the Workplace: The Bullying Boss," *The New York Times*, June 22, 2004.

Champion, Dean (2003). *Administration of Criminal Justice*, 1st ed. Upper Saddle River, NJ: Prentice Hall.

Cohen, Michael D., and James G. March (1974). *Leadership and Ambiguity*. Stanford, CA: Carnegie Foundation for the Advancement of Teaching. Extract reprinted as "Leadership in an Organized Anarchy," pages 432-448 in *Classics of Organizational Theory*, 3rd ed., edited by Jay M. Shafritz and J. Steven Ott (1992), Pacific Grove, CA: Brooks/Cole.

Cyert, Richard M., and James G. March (1959) [1992]. "A Behavioral Theory of Organizational Objectives," pages 133-142 in *Classics of Organizational Theory*, 3rd edition, edited by Jay M. Shafritz and J. Steven Ott, Pacific Grove, CA: Brooks/Cole.

Etzioni, Amitai (1961). *A Comparative Analysis of Complex Organizations*. New York: The Free Press, Macmillan.

Fisher College of Business, Ohio State University (2008). *Leader Behavior Description Questionnaire (LBDQ)*. Accessed online at https://fisher.osu.edu/offices/fiscal/lbdq/

Fiedler, Fred E. (1967). *A Theory of Leadership Effectiveness*. New York: McGraw-Hill.

Follett, Mary Parker (1926). "The Giving of Orders," in *Scientific Foundations of Business Administration*, edited by Henry C. Metcalf, et. al. Baltimore: Williams and Wilkins.

Gulick, Luther (1937). "Notes on the Theory of Organization," *Papers on the Science of Administration*, edited by Luther Gulick and Lyndall Urwick. New York: Institute of Public Administration.

Herzberg, Frederick (1966). *Work and the Nature of Man*. New York: Ty Crowell.

Herzberg, Frederick (1968). "One More Time: How Do You Motivate Employees?" *Harvard Business Review*, 46(1): 53-62, reprinted in the *Harvard Business Review*, 65(5): 109-120.

Katz, Robert (1974). "Skills of an Effective Administrator," *Harvard Business Review*, 52(5): 90-101.

Klofas, John, Stan Stojkovic, and David Kalinich (1990). *Criminal Justice Organizations: Administration and Management*. Pacific Grove, CA: Brooks/Cole.

Luthans, Fred (1976). *Introduction to Management: A Contingency Approach*. New York: McGraw-Hill.

Madsen, K.B. (1973). "Theories of Motivation," pages 673-706 in *Handbook of General Psychology*. Englewood Cliffs, NJ: Prentice Hall.

Maslow, Abraham H. (1943). "A Theory of Human Motivation," *Psychological Review*, 50: 370-396.

Maslow, Abraham H. (1954). *Motivation and Personality*. New York: Harper and Row.

Maslow, Abraham H. (1970). *Motivation and Personality*, 2nd ed. New York: Harper and Row.

Massie, Joseph L. (1987). *Essentials of Management*, 4th ed. Englewood Cliffs, NJ: Prentice Hall.

Mayo, Elton (1933). *The Human Problems of an Industrial Civilization*. Cambridge, MA: Harvard University Press.

Mayo, Elton (1945). *The Social Problems of an Industrial Civilization*. Cambridge, MA: Harvard University Press.

Patton, George S. (2008). "General George S. Patton, Jr." CMG Worldwide, Estate of George S. Patton, Jr. Accessed online at http://www.generalpatton.com/quotes.html.

Roethlisberger, F.J. (1941). *Management and Morale*. Cambridge, MA: Harvard University Press.

Roethlisberger, F.J., and William J. Dixon (1939). *Management and the Worker*. Cambridge, MA: Harvard University Press.

Schubert, James N. (1988). "Age and Active-Passive Leadership Style," *American Political Science Review*, 82(3): 763-772.

Shafritz, Jay M., and J. Steven Ott, editors (1992). *Classics of Organizational Theory*, 3rd ed. Pacific Grove, CA: Brooks/Cole.

Souryal, Sam S. (1985). *Police Organization and Administration* Cincinnati: Pilgrimage/Anderson.

Souryal, Sam S. (1995). *Police Organization and Administration*, 2nd ed. Cincinnati: Anderson.

Tannenbaum, Robert, and Warren H. Schmidt (1958). "How to Choose a Leadership Pattern," *Harvard Business Review*, 36(2): 95-101.

Tannenbaum, Robert, and Warren H. Schmidt (1973). "How to Choose a Leadership Pattern," *Harvard Business Review*, 51(3): 162-180, reprinting the original article as a Harvard Business Review Classic.

Taylor, Frederick Winslow (1911; 1967). *The Principles of Scientific Management*. New York: Norton Library, Harper and Row.

Wilson, Woodrow (1887). "The Study of Administration," *Political Science Quarterly*, 2(2): 197-222.

5
Organizing Criminal Justice

The "O" in LODESTAR and the first "O" in POSDCORB both stand for "organizing." Organizing the work force is one of the essential responsibilities of a criminal justice manager. In Chapter 1 we considered how the study of organization and management has been complicated by popular misunderstandings of the key terms. It is easy to limit the conceptualization of "organization" to only its corporate-entity meaning, a synonym for "agency" (e.g., the organization, as in the FBI), thereby ignoring its process meaning (e.g., organization is the process of arranging and structuring cooperative human effort). The study of "organization" is not the study of an "organization" but the science of how organizations are best organized, structured, and arranged.

Often people join organizations and function within them with the assumption that they always have been as they are—that their structure is "set in stone" and immutable. This is absolutely false. Agency managers have both the authority (subject to laws) and the responsibility to alter and modify organizational arrangements to respond to new demands and changes in the work environment.

Bureaucracies

Most modern criminal justice agencies are bureaucracies. In the course of human history a criminal justice bureaucracy is a relatively new concept, not yet 400 years old. Until the time of Cardinal Richelieu in France (1585-1642), there were no governmental or criminal justice bureaucracies in Europe. The Roman Catholic Church, a large and widely dispersed organization, did have a system of self-governance that approximated a bureaucracy, and Richelieu applied many of those concepts to French government. He selected government officials on the basis of objective merit, naming judges who were formally trained in law to replace some of the feudal nobles who had been judges by birthright. By the time of Emperor Napoleon Bonaparte (1769-1821), France possessed an advanced governmental bureaucracy that included the management of the courts, the police, and the prisons by trained, merit-selected officials. The occupying French forces replaced the governing institutions of conquered nations with bureaucrats trained by the French. The consequence was the rapid spread of bureaucracy across Europe in the first years of the nineteenth century. Even the final, total defeat of the French in 1815 did not set back the progress of bureaucracy as an institution of governance in Europe. In the German states it was especially successful in taking hold.

Bureaucracy therefore is an essential element to consider as we study organization in contemporary criminal justice organizations. German scholar Max Weber was the first to recognize and examine the key features of a modern **bureaucracy**. Nicely summarized by Sam Souryal (1995: 10-11), its features include:

- a system of fixed jurisdictions
- enumerated tasks and duties
- predetermined goals and objectives
- explicit rules and procedures
- integration of the labors of large numbers of people
- hierarchical system of authority (chain of command)
- delegation of authority with supervised span of control
- career officials (bureaucrats)
- probationary appointments
- fixed salaries and benefits
- in-service training
- code of discipline
- information systems of internal communication, written records, and files

Maximilian Carl Emil Weber: Max Weber (1864-1920) was a German social scientist credited with being one of the founders of both sociology and public administration. Although best known today as a scholar and professor, he was active in German politics after World War I and served on the commission that drafted the Weimar Constitution.

Weber was a prolific writer on a wide range of subjects. His last work was *Economy and Society* (1922), published posthumously. Among his most important theoretical contributions were his analysis of power and authority and his detailed explanation of bureaucracy. He employed the concept of the **ideal type** as an explanatory device, and his description of bureaucracy was an example of an ideal type. In his day the concept of bureaucracy was seen as a positive development, as a superior way of managing and conducting public affairs. Its dependence upon merit selection of public officials was a major improvement on earlier ways of appointing government officials from the petty nobility.

When Weber wrote about "bureaucracy," he introduced us to some of the key organizational principles of modern bureaucratic organizations:

en.wikipedia.com

Max Weber was a German social philosopher who approached the study of bureaucracy both historically and analytically, identifying within it the features that have given it its great strength in public service. He also studied the origins and exercise of noncoercive power as an aspect of leadership.

1. fixed jurisdictional areas
2. hierarchal principle
3. documentation (the files)
4. trained office management
5. career commitment (official duties, a "vocation")
6. official, stable learnable rules.

Some of the elements of bureaucracy had their conceptual origins in earlier ideas. A system of fixed jurisdictions, enumerated tasks and duties, and predetermined goals and objectives are aspects of "the division of labor," attributed first to Adam Smith (1776) and a key feature of the scientific managerial principles of Henri Fayol.

Hierarchal arrangements have been part of human social structure since ancient times. The delegation of authority with supervised span of control also is quite ancient, being a feature of armies in the earliest historical records. But there were new features to be found in bureaucracy. The merit selection of career officials, chosen objectively for their educational preparations, talents, and skills; initially giving probationary appointments; and entitling them to fixed salaries and benefits all were original ideas. The keeping of comprehensive files, the establishment of rules and procedures for the conduct of the work, and the system of internal discipline required to follow them all were new as well. Bureaucratic work ceased to be the responsibility of an individual practitioner and became instead the responsibility of the office he or she occupied. In this way an incumbent in the office could share the duties, responsibilities, and records of the office with associates and subordinates, and pass them on to successor.

In Weber's mind, bureaucracy was the solution to many problems of governance and human organization. Today, however, bureaucracy is seen by many as a problem. Bureaucracy has developed a reputation for being cumbersome, slow, inefficient, and officious.

Box 5.1 • Asterix the Gaul versus Bureaucracy

The French, who did so much to spread bureaucracy across Europe, often ridicule their own bureaucrats. The popular French-Belgian cartoon character Asterix must deal with the entrenched and unresponsive bureaucracy as one of the most difficult of *Les Douze Travaux d'Asterix [The Twelve Labors of Asterix]*, a parody of the "Twelve Labors of Hercules." In his eighth labor Asterix must secure "Permit A-38," contending with a multitude of bureaucrats and offices in an almost hopeless effort to secure this document. He only does so by playing the bureaucratic game against the bureaucrats themselves, demanding from them an imaginary permit to which he claims an entitlement.

While bureaucracy has become tainted by its abuses, done right, it still works better than most means for managing a large organization. Elliott Jaques wrote "In Praise of Hierarchy" as a defense of this essential aspect of bureaucracy (1990), yet Jaques too identifies real problems in hierarchal arrangements:

1. There are too many layers and too much distance between managers and labor, poor communication, deflection of responsibility, stress and conflict.

2. Mid-level managers rarely add to the productivity of their line subordinates; and even can reduce its value.

3. Bureaucracies often play into the nasty aspects of human behavior, greed, insensitivity, selfish careerism, unhealthy competition.

Jaques finds that hierarchy, like bureaucracy, when done right, works well. Both responsibility and accountability must be defined unambiguously. Someone must be held accountable for each of the tasks assigned to the organization—both for doing them and for seeing that they are being done. The focus must be on getting the job done; exercising authority is a very distant secondary aspect. If getting the job done can be made easier by distributing authority, then that is the way to go; if centralization gets more done, then centralize. However, "group decisions" must still be the manager's decision. The manager is responsible for buying into the decision, or into the decision-making process. To make **hierarchy** (which arranges the performers of tasks in a ranked or graduated series) actually work, several powers must be vested in the leadership:

1. The manager needs to retain the right to veto the employment or placement of any person not up the standards of the organization or of the tasks to be performed.

2. The manager needs to have the right to make work assignments.

3. The manager needs the power to conduct performance appraisals and to allocate or withhold rewards based on them; not just to make inconsequential recommendations.

4. The manager needs the authority to initiate removal procedures for nonfunctional or low-productivity staff.

Organizational Principles and the Courts: There are organizations that do not fit the bureaucratic pattern well (for example, the courts). Court officials are elected in many of the states, both judges and clerks of court. The courts are a meeting place for multiple bureaucracies with competing goals and objectives. Here the court staff, the police, the prosecutor, the public defender, and representatives of the probation office meet to determine complex questions of law, innocence or guilt, and consequences of convictions. Each of these represented bureaucracies has a different interest in the case before the court. Nevertheless, leaders in the judiciary have made significant organizational improvements in the courts. Among the most noteworthy of these court reformers was Arthur Vanderbilt.

Arthur T. Vanderbilt: In the area of the courts, major organizational innovations were introduced by Arthur Vanderbilt (1888-1957). A New Jersey native and politically active community leader, Vanderbilt helped bring about major constitutional changes in the organization of the New Jersey court system, and thereafter became its Chief Justice (1948-1957). In that capacity he also served as the director of the newly created Administrative Office of the Courts, the first such entity in the United States. Previously Vanderbilt was the president of the American Bar Association (1937-1938). He had served as Dean of New York University Law School and founded the Institute of Judicial Administration at New York University in 1950. He was a strong advocate of states establishing court administration agencies in a period when judges expected virtual autonomy in running their courts (Vanderbilt II, 1976). He wrote *Minimum Standards of Judicial Administration* (1949) (standardizing court practices) and *The Challenge of Legal Reform* (1955). Today his ideas form the basis of modern court administration. State agencies assure that their courts are consistent and uniform in their documentation, record-keeping, and routine procedural matters. Judges get training on routine judicial administration upon entering office.

Organizational Principles and Law Enforcement: Introducing the concepts of organizational theory to law enforcement were Leonhard F. Fuld, August Vollmer, and Orlando W. Wilson. Fuld penned the first American book on police administration (1910), intended primarily for police executives. Vollmer and Wilson were mentor and protégé. Together these two men substantially altered the path of law enforcement in the United States in the first half of the twentieth century. Both were prolific writers on police organization and administration (Vollmer, 1936; Wilson, 1950). Raymond Fosdick (1920), Elmer Graper (1921), and Bruce P. Smith (1940) were other pioneers in the application of scientific management principles to law enforcement.

en.wikipedia.org

August Vollmer: The first law enforcement position held by August Vollmer (1876-1955) was as an elected town marshal in 1907. Vollmer had earned a national reputation as an innovator and publicist of new ideas while serving as police chief in Berkeley, California. He was an advocate of the selection of college-educated men for police work. In an age when many police departments still did not even require a high school diploma, the need for college-educated police was not immediately appreciated.

Often called the "father of modern law enforcement," Vollmer reorganized the Berkeley Police Department, created new units within it, and increased its capacities with motor vehicles outfitted with one-way radios that could monitor the police dispatchers (but could not at that time reply to them). Never feeling bound by the old ways of doing things, he was willing to experiment with organizational experiments. He wrote many articles about his innovations, and in 1936 published a compilation of his progressive ideas in *The Police and Modern Society*.

August Vollmer was a leading American law enforcement innovator and reformer. He introduced many ideas into policing we now take for granted: patrol cars, radio dispatch, MO files, and criminal profiling among them. He also recruited and hired the first college-educated police officers, and helped create criminal justice education in the United States.

Orlando W. Wilson: Orlando W. Wilson (1900-1972) was a police chief and educator who was instrumental in applying managerial concepts to police agencies. His book, *Police Administration*, is a classic in the application of scientific management concepts to police practices. Wilson was one of the first college-educated police officers (a street cop, not a college-educated police executive).

Wilson was hired by another great leader in law enforcement, August Vollmer, to be an officer in the Berkeley Police Department in 1921. He earned his bachelor's degree while a police officer and then took his first chief of police post in Fullerton, California, in 1925. In later years he directed police departments in Wichita, Kansas, and Chicago, Illinois, and was involved in public safety in Italy and Germany in the war-time occupations of those nations.

Wilson created the School of Criminology at U.C.-Berkeley in 1950 and served as its first dean. As a police manager and as an academic, he sought to apply the basic principles of good management to law enforcement and did much to create the emphasis on "professionalism" in policing that has characterized its development in the last half century (R.C. McLaren, 1977; in Wilson and McLaren, 1977).

Bruce P. Smith: Bruce Smith (1892-1955) was a leading advocate of **economies of scale**, arguing that the consolidation of smaller police forces into larger ones, replacing sheriffs with state police, and other centralizing efforts would provide for greater efficiency in law enforcement. He helped develop the Uniform Crime Reports (UCR) for the International Association of Chiefs of Police (IACP) and the FBI (Wilson, 1956: 235). His book, *Police Systems in the United States* (1940), was the peak expression of the reform ideal merging with the rising focus on better managerial practices.

Organizational Principles and Corrections: Leaders in correctional management began making contributions to the better organization of prisons and jails in the nineteenth century. Such early leaders as John Howard, Jeremy Bentham, Alexander Maconochie, Dorothea Lynde Dix, Elam Lynds, and Zebulon Reed Brockway already were mentioned in Chapter 3 on the historical antecedents to criminal justice management. In the twentieth century, new ideas were offered by reform-minded leaders seeking to further improve upon prison and jail organization. Three famous twentieth-century correctional reformers were Katharine Bement Davis, Mary Belle Harris, and George Beto.

Katharine Bement Davis: Katharine Bement Davis (1860-1935) was the first woman to be appointed New York City Correction Commissioner (1914), and her selection made news around the world. She was the first woman to run a major municipal agency in New York. She managed an agency with 650 uniformed and civilian employees; 5,500 inmates in nine city prisons and jails; and a $2 million annual budget. Between 1918 and 1928 she served as the head of the Bureau of Social Hygiene, funded by the Rockefeller Foundation. With her sponsorship, the Bureau published *Women Police* and Edith Spaulding's *Experimental Study of Psychopathic Delinquent Women*. Having earned a Ph.D. at the University of Chicago in 1900, she was a social reformer and activist for much of her life. She undertook a highly controversial sex study of 2,200 women, which began in 1920. Among her achievements was the recruiting of Mary Belle Harris, another prison reformer (McCarthy, 1997).

Mary Belle Harris: Mary Belle Harris (1874-1957) was appointed superintendent of the women's workhouse on Blackwell's Island, New York, by Katharine Davis. She revised institutional rules to transform the workhouse, which was badly overcrowded and one of the worst on Blackwell's Island, into a model institution, with a library, an exercise yard, and an inmate classification system. Harris later moved to New Jersey to head the State Reformatory for Women at Clinton. Harris later served in corrections posts in Pennsylvania and the U.S. Bureau of Prisons women's prison in Alderson, West Virginia, where she was the first woman to be a warden in the federal system. She also earned a Ph.D. at the University of Chicago. In a 1936 book about her career in penology, *I Knew Them in Prison*, Harris recounted her life, accomplishments, and penal reforms, and credited Davis with having a major influence on her correctional career (McCarthy, 1997; Rogers, 2000).

George John Beto: George John Beto (1916-1991) was appointed to the Texas Prison Board in 1953 (later renamed the Texas Board of Corrections), serving until 1959. Soon after that he served on the Illinois Parole and Pardon Board. In 1962 he returned to the Texas Department of Corrections. The prisoners called him "Walking George" because he unexpectedly visited the prisons to observe them. He helped secure legislative approval and funds for prison system reforms. Among the reforms he helped bring about were an eight-week prerelease program, giving prisoners counseling and education. In 1969 he helped institute a special work-release program, and also expanded college-education programs at prisons in cooperation with Sam Houston State University. He helped the university develop its criminology program, and the American Correctional Association elected him its president for 1969-1970. Though a reformer, Beto favored authoritarian disciplinary practices.

After he retired as director of the Texas Department of Corrections Beto was a professor of criminology and corrections at Sam Houston State University (1972-1991). He is described as being "one of the visionaries who brought about the building of the Criminal Justice Center" at Sam Houston State University (Roth, 1997: 46). He was member of the National Advisory Commission on Criminal Justice Standard and Goals, 1972-1973 (Horton and Nielsen, 2005; Lucko, 2007).

Each of these leaders and reformers—and many others—have found creative ways to reorganize and revitalize criminal justice agencies to better provide the services they were created to deliver. In various ways they each applied the principles of organization to achieve these innovations and improvements.

Principles of Organization

In the fourth edition of *Police Administration*, by O.W. Wilson and Roy C. McLaren (1977: 73-74), the following principles were set down, with application to police work first in Wilson's mind. However, the principles have much more general application in all public service organizational contexts:

1. Tasks should be grouped together in one or more units under the control of one person. In order to facilitate their assignment, these tasks may be divided according to:

    (a) similarity in purpose, process, method, or clientele (functional),

    (b) the time (temporal),

    (c) the place of their performance (spatial), and

    (d) the level of authority needed in their accomplishment.

2. Specialized units should be created only when overall departmental capability is thus significantly increased; they should not be created at the expense of reduced control and decreased general interest.

3. Lines of demarcation between the responsibilities of units should be clearly drawn by a precise definition of the duties of each,

    (a) duties of a unit should be made known to all members of the unit.

    (b) responsibility within the unit and between units should be placed exactly.

    (c) such definition should avoid duplication in execution and neglect resulting from the nonassignment of a duty.

4. Channels should be established through which information flows up and down and through which authority is delegated.

    (a) These lines of control should correspond to the delegation of authority, the placement of responsibility, the supervision of work, and the coordination of effort.

    (b) Lines of control should be clearly defined and well understood by all members so that all may know to whom they are responsible and who, in turn, is responsible to them.

    (c) Exceptions to routine communication of information through channels should be provided for emergency and unusual situations.

5. Structure and terminology should facilitate the understanding of the purposes and responsibilities of the organization by all its members. Avoid exotic arrangements and obscure jargon.

6. Each individual, unit, and situation should be under the immediate control of one, and only one, person, thus achieving the principle of unity of command and avoiding the friction that results from duplication of direction and supervision.

7. The span of control of a supervisor should be large enough to provide economical supervision, but no more units or persons should be placed under the direct control of one person than he or she is able to manage.

8. Each task should be made the unmistakable duty of someone; responsibility for planning, execution, and control should be definitely placed on designated persons.

9. Supervision should be provided for every member of the organization and for every function or activity. (If the supervision is not immediately available at the actual level of execution, it should be obtainable through referral to a predesignated authority.)

10. Each assignment or duty should carry with it commensurate authority to fulfill the responsibility.

11. Persons to whom authority is delegated should be held accountable for the use made of it and for the failure to use it.

These principles of organization often are depicted in the form of the organizational chart. Known by such terms as a "block chart," "plumbing chart," or a "wiring diagram," the organizational chart is the embodiment of the ancient adage that a picture is worth 1,000 words. These box charts use rectangular boxes to represent offices, units, or important individual officers in an agency. One of the learning objectives of this unit is teaching each student how to read, use, and later how to draw a correct organization chart.

Police patrol units take messages from the 911-dispatch center and respond to them as if they were taking orders (e.g., "Unit B-57, respond to a disorder at 123 4th Avenue"). Such a communication sounds like an order being given by a dispatcher to a uniformed officer. In organizational practice it is not. The dispatcher is "sharing information" with the officer. If the officer feels he or she should not respond to the call, the officer can decline it or request direction from his or her direct supervisor (e.g., "Unit B-03, this is B-57. I am monitoring a suspicious activity at 8th and Market Street. Request that another until respond to the disorder on 4th Avenue"). The field supervisor, shown as the solid line on the organization chart, has the authority to reassign the officer to take the call or assign another patrol unit to respond to it.

Figure 5.1 • Sample Organization Chart

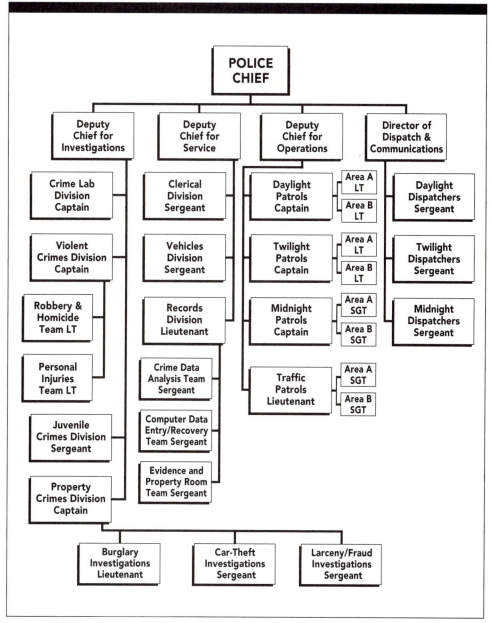

Box 5.2 • Reading an Organization Chart

Solid lines represent command and supervisory relationships.

Dashed or dotted lines represent communications and coordination channels and interrelationships such as relationships as attachment, operational control (Op Con), liaison, and detail.

Boxes represent an "office," "department," or some other unit with a functional, temporal, or spatial division of labor.

Very similar units are often merged, by overlapping (stack) or "**comb**" **arrangements**, meaning that all such units are very similar in their organization/function.

The chart should show all elements supervised by a superior element/person with a single clear path from top to bottom.

A chart ought not create fictional relationships (yet some do, leading to people saying "I don't report to him!").

No box should be unconnected, but some will be in reality because of managerial or political compromises; e.g., the "independent" agency such as the office of the ombudsman, the "special prosecutor," or the "independent counsel."

No box should be connected to two or more supervisory boxes with a solid line, yet some can linked by a dotted or dashed line, reflecting such relationships as attachment, operational control (Op Con), liaison, detail, or pre-authorized direct communication channels.

The way dotted-line, dual relationships can be handled includes concepts of *attached*, *operational control* (OPCON), *liaison*, and *detailed*.

Attached: When a unit (or an individual) is detached from its own agency and attached to a different organization, the receiving organization becomes responsible for that unit, providing its logistics, supervision, and duty assignments. A criminal justice example would be a judge, temporarily transferred from his or her home district to a different district to help reduce case backlogs in the receiving court district. For most purposes, that judge functions as if he or she had been transferred to the new district. Logistics support, such as office space, a courtroom, clerical support, and a wide range of other support activities, is provided by the receiving district. Eventually the attachment will end and the judge will return to his or her home district.

Operational Control (OPCON): When an entire unit from one organization takes its direction from another organization that is not normally part of its chain of command, it can be considered under operational control. Common examples in law enforcement are combined task forces of federal, state, and local law enforcement agencies

Figure 5.2 • Common Organization Chart Error

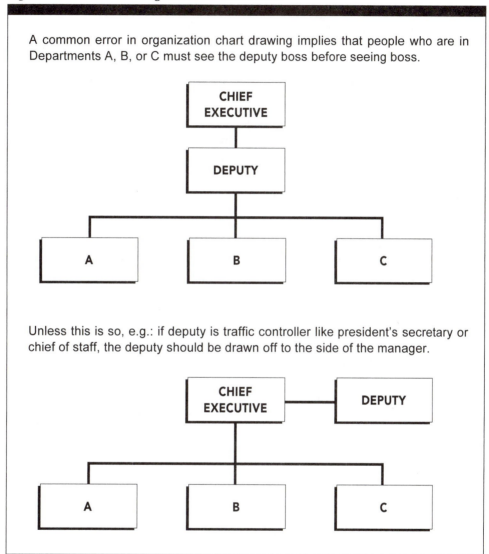

A common error in organization chart drawing implies that people who are in Departments A, B, or C must see the deputy boss before seeing boss.

Unless this is so, e.g.: if deputy is traffic controller like president's secretary or chief of staff, the deputy should be drawn off to the side of the manager.

that agree to protocols that place one of them in charge of the activities of the others. The Drug Enforcement Agency (DEA) often has operational control of drug investigations that have the full participation of state and local anti-drug agencies. The state and local units remain the "property" of their larger organizations, which provide most of their support and logistics, but their actual task assignments, direction, and supervision are transferred to the DEA agent in charge.

Liaison: A liaison officer is an official of one agency who is assigned to work with a different agency as a means of facilitating coordination and communication between or among agencies. A common criminal justice example would be police, fire, rescue, and public health officials assigned to an emergency operations center established to respond to a major community crisis. They interact with each other and inform each other of what their home agency can contribute to the joint operation. Some liaison relationship are long-lasting; others very temporary. The long-lasting relationships take on the features of a detail.

Detailed: When a unit or an individual is detailed, that person or unit works for one department or agency but is "detailed" to support a different department for a specific function or a limited time. A common criminal justice example is an experienced police investigator being detailed to the prosecutor's office to conduct further investigation into a case being prepared for trial. Such an investigator remains an employee of the police department and will eventually return to the police department, but for the duration of the detail will work under the direct supervision of the prosecutor's office.

It might be worthwhile to clarify some of the terminology in common use in criminal justice agencies. An **officer** is an employee empowered to act on behalf of the agency or organization, and can be a part of the management team, having some supervisory duties. Formally speaking, a "police officer" would not be an "officer" within the police department in this sense, but a police sergeant or lieutenant with managerial duties would be. On the street, though, a police officer is authorized to act independently and takes on duties in his or her relationship to the public that imply being an "officer" of the police department. An "employee" need not be an officer. A clerk has a task to do but no supervisory or managerial powers to exercise in behalf of the agency. An agent will include a nonemployee engaged for specific acts (e.g., a lawyer hired to represent the agency or organization on a limited question or case). Agents who are not employees often do not appear on the organizational charts.

Organizational Structure and Function

Weber and Wilson both approached organization as a rational exercise, with an underlying assumption that workers are analogous to identical replacement parts in a working machine. This was also evident in Frederick Taylor's writings. However, the Hawthorne Studies invited questions about this assumption. Workers were "vital engines" even more than Robert Owen might have assumed. This gave rise to the human relations school and its model of human organizational behavior. In time other models have been proposed, so that now we can consider three major options that a leader may employ in organizing his or her agency:

1.   **Bureaucratic-Scientific Management Model** (Gulick, 1937; Taylor, 1911; Weber, 1920; Wilson, 1950): Organizational principles are applied somewhat rigidly, with the hierarchy

principle given very high priority. Authority is very pre-cisely allocated, with those higher up in the hierarchy having more power. Rules are explicit, and organizational discipline is enforced. The agency's organizational chart clearly defines areas of jurisdiction and command-control relationships. Organizational communications, command, and control are expected to follow the chain of command. This approach dominated organization in criminal justice well into the middle of the twentieth century.

2. **Human Relations Model** (Herzberg, 1968; Maslow, 1970; Mayo, 1923; Roethlisberger 1941): Preceded by the ideas of Mary Parker Follett, and arising with the discover-ies of the Hawthorne group (Mayo and Roethlisberger), older scientific management organizational principles were called into question. Hierarchy and command aspects were not abandoned, but their importance declined. Lines of command, control, and communication were often ignored in favor of work groups, operating as co-equals, even when they were comprised of different ranks. Rules were replaced by flexible guidelines. Rising in popularity in the 1960s, these ideas never fully replaced scientific management organization in criminal justice. They found expression in the 1970s as team policing, community policing, and empowerment of client populations in crimi-nal justice priority-setting became popular.

3. **Situational and Contingency Models** (Fiedler, 1967; Luthans, 1976): these models promoted flexibility and situational management, and revived Mary Parker Follett's 1926 recommendation that leaders should take their orders from the situation. The application of CompStat in law enforcement and problem-oriented policing are both expressions of this approach. Criminal justice work-teams are created, reorganized, and disbanded as needed. There is more use of delegation and operational control practices than in scientific management, but less workplace democ-racy than was the case in human relations applications. The older scientific management-based principles reemerged as good practices, but not rigid formulae, for organizing criminal justice agencies.

Applying Organizational Principles

The **division of labor** in a criminal justice organization must reflect functional, temporal, and spatial demands placed upon it by its mission.

Functional Divisions of Labor: The tasks or functions a criminal justice agency has will be reflected by the internal divisions it adapts.

Souryal (1985: 12-13) identified several factors to be considered, among them major purposes (missions), processes employed, subjects (specific services to be provided), and clientele.

A municipal police department needs to provide crime prevention, public safety, order maintenance, public service, and crime investigation services to the public. If the workload justifies it, there can be functional divisions to reflect each of these. Even a smaller police department will have patrol, services, and investigative units. The courts are called upon to hold bail and bond hearings, conduct civil and criminal trials, sentence people, collect fines, supervise probation conditions, hear appeals, and perform many other judicial functions. Court managers create units within the court system to provide these services. Corrections managers must classify, house, educate, medicate, treat, and release inmates. They will pay attention to classifications of inmates based upon their danger to correctional staffs and society at large, and thus correctional units will be developed that are maximum-security, medium-security, and minimum-security. There will be classification units. There will be medical, counseling, education and vocational training, parole-hearing, and other correctional units.

Clientele will include the aforementioned security grades in a prison population, youth offenders, victims, witnesses, the public at large, the staffs of the agencies, and many others. Specific units can be established to deal with the special requirements of various client groups. Police, court, and corrections units exist to meet the needs of juveniles. Prosecutors need to handle offenders, witnesses, and victims in different ways, and may choose to create divisions within their offices to provide those services.

The processes employed by modern criminal justice agencies often rely upon complex technologies the average agency employee simply will not possess. Police will reply upon crime scene investigation (CSI) experts and other advanced scientific elements to provide such technical support. Computers are very important in all the components of the criminal justice system, and having support staffs who can manipulate data efficiently on computer platforms is critical to all criminal justice agencies. Highly sophisticated communications equipment can be entrusted to centralized 911 dispatch and communications centers.

Henry Mintzberg identified five basic parts of an organization, and these are a modern reflection of the functional divisions of labor (1979):

1. **apex** — the top leadership and management team

2. **middle line** — mid-level managers and supervisors

3. **techno-structure** — specialists in the applications of complex technologies

4. **support staff** — clerical-administrative personnel who deal with internal matters

5. **operating core** — the actual workforce to do the labor of the organization

Temporal Divisions of Labor: Municipal police agencies, 911 centers, and correctional units operate 24 hours a day, seven days a week. In some larger cities magistrates also are available 24/7, and lower courts hold night sessions. Juvenile justice units have to respond to cases whenever they arise, not just between 9 A.M. and 5 P.M., Monday through Friday. On the other hand, state and federal investigative agencies and higher courts often can maintain "banker's hours" with 40-hour-a-week work schedules, so the organization of the criminal justice agency must reflect accurately the times when their services are needed.

Spatial Divisions of Labor: Many criminal justice agencies serve large geographical areas. Federal agencies need field offices across the entire nation. State agencies must be present state-wide. Police in large cities need to operate divisions or precincts to provide police services city-wide. Patrol operations must be provided over the entire jurisdiction being served. The courts have established districts so that every community has local or regional access to judicial services.

The **span of control** refers to the number of individuals routinely supervised by an officer of the agency. Tight control exists when a supervisor oversees only two or three subordinates. Loose control exists when a supervisor oversees a large number of subordinates. Therefore, span of control exists in inverse relation to intensity of supervision. When supervision does not need to be intense, the span may be increased without loss of manageability and productivity. This is often the ideal case in Theory Y scenarios. When supervision must be intense, span of control must be left small to achieve manageability and productivity. This is the case when Theory X is applied.

Span of control and the number of steps or layers in the command hierarchy exist in an inverse relation with affect on manageability and productivity. If an agency has each supervisor overseeing only a few subordinates, it will require many more layers of supervision. An increased span of control will produce a decrease in communication time and efficiency. This occurs because an increase in the hierarchy adds additional layers or links in the communication chain, and this produces delays and a decrease in communication transfer. The more extenuated the command-control chain, the more information is lost.

When does supervision need to be intense? Theory X-Scientific Management and Contingency models would recommend it with a work force that has low skills and little motivation.

When does communication "line-loss" need to be kept at a minimum? Theory Y-Human Relations and Contingent models would advise it when criticality, responsiveness, discipline, or control are critical to managerial situations.

There is an inherent paradox to all of this: an abbreviated chain of command can produce a greater span of control but also can enhance internal communication. However, this is not guaranteed. A greater span of control can reduce the communication line-loss in two ways:

1. more face-to-face communications will be necessary
2. fewer transmission links will be required from top down

A greater span of control also can reduce overall internal communications effectiveness by:

1. reducing the time a manager has with each subordinate
2. increasing likelihood that manager will miss someone

Management Theorists Consider the Three Models

Philip Selznick (1948; 1992) sees an organization as a social entity existing to accomplish an "agreed purpose through the allocation of functions and responsibilities" (1992: 114). The maintenance of the system is an implicit agreed purpose; hence, his five "imperatives" (1992: 118-119):

1. The security of the organization as a whole in relation to the social forces in its environment.
2. The stability of lines of authority and communication.
3. The stability of informal relations within the organization.
4. The continuity of policy and of the sources of its determination.
5. A homogeneity of outlook with respect to the meaning and role of the organization.

The imperatives cross-cut the three models. However the criminal justice manager approaches the organization of his or her agency, these concerns must be met. It is the duty of the manager to select the appropriate organizational structure and the organizational model that will best enable the agency to meet its mission and responsibilities to the public.

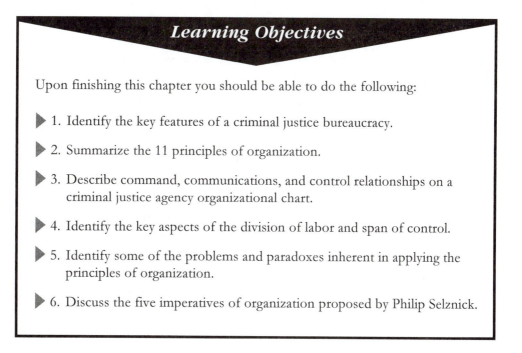

Learning Objectives

Upon finishing this chapter you should be able to do the following:

▶ 1. Identify the key features of a criminal justice bureaucracy.

▶ 2. Summarize the 11 principles of organization.

▶ 3. Describe command, communications, and control relationships on a criminal justice agency organizational chart.

▶ 4. Identify the key aspects of the division of labor and span of control.

▶ 5. Identify some of the problems and paradoxes inherent in applying the principles of organization.

▶ 6. Discuss the five imperatives of organization proposed by Philip Selznick.

IMPORTANT TERMS AND NAMES

- agent
- apex
- attached
- bureaucracy
- chain of command
- "comb" arrangements
- detailed
- division of labor
- economies of scale
- functional divisions of labor
- hierarchy
- ideal type
- liaison
- middle line
- officer
- operating core
- operational control
- span of control
- spatial divisions of labor
- support staff
- techno-structure
- temporal divisions of labor

References and Supplemental Sources

Fiedler, Fred E. (1967). *A Theory of Leadership Effectiveness*. New York: McGraw-Hill.

Fosdick, Raymond B. (1920). *American Police Systems*. New York: Century.

Fuld, Leonard Felix (1910). *Police Administration: A Critical Study of Police Organizations in the United States and Abroad*. New York: Putnam.

Graper, Elmer Diedrich (1921). *American Police Administration*. New York: Macmillan.

Herzberg, Frederick (1968). "One More Time: How Do You Motivate Employees?" *Harvard Business Review*, 46(1): 53-62, reprinted in the *Harvard Business Review*, 65(5): 109-120.

Horton, David M., and George R. Nielsen (2005). *Walking George: The Life of George John Beto and the Rise of the Modern Texas Prison System*. Denton, TX: University of North Texas Press.

Jaques, Elliott (1990). "In Praise of Hierarchy," *Harvard Business Review*, 68(1): 127-134.

Lucko, Paul M. (2007). "Beto, George John," The Handbook of Texas on Line. Found at http://www.tsha.utexas.edu/handbook/online/articles/BB/fbenm.html

Luthans, Fred (1976). *Introduction to Management: A Contingency Approach*. New York: McGraw-Hill.

March, James G., and Herbert A. Simon (1958). *Organizations*. New York: John Wiley and Sons.

Maslow, Abraham H. (1970). *Motivation and Personality*, 2nd ed. New York: Harper and Row.

Mayo, Elton (1933). *The Human Problems of an Industrial Civilization*. Cambridge, MA: Harvard University Press.

McCarthy, Thomas C. (1997). "Correction's Katharine Bement Davis: New York City's Suffragist Commissioner." KBD Bio. New York City Department of Correction. Found at http://www.correctionhistory.org/html/chronicl/kbd/kbd_15.html

McGregor, Douglas (1960). *The Human Side of Enterprise*. New York: McGraw-Hill.

Mintzberg, Henry (1979). *The Structure of Organizations*. Englewood Cliffs, NJ: Prentice Hall.

Roethlisberger, F.J. (1941). *Management and Morale*. Cambridge, MA: Harvard University Press.

Rogers, Joseph W. (2000). "Mary Belle Harris: Warden and Rehabilitation Pioneer," *Women and Criminal Justice*, 11(4): 5-28.

Roth, Mitchel (1997). *Fulfilling a Mandate: A History of the Criminal Justice Center at Sam Houston State University*. Huntsville, TX: Sam Houston Press.

Selznick, Philip (1948). "Foundations of the Theory of Organization," *American Sociological Review* 13(1): 25-35.

Selznick, Philip (1992). "Foundations of the Theory of Organization," pages 114-123 in *Classics of Organizational Theory*, 3rd ed., edited by Jay M. Shafritz and J. Steven Ott. Pacific Grove, CA: Brooks/Cole.

Smith, Adam (1776) [1937]. *The Wealth of Nations*. New York: Random House, Modern Library.

Smith, Bruce P. (1940). *Police Systems in the United States*. New York: Harper and Brothers.

Souryal, Sam S. (1995). *Police Organization and Administration*, 2nd ed. Cincinnati: Anderson.

Vanderbilt, Arthur T., editor (1949). *Minimum Standards of Judicial Administration*. New York: The Law Center of New York University.

Vanderbilt, Arthur T. (1955). *The Challenge of Legal Reform*. Princeton, NJ: Princeton University Press.

Vanderbilt, Arthur T., II. (1976). *Changing Law: A Biography of Arthur T. Vanderbilt*. New Brunswick, NJ: Rutgers University Press.

Vollmer, August (1936). *The Police and Modern Society*. Berkeley, CA: University of California Press.

Weber, Max (1922). *Economy and Society*, 2 volumes, edited by Guenther Roth and Claus Wittich. Berkeley, CA: University of California Press.

Wilson, Orlando W. (1950). *Police Administration*. New York: McGraw-Hill.

Wilson, Orlando W. (1956). "Bruce Smith," *Journal of Criminal Law, Criminology, and Police Science*, 47(2): 235-237.

Wilson, Orlando W., and Roy C. McLaren (1977). *Police Administration*, 4th ed. New York: McGraw-Hill.

6
Decisionmaking and Planning

Decisionmaking or "deciding" is the "D" in LODESTAR, and is different from the "D" in POSDCORB, which stands for "directing." Making decisions is a major managerial responsibility and will be significantly influenced by the leadership style of the manager. Type A managers are more likely to decide autocratically and give orders, direct subordinates, and expect compliance to those orders. Type B managers are more likely to decide democratically and enter into discussions (reciprocal communication and joint study of the issue).

We will merge the study of deciding with "planning," the "P" of POSDCORB, noting that both deciding and planning share many common features. Some authorities separate decisionmaking from planning, as does Joseph L. Massie (1987), but others (including this author) disagree. A plan is a type of decision, and planning uses a decision-making process. As Massie points out, decisionmaking is a process involving three components (1987: 42):

1. choice—the manager considers options and alternatives.

2. thought—the manager exercises what Massie calls a conscious mental process.

3. purpose—the manager determines missions, goals, objectives, and end states.

Each of those three components also are present in planning. Massie identifies five steps to sound managerial decisionmaking (1987: 42-45), and these too are essential in good managerial planning:

1. understanding the situation
2. recognition of the right problem
3. identification and analysis of available alternatives
4. selection of the solution
5. organizational acceptance

Decisionmaking is found at every process-stage in the justice system, often with lower-level officials making critical decisions the whole organization must live with. Police officers in the field and correctional officers often make life-and-death decisions with little opportunity for deliberation, guidance, or option evaluation. In comparison, judges also make life-and-death decisions, but do so after a lengthy process of fact-gathering and deliberation, with input from prosecutors, defense attorneys, and even juries.

It is absolutely essential that criminal justice practitioners have and exercise discretion in the performance of their duties. **Discretion** is an expression of decision-making authority and it exists throughout the entire justice system. For example, a police officer is expected to decide when to make an arrest and when to issue only a warning—when to employ force and what level of force to use. A prosecutor must decide which cases to prosecute, what specific charges to bring, whether to accept or reject a plea bargain, and what sentence to recommend. Judges are expected to rule on motions, make verdicts, and sentence those who have been convicted. Corrections officials need to decide how to classify inmates, what treatment options to employ with them; how to respond to indiscipline, escape attempts, and riots; and when to approve inmates for parole. However, these kinds of decisions are *operational decisions*, not *managerial decisions*.

Managerial Decisionmaking

Managerial decisions are those that involve the mission, goals, objectives, policies, and end states desired for the organization. These decisions may modify or refine the mission, goals, and objectives, and most certainly will influence the policies that will subsequently influence the operational decisions made by the workforce. Major figures in the development of planning and decisionmaking include Chester Barnard (*The Functions of the Executive*, 1938), Herbert Simon (*Administrative Behavior*, 1957), Fred Luthans (*Introduction to Management: A Contingency Approach*, 1976), Chris Argyris (*Personality and Organization*, 1957), and Wendell French and Cecil Bell (*Organizational Development*, 1973).

From these experts we learn that the manager must compromise rational, goal-oriented behavior with economically nonrational (but socially rational) requirements of employees and client populations. In their decisionmaking and implementation, modern criminal justice managers make exchanges with workers, and do not simply command them to perform. This is the transition from scientific management, which *directed*, to human relations, which *leads and negotiates*. Actors at all levels in the criminal justice organization are decisionmakers, as was pointed out previously, but managerial decisionmakers are making policy for their agencies, not making operational decisions.

Managerial decisionmaking concerns include rationality, efficiency, and productivity. Good decisionmaking requires data collection, analysis, action planning, implementation, and evaluation.

Decisionmaking Theory: There are four models of managerial decisionmaking:

1. rational choice
2. bureaucratic
3. decision process (decision-tree)
4. political

The traditional view of decisionmaking is that decisions are made following a **rational choice model** (Pfeffer, 1981), in which:

1. all alternatives are identified
2. advantages and disadvantages of each are itemized
3. projected costs, consequences, and outcomes are anticipated
4. the best option stands out from the others and is chosen

Yet Herbert Simon was quick to observe that this usually was not the way decisions are made. He looked at decisionmaking empirically, and observed that, "Few managers actually decided things by rational searches for alternative solutions for anticipated problems." Instead, they rely upon "bounded rationality" and "satisficing," two terms that are associated with Simon's critical analysis of formal decisionmaking. **Bounded rationality** is rational choice that takes into account the cognitive limitations of both knowledge and cognitive capacity. **Satisficing** is Simon's term for the all too common managerial practice of treating as sufficient (*sufficing*) the first solution to emerge that will meet (*satisfy*) the necessary criteria for a solution, even if there might be other, better solutions that could be discovered by further study and consideration of the problem.

Rather than follow the rational choice model faithfully, typically managers simply follow **programmed decisions**. These are the rituals, routines, and traditional practices of criminal justice agencies, which require minimal discretion and very little actual deciding but generally assure organizational norm maintenance. The key managerial role in this model is establishing routines, and promulgating and maintaining the norms and values that sustain them. This is done using such "premises" as previous decisions, the preferences of supervisors, and pre-existing **standard operating procedures** (SOPs), all of which supplant rational decisionmaking.

This leads Pfeffer to identify the second managerial decision model: the bureaucratic. Best explained by March and Simon (1958) and Cyert and March (1959), this approach tends to be low-risk, but also unoriginal, and limits choices open to the decisionmaker (Pfeffer, 1981). The bureaucratic model relies upon the procedures and precedents of the past, as found in the much cherished rules of the organization. This is the famous "by the book" behavior of some managers. It assumes that the rules, that is, "the book," were formulated by a rational decision process in the past, so they remain rational still. Not everyone would agree. As far back as the 1920s, Mary Parker Follett was identifying problems with predetermined decisions that were passed along to the workforce in the form of orders or rules (1995: 132-134). This led her to propose that managers not rely upon orders but the law of the situation—the recognition that situations are always evolving, so that rigid orders (the established rules of the organization) will be out of place much of the time.

The third approach employs a **decision process model** and assumes that the outputs (the decisions) are products of multiple actors, each having inputs into the process. Pfeffer (1981) refers to this also as "organized anarchy." **Decision trees** often are employed to help the process, and there is an aspect of computer modeling implicit (e.g., If "A," then "B"; if not "A," then Path C). The LEAA flowchart depicted in Chapter 2 is an example of a decision tree.

The fourth model relies upon *political power* and is commonly exemplified in the decisions made in an election year, when the use of an economic rational choice or bureaucratic model would consider other courses of action to be preferable. The U.S. Congress and state legislatures change laws for many reasons—some rational, others for ideological reasons, and still others for political expedience. Once a political decision has been made by the legislature or a lawful executive order is issued by the president, governor, or mayor, the criminal justice executives and mid-level managers must make their decisions in harmony with those political policies.

Decisionmaking: General Principles and External Planning Factors

Just as Tannenbaum and Schmidt (1958) identified different managerial leadership styles, there are corresponding decision-making styles. These and other factors will help determine how a decision is made. Reminiscent of the contingency models favored by Fred Fiedler (1967) and Fred Luthans (1976), and as exemplified in *The Managerial Grid* (1964), a wise decisionmaker will not adhere to just one approach but will consider several ways of coming to a decision. There are five key factors a manager should consider in selecting a managerial decision-making method.

1. What is the managerial style preferred by the decisionmaker?

2. Time? Does the situation require quick action, or is there time for deliberation?

3. Significance and severity? How important or serious is the problem? How much effort does it justify?

4. Frequency? Will the problem arise again?

5. What are the ripple effects and outside consequences of the decision?

Theorists and experienced decisionmakers adhere to different models and have different leadership styles. Some may prefer solo decisionmaking; others prefer group decision-making processes. It would seem that they agree upon few things, but there is a consensus on three points:

1. Come to a decision ("make the decision"; this is in keeping with Theory X).

2. Do not worry about the decision (it proves itself; somewhat laissez-faire).

3. Do not try to satisfy everyone. It can't be done (more in keeping with Theory X) .

Box 6.1 • Means-End Analysis and the Managerial Decision-making Proccess

1. Set the objective.
2. Identify obstacles.
3. Collect and analyze data.
4. Develop alternative solutions.
5. Select preferred alternatives.
6. Develop and implement a plan.
7. Evaluate results.

Criminal Justice Managerial Planning

Orlando W. Wilson (1950) and John P. Kenney (1959) were among the first to apply planning to police management. In court administration Arthur Vanderbilt planned the overhaul of the New Jersey court system and saw that plan implemented. He then applied his experiences to advising courts nationally. Planning is an extension of the decision-making process. It is future-oriented decisionmaking in which a manager anticipates and visualizes the future and makes decisions based upon that vision of the future. "A plan is a predetermined course of action" (Massie, 1987: 83). It consists of five distinct elements (Massie, 1987: 84-85):

1. setting goals

2. searching for opportunities (data collection, forecasting, research and development activities)

3. formulating plans (program development)

4. setting targets (defining desired end states)

5. following up

Long-Range, Intermediate, or Short-Range Planning: The time dimension is a factor in planning. Planning can be long-range, intermediate, or short-range (Kenney, 1959: 15-16). There is no definition with regard to which is which, but as a general guide, long-range planning involves multiple operational cycles that are usually defined in terms of the budget cycle for the agency (e.g., in a state using a two-year budget, the operational cycle is two years). An intermediate or short-range plan involves one operational cycle or just part of one cycle. Typically a short-range plan is a response to an immediate problem or the one-time application of some new methods, procedures, or technologies. Planning a police response to a major public event, like a presidential visit to the city, would be a short-term plan. In court administration, implementing a new court procedure also would involve short-term planning. Preparing to train correctional officers in use of a new communications system also would be short-term planning. An intermediate plan might be developed to develop, implement, and evaluate a comprehensive community-oriented policing program or a new correctional treatment program. Most strategic planning in criminal justice is long-range planning.

Strategic (Large-Scale) Planning: Strategic managerial planning was a key feature of large-scale military planning in the two World Wars. It first became popular in commercial management in the 1950s (Gilmore and Brandenburg, 1962), and was applied in the public sector in the late 1980s. The Law Enforcement Assistance Administration (LEAA) required comprehensive statewide strategic plans for states to become eligible for LEAA grants in the 1970s. In turn, the states required regions, counties, and cities to develop their own strategic plans to qualify for pass-through grants. The LEAA is long gone, but strategic planning has endured. Thus, strategic planning became part of criminal justice management in localities across the United States, and urban planners became a common feature of local government (Gordon, 2005). Newer federal criminal justice programs also called for strategic planning, including Community Oriented Policing (COP) programs (Cordner, 1997; Zhao, Thurman, and Ren, 2008). In criminal justice applications, strategic planning will involve the political leadership of the jurisdiction, the chief executives of the criminal justice agencies involved in the plan, and representation of community and client populations.

The plans can be either market-oriented (externally oriented) or centralized (internally oriented) approaches (Stewart and Garson: 123-129), determined by whose interests, needs, and opinions are being considered. Large-scale strategic planning can be national, statewide, or community-wide in scope. It is broad in application, influencing the lives of many people and representing multiple agencies and client groups both within and outside the organization (Stewart and Garson, 1983: Chapter 6). Zhao, Thurman, and Ren (2008: 20-23) have developed a four-part model for strategic planning in COP programs. It is derivative of the leadership style models discussed in Chapter 4. With dimensions of participation ("ranks involved") and "extent of application," their model reflects the contrast of hierarchal scientific management planning and more democratic, full-participation human relations planning in the implementation and continuation of COP programs. These are large-scale plans because they integrate efforts of the police with a wide range of community interests and agencies, both within criminal justice and beyond it.

In recent years we have observed a vivid example of strategic planning: the national responses to 9/11. In the months after the September 11th attack on the United States, the federal government, the states, localities, and private organizations were brought together to develop a national response to the threat of terrorism. Among the obvious products were the creation of the Department of Homeland Security (DHS), the passage of the USA PATRIOT Act (officially the Uniting and Strengthening America by Providing Appropriate Tools Required to Intercept and Obstruct Terrorism Act), and the undertaking of aggressive anti-terror operations worldwide. These plans involved and integrated the efforts and resources of many entities, including the Department of Defense (DOD), including the Army, Navy, Marines, Air Force, Defense Intelligence Agency (DIA), and National Security Agency (NSA); the Department of Justice (DOJ), including the U.S. Marshal's Service; the Drug Enforcement Agency (DEA); the Federal Bureau of Investigation (FBI) (with its Joint Terrorism Task Force (JTTF); the Department of Energy (DOE); the Central Intelligence Agency (CIA); the Centers for Disease Control and Prevention (CDC); and many others at both the federal and state levels. Also involved in national security planning have been nongovernmental organizations (NGOs) such as the International Association of Chiefs of Police (IACP) and the International City/County Management Association (ICMA) (Oliver, 2007).

Small-Scale/Operational/Tactical Planning: Tactical or operational planning is used to develop a project or program, carry out some anticipated new activity, prepare for future developments, and so on. Operational or tactical planning is centered on the organization itself and involves implementation of tasks clearly associated with that organization. Other agencies or client populations may be impacted, but not in so significant a way as to disrupt their own continuing operations. For example, a police crackdown on some particular traffic violation may result in more traffic cases in court, but not so many more as to require special court responses. A court plan to improve case docketing will bear upon the schedules of witness programs, the prosecutor's office, and defense attorneys, but will not introduce any new burdens upon them.

Forecasting is an important feature of planning. When forecasting, a manager makes certain informed, empirical assumptions about what the future is likely to bring. It employs several processes (Massie, 1987: 87-88):

1. quantitative time series analysis—using data on existing patterns to project future patterns

2. derived forecasts—using forecasts from similar situations as models for the one under consideration (e.g., How has another state achieved the same objectives our state aims to achieve?)

3. causal models—using mathematical models to express relationships among interactive variables

4. surveys of individual plans and attitudes—a survey of individuals can anticipate what they hope to achieve, and thus provide a model for where the whole organization should be moving (e.g., by asking how many of their employees want to continue their formal educations in the next five years, and in what specialties, management can develop coordinated staff development training plans)

5. brainstorming—a group comes together to discuss options under some pre-agreed conditions, such as:

    a. no criticizing the ideas of others

    b. encouraging support for the ideas of others

    c. recording all comments for future consideration

6. Delphi method—RAND Corporation method using expert opinions collected independently by questionnaire

7. contingent forecasting scenarios—developing a likely narrative of how events might unfold, as in writing a novel or short story

Planning is absolutely necessary in certain situations. According to James Thompson (1967), plans are needed for:

1. Buffering (protection from environment with input/output structures)

2. Leveling (balancing the inputs and outputs to reduce fluctuations)

3. Adaptation (dealing with changes that cannot be leveled or buffered)

4. Rationing (restricting input or output to match capacity)

The Products of Planning

Types of Decisions: Decisions fall within three broad categories: (1) routine (assigning leaves, days off, etc.), (2) problem solving—crisis, emergencies, and challenges, and (3) innovative future-oriented decisions. These will result in the following four products:

1. *Policy:* a guide for making decisions.

2. *Rule:* a precise statement of what is required with minimal discretion.

3. *Procedure:* a detailed system of actions (steps) to be followed to accomplish a task.

4. *Tasks:* specific actions to be taken to carry out the plan.

Methods of Group Decisionmaking: Cooperation and Consensus versus Competition

Group decisionmaking is thought to be better than making "individualized" decisions for several reasons (Shermer, 2004):

1. Groups have "broader fund of knowledge," that is, they have more experience collectively than any one manager is likely to possess on his or her own.

2. Groups are likely to identify far more alternatives.

3. Groups are likely to be more critical of alternatives than a solo manager.

4. Groups will take more risks, "think outside of the box" more readily, and be more creative (as potential blame is shared).

5. Group decisions are more likely to be accepted when they are the product of multiple authors rather than a single author.

There are potential flaws in group decisionmaking. We are cautioned that: "Group decision making is rarely of as high quality as the decisions of the organization's most proficient member" (Stewart and Garson, 1983: 138). There are several reasons for this:

1. Group discussion inhibits some people.

2. There is a general desire to "get along" in a group setting.

3. Dominance by a few vocal opinion-setters can determine the outcome.

4. The desire to incorporate ideas from all participants in order to avoid leaving anyone out can produce unsatisfactory results. This infamous committee malaise is humorously exemplified by the camel: "The camel is a racehorse designed by a committee."

There are other potential problems to be considered:

1. *Personalities* within the decision group sometimes will clash with disruptive results. Egos will clash when some members of the decision group seek to promote agendas and ideas in competition with others having strongly held opposing views.

2. The *homogeneity versus heterogeneity* of the group can be a factor. Multiple individuals sharing the same viewpoint (a homogenous group) will be far less likely to propose or consider a wide-range of options.

3. The *setting* can either facilitate or retard deliberation. The talk circle usually will work better than other arrangements. It is important to avoid prominent seating [thrones] and cross-table barriers when free and open discussion is desired. A meeting in the senior manager's office will be dominated by him or her, whereas a meeting in a conference room used by them all usually will encourage freer flow of ideas.

4. The *group size* will influence the deliberations. Too small a group will limit ideas, and too many participants will be unmanageable, circumstantially limiting the opportunities for all to take part. An ideal group size will be in the five- to 12-person range, the actual number reflecting the interests to be represented in the deliberations. When the group must be large because of other considerations, either voting or parliamentary procedures will be employed. There are, however, problems with them as well.

Democratic, Nondivisive Group Decisionmaking: Voting and parliamentary procedure may be democratic, but often they are also competitive and divisive. Various alternatives to traditional voting methods have been offered (Dasgupta and Maskin, 2004). Two decision-making techniques using a mix of democratic principles and expertise are the *Delphi method* and the *nominal group technique*. Both are now widely used.

Delphi Method: Developed by the RAND Corporation in the 1950s, the method allows the manager the advantage of using many of the best minds in the country on an issue, technology, or area of expertise, without having to put them on the payroll for an extended period. The process includes the following:

1. Identify and enlist outside experts.

2. Administer questionnaires on the issue by mail asking:

    a. direction

    b. degree

    c. time frame

    d. likelihood

3. Aggregate results from survey and re-edit questionnaire.

4. Resubmit revised questionnaire.

5. Repeat cycle until new responses decline to negligible level.

6. Arrange a face-to-face analysis session.

7. Define the explicit group consensus.

Nominal Group Technique: Developed by Andre L. Delbecq, Andrew H. Van De Ven, and David H. Gustafson (1975), the nominal group technique uses the expertise of those already in the organization. It is less costly than hiring dozens or hundred of consultants, and has the additional advantage of involving those who are or will be affected by the decisions reached.

1. Hold a face-to-face meeting of experts and involved in-house staff on the given problem.

2. Invite all participants to offer ideas on the issue.

3. List ideas on paper, one idea at a time, as an analyst records all.

4. After all ideas are recorded, each is discussed for:

   a. clarification,

   b. agreement, and

   c. disagreement.

5. Conduct anonymous balloting to rank order suggestions.

6. Lead a further discussion of rank-order results to eliminate duplication and to consolidate similar ideas, dropping low-priority, low-regard items.

7. Conduct anonymous final ranking, with average ranks calculated, to select the preferred solution.

Systems Management and Planning

In criminal justice planning generally, social planning models have been employed reflecting the rise of "the systems management" philosophy and the rise of Management by Objectives (MBO) (Lynch and Lynch, 2005: Chapter 13). Recall that Souryal (1985; 1995) views "systems" as a school of thought in management science on par with either scientific management or human relations.

The growth of computer modeling has required a method for managerial planning that conforms to the "path models" of computer analysis. This reinforces the systems approach by indicating the concern for the system as an entire thing, rather than the particularizing of "task mission" planning.

Box 6.2 • Management Decision-Making and Planning Models and Styles

Different authors have presented various models and proposed differing styles used by decisionmakers and planners. Klofas, Stojkovic, and Kalinich (1998: 300-301) list the following:

Sequentialists use experience to select key information, then proceed to examine these in prioritized, sequential, and detailed fashion.

Ah, Yes! People: amass a great body of information, infer a pattern, and then make a decision that unsystematically fits this pattern.

Simplifiers seek to reduce the problem to its simplest expression, then decide based on that simplification.

Ratifiers wait to see what other are thinking, then join the apparent majority.

Planners also have been classified according to their styles. Ronald Lynch notes that most try to create a balance of risk and concern for system (Lynch and Lynch, 2005: 160-163). Lynch classifies planners into one of four categories:

Purposeful: High concern for continuity of the system, yet willing to take risks (objective-oriented);

Traditional: High concern for continuity of the system and preferring to be low-risk (status-quo oriented);

Crisis: Low concern for the continuity of the system; unwilling to take risks, but forced into crisis problem-solving (beset by emergencies; not a planner at all, a reactor) [This is not the planner who anticipates crises and does what he or she can to avoid their disruptions.]

Entrepreneurial: Low concern for continuity of the system; willing to take risks (objective-oriented), willing to attempt exploration and speculation (action-oriented).

Program Planning

The key elements to program planning include:

1. Objective setting
2. Data collection — fully exploit "historical data" identify available resources, project requirements to be served, seek out working examples (models)
3. Simulation — mentally track each actor's role in the events sequentially (chronologically) (PERT/CPM will illustrate), scenario-building
4. Circulate the plan to interested parties — solicit suggestions
5. Synthesize suggestions — especially those that are most critical and negative—these will best predict problems

6. Seek approval for revised plan.

7. Implement plan.

8. Revise continuously, even when implemented, to reflect new information and status reports, problems encountered, solved, and so on.

Box 6.3 • Analytical Dimensions for Planning Purposes

- goals
- functions
- administration and policy
- information systems and data requirements
- procedures and practices
- human-labor resources
- clients
- physical facilities
- cost and budgetary considerations

Problem Analysis

According to Lynch and Lynch(2005: 168-171), there are five steps to **problem analysis**:

1. Recognize and identify the problems of the organization.

2. Separate into their component areas, answering several key questions. Where? When? Who is most concerned? What is the extent, magnitude and seriousness of the problem? Are there any trends in evidence?

3. Prioritize by component area, and among components.

4. Select and analyze the priority problems in detail.

5 Test for true causes. What really is producing the problem? Avoid treating only the symptoms when the disease itself is left unremedied.

The armed services of the United States long ago realized the critical importance of detailed planning for complex operations. Beginning in 1917 during World War I, army staff officers were provided a manual to help them with performing their staff functions, including problem analysis and planning. The staff study format in Box 6.4 was developed for the manual to assist in problem analysis. Various editions and revisions of what is known in the army as *FM-101-5* were prepared as the army faced other wars and periods of conflict—in 1940 for World

Box 6.4 • Staff Study Format

1. Statement of the problem or issue under study.

2. Assumptions, theories, and inferences being considered.

3. Summary of data and relevant facts (appendices may be attached).

4. Discussion of the options available.

5. Conclusions based upon the assumptions and supported by the data.

6. Actions recommended for the agency.

7. Concurrences and nonconcurrences from others.

8. Appendices with detailed data.

War II, in 1954 and 1960 for the Cold War, in 1972 for Vietnam, and in 1984 and 1997 for contemporary global challenges including the current "War on Terror" (Military/Info, 2008). In these evolving manuals, a process for carrying out comprehensive large-scale planning and operational decisionmaking was developed that involves staff input and joint decisionmaking by the lead manager and his or her staff. This "military decisionmaking process" has been proven by the test of time. This is modified for nonmilitary applications and provided in Box 6.5 as the "manager-staff decision-making process."

Box 6.5 • Military or Manager-Staff Decision-making Process

The U.S. military has done complex operational planning and decisionmaking, involving thousands and even millions of persons for much of its history. The armed services have developed a procedure for this, adapted here for criminal justice organizations doing large-scale planning and operational decisionmaking as the "manager-staff decision-making process."

1. Mission (Objective) Determined — by the manager or by the manager's superior.

2. Estimate of the Situation — initial estimate from information immediately available and/or from experience.

3. Planning Guidance — given by the manager to his or her staff (omitted if the manager is coming to his or her decision without staff input), including such elements as:

    A. Specified tasks contained within the general mission.

    B. Implied tasks essential to the mission.

    C. Preferences, options, possible course of action.

Box 6.5 *(continued)*

    D. Potential sources of information and data.

    E. Staff's functional organization — if not already delineated (who will work on what aspects of the planning).

    F. Timetables, deadlines, reports, and inputs requested.

4. Staff Estimates (staff work rising from the planning guidance [omitted if there is no staff], uses the Staff Study (see Box 6.3):

    A. Problem statement

    B. Assumptions (derived from above)

    C. Facts Bearing on the Problem

    D. Discussion of Options

    E. Conclusions (original staff work)

    F. Actions Recommended
       See: the Staff Study (see Box 6.3)

5. Manager's Estimate/Decisions

    A. Mission

    B. Situation

    C. Courses of Action (options)

    D. Analysis of Opposing Courses of Action — factors to overcome

    E. Comparison of our Courses of Actions — the agency's options

    F. Decision/Recommendation

6. Preparation of Plans/Orders — done by either the manager himself/herself or by the staff:

    A. Situation Statement: opposition; assets

    B. Mission: what specifically is to be done

    C. Execution: the concept of the operation and submissions for each participant

    D. Support: material, services, personnel needs to sustain the activities.

    E. Control/Coordination: supervisory activities.

7. Approval of Plans/Orders by the manager (omitted if no staff work is involved).

8. Issuances of Plans/Orders: Communications

9. Supervision by the manager and managerial staff

10. Mission Completion — concluding step, confirming that the mission has been accomplished, crediting the contributions of participants, and usually including a follow-up report with lessons learned.

Organizational Development

Organizational development is planned, organization-wide, long-term change. It applies principles of the behavioral sciences and requires changes in attitudes, behavior, and organizational structure to achieve greater individual and organizational effectiveness (French and Bell, 1999: 1, 24). There are eight features of organizational development:

1. It is ongoing and dynamic, a continuous process.

2. It is applied behavioral/social sciences, employing
   - psychology
   - sociology
   - economics
   - political science
   - business administration.

3. It is a re-education process.

4. It is a "systems approach" that treats agency activities as interactive operations.

5. It is a rational process based upon data acquisition evaluation and verification.

6. It is experienced-based.

7. It uses planning and decision-making processes such as means-ends analysis.

8. It uses work teams or task forces to achieve its implementation.

Forming the Work Teams: Task forces and T-Groups (also called *T-Teams* and *tiger teams*) are small working committees or training groups that study, make collective decisions, and implement action programs to effect major changes. Typically the T-Group leader is a "passive facilitator" and "resource person" who guides the group to help it find its own change solutions.

Management workshops are especially useful when outside consultants are employed to facilitate and control the process. A facilitator administers a questionnaire to the management group of the organization, asking them what their organization does well (getting the process thinking positively), what it can improve upon, and what new things it should consider. The facilitator then will conduct follow-up interviews with key submanagers to develop an agenda for the upcoming workshop. This agenda should be discussed with the senior manager to include his or her inputs. The workshop is scheduled, and the key decisionmakers in the management team are brought together. Notes are taken, and a synthesis of contributions is prepared. These are shared in a report distributed afterward.

Retreats are similar to management workshops. The planners of the retreat take the key people away from the workplace to a relaxing setting where the key manager and staff can learn to interact constructively.

Box 6.6 • Problems in Managerial Decisionmaking (A Little Humor)

Dead Pony Principles of Management: The origins of this item have been lost, for it has been circulating on the Internet in one form or another for many years with the authorship long since deleted. The humorist who penned the original version was expressing the cynicism that surrounds the failures of modern management.

In the version shared here, we are informed that Dakota Amerind tribal wisdom says that when you discover you are riding a dead pony, the best strategy is to dismount. However, managers often try other strategies with dead ponies, including the following:

1. Buying a stronger whip.
2. Changing riders.
3. Saying "This is the way we always have ridden this pony."
4. Appointing a committee to study the pony.
5. Arranging to visit other sites to see how they ride dead ponies.
6. Increasing the standards to ride dead ponies.
7. Appointing a "tiger team" to revive the dead pony.
8. Creating a training session to increase our riding ability.
9. Comparing the state of dead ponies in today's environment.
10. Changing the requirements, declaring that "this pony is not dead."
11. Hiring contractors to ride the dead pony.
12. Harnessing several dead ponies together for increased speed.
13. Declaring that "no pony is too dead to beat."
14. Providing additional funding to increase the pony's performance.
15. Doing a cost-effectiveness study to see if contractors can ride it cheaper.
16. Purchasing a product to make dead ponies run faster.
17. Declaring that the pony is "better, faster, and cheaper" dead.
18. Forming a quality circle to find uses for dead ponies.
19. Revisiting the performance requirements for ponies.
20. Saying this pony was procured with cost as an independent variable.
21. Promoting the dead pony to a supervisory position.

Summary

Mastering decisionmaking and planning is something of an art. Some managers excel at both; some have to work hard at them. Making decisions and planning ahead will be a chore faced by all criminal justice managers. It is important that the manager be flexible rather than taking up one style and rigidly sticking to it.

Learning Objectives

Upon finishing this chapter you should be able to do the following:

▶ 1. Discuss the features of the four models of managerial decisionmaking: rational choice, bureaucratic, decision trees, and political.

▶ 2. Distinguish between operational decisions and managerial decisions.

▶ 3. Contrast long-range and short-range planning in terms of the planning cycles of criminal justice organizations.

▶ 4. Discuss the five key factors a manager should consider in selecting a managerial decision-making method.

IMPORTANT TERMS AND NAMES

- bounded rationality
- decision process model
- decision trees
- Delphi method
- discretion
- forecasting
- management workshops
- nominal group technique
- organizational development
- policy
- problem analysis

- procedure
- programmed decisions
- rational choice model
- retreats
- rule
- satisficing
- standard operating procedures (SOPs)
- T-Groups
- tasks
- task forces

References and Supplemental Sources

Argyris, Chris (1957). *Personality and Organization*. New York: Harper Collins.

Barnard, Chester (1938) [1989]. "Economy of Incentives" in *Classic Readings in Organizational Behavior*, edited by J. Steven Ott (1989). Pacific Grove, CA: Brooks/Cole.

Cyert, Richard M., and March, James G. (1959). *Modern Organization Theory*. New York: Wiley.

Dasgupta, Partha, and Eric Maskin (2004). "The Fairest Vote of All," *Scientific American*, 290(3): 92-97.

French, Wendell L., and Cecil H. Bell, Jr. (1973). *Organizational Development*. Englewood Cliffs, NJ: Prentice Hall.

French, Wendell L., and Cecil H. Bell, Jr. (1999). *Organizational Development*, 6th ed. Upper Saddle River, NJ: Prentice Hall.

Gilmore Frank F., and Richard G. Brandenburg (1962). *Harvard Business Review*, 4(6): 61-69.

Gordon, Gerald L. (2005). *Strategic Planning for Local Government*, 2nd ed. Washington, DC: International City/County Management Association.

Harvey, Jerry B. (1974). "The Abilene Paradox: The Management of Agreement," *Organizational Dynamics* (Summer): 63-80.

Kenney, John P. (1959). *Police Management Planning*. Springfield, IL: Charles C Thomas.

Klofas, John, Stan Stojkovic, and David Kalinich (1998). *Criminal Justice Organizations: Administration and Management*, 2nd ed. Belmont, CA: West-Wadsworth.

Lynch, Ronald G., and Scott Lynch (2005). *The Police Manager*, 6th ed. Newark, NJ: LexisNexis Matthew Bender.

March, James G., and Herbert A. Simon (1958). *Organizations*. New York: Wiley.

Massie, Joseph L. (1987). *Essentials of Management*, 4th ed. Englewood Cliffs, NJ: Prentice Hall.

Military/Info (2008) "Staff Operations." Plymouth, MN: Military/Info. Found at http://www.military-info.com/MPHOTO/p054.htm

Oliver, William M. (2007). *Homeland Security for Policing*. Upper Saddle River, NJ: Prentice Hall.

Pfeffer, Jeffrey (1981). *Power in Organizations*. London: Pitman.

Shafritz, Jay M., and J. Steven Ott, eds. (1996). *Classics of Organizational Theory*, 3rd ed. Pacific Grove, CA: Brooks/Cole.

Shermer, Michael (2004). "Common Sense: Surprising New Research That Crowds Are Often Smarter Than Individuals," *Scientific American*, 291(6): 38.

Simon, Herbert (1997). *Administrative Behavior: A Study of Decision-Making Processes in Administrative Organizations*. New York: Free Press.

Souryal, Sam S. (1985). *Police Organization and Administration*. Cincinnati: Pilgrimage/Anderson.

Souryal, Sam S. (1995). *Police Organization and Administration*, 2nd ed. Cincinnati: Anderson.

Stewart, Debra, and G. David Garson (1983). *Organizational Behavior and Public Management*. New York: Marcel Dekker.

Thompson, James D. (1967). *Organizations in Action: Social Science Bases of Administrative Theory*. New York: McGraw-Hill.

Thompson, James D. (2003). *Organizations in Action: Social Science Bases of Administrative Theory*, with a new preface by Mayer N. Zald and new introduction by W. Richard Scott. New Brunswick, NJ: Transaction.

Delbecq, Andre L., Andrew H. Van de Ven, and David H. Gustafson (1975). *Group Techniques for Program Planning: A Guide to Nominal Group and Delphi Processes*. Glenview, IL: Scott, Foresman.

Vanderbilt, Arthur T. (1947). *Minimum Standards of Judicial Administration*. Washington, DC: American Bar Association.

Wildavsky, Aaron (1973). "If Planning Is Everything, Maybe It's Nothing," *Policy Sciences*, 4: 127-153.

Wilson, Orlando W. (1950). *Police Administration*. New York: McGraw-Hill.

Zhao, Jihong "Solomon," Quint C. Thurman, and Ling Ren (2008). "An Examination of Strategic Planning in American Law Enforcement Agencies: A National Study," *Police Quarterly*, 11(1): 3-26.

7
Evaluating, Appraising, and Assessing Performance

The "E" in LODESTAR is for evaluating. Evaluation and the closely related concepts of *appraisal* and *assessment* are major managerial tasks, and often are very troubling for the manager. The terms "evaluation," "appraisal," and "assessment" are often used interchangeably in the management literature and in criminal justice workplaces. **Assessment** focuses on the process of determining performance of individuals and organizations. Management theorists will speak of tools and instruments used in the assessment process. Evaluation uses assessment processes to produce evaluations of individuals and work groups. Appraisal is the final aspect of the assessment-evaluation process. An **appraisal** is the score, rating, or ranking given an individual or organization. Because performance appraisals are the products of assessment and evaluation processes, the three are closely entwined, and one is difficult to distinguish from the other in practice. For the purposes of this chapter, the distinctions among them will not be developed further. Evaluation activities are needed both for individuals in the organization and for the organization as a whole, as well as for each of its operational subunits.

Individual Evaluation

Individual evaluation is sometimes referred to as **performance appraisal**. It often involves managers and supervisors assigning ratings to subordinates. Individuals often are given ratings by which they may be compared to other coworkers. The chief criminal justice manager should develop an evaluation plan, if one does not already exist. If there is an existing evaluation plan, the manager should review it occasionally to determine if it addresses the needs of the organization and its employees. An example of an evaluation plan is found in Box 7.1.

Box 7.1 • Individual Performance Evaluation Plan

1. The evaluation process and criteria employed will be explained to and discussed with all new personnel upon reporting for employment, and annually thereafter.

2. The evaluation of each staff member will be prepared by the immediate supervisor of the employee.

3. All employees shall develop and submit to their supervisors an individual professional development plan that will comply with the employees' job descriptions and the mission, goals, and objectives of the organization.

4. The individual professional development plan will be reviewed annually by the supervisor and updates as required.

5. All employees will be evaluated (annually, semi-annually, quarterly).

6. Each supervisor preparing evaluations will be trained on evaluation techniques and standards, and on the use of the evaluation instruments.

7. Each person evaluated shall be given a copy of the evaluation, and will acknowledge receiving it in writing.

8. An evaluated employee will be provided an opportunity for submitting a rebuttal or appeal.

9. The organization shall have an evaluation appeals panel composed of experienced supervisory personnel of the agency.

10. The employee exercising the right to file an appeal will be given an opportunity to review all documents to be presented to the evaluation appeals panel.

11. The appeals panel shall prepare a statement of its findings and attach this to the original evaluation if that evaluation is upheld.

12. The appeals panel may direct that an inappropriate evaluation be revised and resubmitted to correct errors or other identified issues.

13. The evaluation plan process will not discriminate on the basis of race, national origin, religion, marital status, sex, or disability.

14. The evaluation shall be filed with the official personnel records of the employee.

15. Individual evaluations, rebuttals, and appellate reports will be kept as permanent documents.

Managerial Issues in Personnel Evaluation

Content and Criteria of Evaluations: "You can't expect what you don't inspect" is the mantra of the police academy drill sergeant. Indeed, evaluation criteria ought to reflect that which is most important in the job description of the employee. Clearly, evaluations should be based upon job descriptions and the expectations of the job. Wilson and McLaren (1972) offer the following categories for police evaluations:

- observance of work hours
- attendance
- grooming and dress
- compliance with rules
- safety practices
- public contacts
- suspect contacts
- employee contacts
- knowledge of work
- work judgments
- planning and organizing
- job skill level
- quality of work
- volume of acceptable work
- meeting deadlines
- accepts responsibility
- accepts direction
- accepts change
- effectiveness under stress
- appearance of work station
- operation and care of equipment
- work coordination
- initiative
- supervisory factors (when appropriate):
    - —scheduling and coordinating
    - —training and instruction
    - —effectiveness
    - —evaluating subordinates
    - —judgments and decisions
    - —leadership
    - —operational economy
    - —supervisory control

They also leave space for additional factors.

Frequency of Evaluations: It is a managerial choice to determine the frequency of performance appraisals. They can be as frequent as monthly or quarterly, but more often are done annually. Novice and probationary employees may be subjected to more frequent evaluation during their probationary period. Veteran employees in highly professional organizations can be evaluated far less frequently.

The Evaluator: The general rule is that the evaluation should be done by the supervisor having direct control over the evaluated subordinate, as defined by the organizational chain of command. The person designated to prepare the evaluation is the **evaluator** or **rater**. Often the next manager in the chain of command is designated as the **endorser**, whose responsibility is to see that the evaluation is timely, reasonable, and appropriate.

Shared or Secret? When employee improvement is an objective in giving evaluations, it is the best policy to require **shared evaluations**. When the evaluation is shared, the evaluator provides the evaluated party a copy of the evaluation. Often the evaluated person is given an opportunity to respond and even appeal.

There are times and places for **secret evaluations**, such as special evaluations rendered to assist in making some kinds of highly sensitive personnel decisions, such as selecting subordinates for further training or schooling, identifying persons having potential for advancement, greater leadership and promotion, or identifying individuals for dismissal when reductions in force are being contemplated.

Some managers prefer secret evaluations simply to avoid sharing their appraisals with the employee. There are several important purposes to evaluations, and most of these are not served by secrecy. Nevertheless, some criminal justice organizations still pursue secrecy practices.

Purposes of Individual Evaluations: Among the purposes for giving formal individual evaluations are:

1. assisting in individual development

2. encouraging and maintaining discipline

3. allocating promotions or compensation

Formats: Many formats are acceptable, and each has its distinctive advantages and disadvantages. Some agencies employ mixed formats, asking for information in several ways.

Means of Assessment: Criminal justice managers will assess work performance of subordinates in several ways:

1. regular observation and routine contact during work

2. visitation to workplaces

Figure 7.1 • Alexander Maconochie Correctional Center Managerial Appraisal

Alexander Maconochie Correctional Center Managerial Appraisal

Manager's Name: _____

Manager's Unit: _____

Time Period: _____

Evaluation Date: _____

1. ADMINISTRATION AND MANAGEMENT FUNCTIONS

Rate the unit manager on the performance factors using the performance definitions:

        1 = truly exceptional outstanding performance
        2 = routinely exceeds expectations
        3 = fully satisfactory
        4 = needs improvement
        5 = unsatisfactory

Performance Factor	Rating	Remarks and Explanations
Organizational Leadership		
Organization of Work		
Planning		
Decision Making		
Organizational Development		
Information Management		
Budgeting and Resource Allocation		

2. INTERPERSONAL SKILLS

Rate the unit manager on the performance factors using the performance definitions:

        1 = truly exceptional outstanding performance
        2 = routinely exceeds expectations
        3 = fully satisfactory
        4 = needs improvement
        5 = unsatisfactory

Performance Factor	Rating	Remarks and Explanations
Oral Communication		
Written Communication		
Coordination and Collaboration		
Supervisory Control		
Commitment to Equal Opportunity		
Staff Appraisal and Development		

3. INDIVIDUAL LEADERSHIP ATTRIBUTES

Rate the unit manager on the performance factors using the performance definitions:

        1 = truly exceptional outstanding performance
        2 = routinely exceeds expectations
        3 = fully satisfactory
        4 = needs improvement
        5 = unsatisfactory

Performance Factor	Rating	Remarks and Explanations
Mentoring of Subordinates		
Empowering Subordinates		
Team Building		
Professionalism		
Vision		
Self-Improvement		
Innovation		
Objectivity		
Credibility		
Flexibility		
Effort and Initiative		

4. OVERALL APPRAISAL (Please check one.)

_____ Exceptional And Outstanding
_____ Routinely Exceeds Expectations
_____ Fully Satisfactory
_____ Needs Improvement
_____ Unsatisfactory

What were the unit manager's performance highlights in the past year?
_____

What could be improved in the unit manager's performance in the next year?
_____

What should be the unit manager's new performance goals for the next year?
_____

Date _____

Evaluator's Signature _____

Evaluated Manager's Signature _____

Date Evaluation Reviewed by the Evaluated Unit Manager: _____

Figure 7.2 • Vanderbilt County District Court Clerical Employee Evaluation Form

Vanderbilt County District Court Clerical Employee Evaluation Form

Employee Name: _____
Employee Title: _____
Period Covered: _____
Date of Evaluation: _____
Days Absent in Rating Period: _____

	Excellent	Very Good	Satisfactory	Needs Improvement	Inadequate
1. Work Quality					
2. Technical Skills					
3. Reliability					
4. Initiative					
5. Versatility					
6. Efficiency					
7. Public Demeanor					
8. Punctuality					

General remarks on employee's performance (The rater must explain and justify all "excellent" and all "inadequate" scores given above):

Rater's goals for the employee in the coming year (These will be mutually discussed by the supervisor and employee, and will be based upon the employee's job description):

Name of Rater: _____   Signature of Rater: _____

Acknowledgement by Employee (signature): _____
The Employee's signature above does not imply agreement with the evaluation received.
The Employee may attach a one-page response to the ratings given if there is disagreement.

Date Acknowledged: _____   Response Attached: _____ yes   _____ no

3. conducting formal inspections

4. reviewing management reports

5. asking the workers to evaluate themselves

6. performance testing, such as:

    a. scores from weapons qualification

    b. results of physical agility and fitness tests

    c. written or orally administered knowledge tests

    d. technical "hands-on" skills tests

The Stress of Personnel Evaluation: Individual evaluations can be highly traumatic events in employee-supervisor relations. Even an overall "good" evaluation can be disappointing to an employee who has a very high self-image. Some managers are quite adept at "damning with faint praise." All too often evaluations are viewed as punitive, backward-looking, and regressive.

Management by Objectives (MBO): MBO provides a useful, forward-looking, and personally enriching approach to individual performance evaluation. MBO can be defined as "a process whereby individual managers and employees identify goals and work toward their completion and evaluation within a specific work period" (Klofas, Stojkovic, and Kalinich, 1990: 96). The key is the "process" (Massie, 1987: 124-125). The concept originated with Peter F. Drucker in *The Practice of Management* (1954: 119, 121-122), and was popularized by George Odiorne in *Management by Objectives* (1965) and many others who were influenced by Drucker's concepts.

Box 7.2 • Doing MBO with a Subordinate

Step 1: The supervisor begins the process as a traditional scientific manager by preparing a comprehensive job description for the subordinate (or updates and uses one already on file). This is given to the subordinate employee who is instructed to:

Step 2: Identify the subordinate's work objectives and their measurement standards in writing. These objectives should include:

> Routine Objectives – the subordinate will express the job in his or her own terms, following job description framework.

> Problem Solving Objectives – these allow the subordinate to make observations and suggestions to improve the organization in its goals.

> Innovative Objectives – these allow the subordinate to propose new ideas for the organization in which the employee wishes to take part.

> Personal Objectives – these allow the subordinate to express personal needs and ambitions as they relate to the job.

Step 3: The manager and subordinate employee spend some time together going over the objectives, creating a dialogue on common objectives. They should produce a common set of objectives upon which they both agree and both will agree to use to evaluate the success of the subordinate.

Step 4: They put the revised objective statement aside and come back to it six months or a year later (whichever is the manager's policy) and the manager will review the objectives with the subordinate to assess the progress of the subordinate toward meeting the enumerated objectives.

Step 5: This review is used by the supervising manager as the basis for periodic individual evaluations. The supervisor will have the subordinate evaluate himself/herself against those objectives, rather than evaluating the employee unilaterally. Together they will agree on what has been achieved and what remains to be done. They prepare a summary report of the prior term's accomplishments and shortfalls, and file it as the performance appraisal for that rated period.

Step 6: Together the supervisor and the subordinate employee identify new and modified objectives for the next period. In essence, they return to Step 2 and start again.

Organizational Evaluation

As important as evaluation is for individuals, it also is a critical managerial activity to help identify ways to improve the entire organization. Statistics on agency performance are essential measures of agency performance. Since the 1930s, police agencies have used the Uniform Crime Reports (UCR), prepared annually by the Federal Bureau of Investigation, to assess their comparative success in dealing with the crime problem, making arrests, and clearing criminal cases. Prosecutors keep statistics on the number of cases presented to grand juries and brought to preliminary hearings and trials. They keep count of the number of cases plea bargained and handled by various alternatives to adjudication. Many prosecutors publicize their conviction records. The courts track the number of cases heard and keep additional statistics on the number of days taken to bring cases to trial, on continuances, and on the number of decisions and sentences issued. Some courts also collect data on the fines levied and funds collected by the courts on behalf of the state and on behalf of crime victims and successful civil litigants. Correctional units keep track of data on the numbers of inmates in their custody; overcrowding; escapes; the average length of time served; participation in furlough, study, and work-release programs; discharge data; and the productivity of their correctional industries. Probation and parole agencies keep track of the number of clients under their supervision; success and failure (recidivism rates); probation violations discovered; parole revocation hearings; and successful discharge from probation or parole supervision. All are appropriate criminal justice performance measures, and such managerial statistics typically are made public.

However, their interpretation is complex. A police department may have low UCR statistics because it successfully prevents and suppresses more crime than other comparable police departments. However, low UCR statistics also could reflect a lack of public confidence in the local police, hence, their reluctance to call the police when criminally victimized. Some police departments have deliberately falsified UCR data to create a false impression of their performance. A high prosecutorial conviction rate can indicate stellar performance in court, or pressure on indicted individuals to accept excessively lenient plea bargains to achieve convictions easily. The number of court decisions and verdicts does not speak to the quality or justice of those verdicts. Correctional data can be interpreted in multiple ways. Early release of unrehabilitated inmates may reduce overcrowding but does not improve public safety. High rates of probation or parole failure actually may indicate very close supervision, while high rates of successful discharge may be explained by a lack of effort in supervising probationers and parolees and failure in detecting their misconduct.

Moreover, there are other aspects of the organization that these managerial performance measures miss entirely. Organizational efficiency cannot be measured easily. Organizational standards of professionalism and integrity are not to be determined from such performance statistics. While commercial managers can look to "the bottom line" of profitability, criminal justice agencies are not created to make profits. Criminal justice managers are wise to develop and look to other measures of agency performance to augment the official statistics. Among the other aspects of a criminal justice agency performance that are especially useful in doing an organizational evaluation are:

1.   efficiency (cost-effectiveness) measures

2.   absenteeism rates

3.   turnover rates

4.   measures of goal consensus and conflict

Doing MBO with the Organization: MBO also can be employed to evaluate entire work units or the whole organization. As Ronald Lynch applied MBO to criminal justice (1986: 152-153, 161-169), it is the duty of the criminal justice manager to recognize the values preset for his or her agency by the community and the law, including the constitutional principles under which all American government must operate. The manager then must articulate for his or her organization the mission statement that is assigned to it by the government and public processes. The manager then sets goals for the agency. These are abstract and long-term statements of what the organization ultimately hopes to achieve. However, it is not supposed that the agency will ever be completely successful in accomplishing its goals, including such ongoing statements as "preventing crime," "protecting the innocent" "identifying the guilty," and "achieving justice." The criminal justice manager then derives the objectives for the agency from such broad and abstract concepts. These objectives define the performance and results the agency hopes to achieve in the near future. While they relate to the goals, the objectives are reasonable, clear, and realistic. They can be achieved in the near term, and typically are integrated into the organizational planning and budgeting cycle (which is usually annual). From the objectives the criminal justice manager will develop projects and action plans. Evaluation follows the implementation of these projects and plans and must (1) be based on measurable objectives, (2) have a detailed and practical evaluation design, (3) establish data-collection procedures, and (4) specify the data analysis methods to be employed.

Pitfalls of MBO: MBO is not a panacea for all management ills. It cannot correct deep, systemic problems that can infect a criminal justice organization. For example, a corrupt agency will not acquire integrity by doing MBO. Low levels of talent or training in the work force will not become upgraded simply by doing MBO with a pool of poorly selected, poorly prepared, or chronically underachieving employees. It also cannot be allowed to replace day-to-day operations. The participation of an entire organization all at one time can disrupt the work of the organization. Therefore, it is best to rotate MBO through each of the units of the larger organization over a lengthy evaluation cycle, returning to the first unit using MBO after all units have been so evaluated.

Box 7.3 • Doing MBO in a Group

Step 1: Schedule the MBO workshop (all day or a weekend) away from the workplace. Supply each participant with a set of the organizational values, beliefs, mission statement, and goals.

Step 2: Designate a workshop coordinator to visit each participant BEFORE the workshop to outline how it works and to develop an agenda; asking each participant:

- what does the organization do well?
- what does the organization do poorly?
- what do you want to discuss at the workshop?

Step 3: The coordinator synthesizes the answers, removes any potential identifiers, thus providing their proponents a degree of anonymity, and develops an general (lightly structured) agenda for the workshop.

Step 4: The secluded workshop is held and NO noncritical interruptions are allowed. The agenda topics are exposed, expanded and hashed out.

Step 5: Objectives for the future are derived from the discussions, are agreed to, and projects are assigned for implementation by the participants when they get back to work.

Step 6: The coordinator compiles "minutes" of accepted objectives and derived projects.This becomes a report which each participant is given soon after the workshop.

Step 7: The manager reassembles the participants six months to a year later to review their accomplishments and evaluate unit performance, vis-à-vis the report prepared after the workshop.

The success of doing MBO for an organization relies upon the recognition of the following articulated concepts:

- Mission
- Goals
- Objectives
- Action plans
- Project implementation
- Evaluation

Law Enforcement Accreditation: An organization also can be evaluated by an outside team of evaluators. In 1984 the first police department in the United States underwent accreditation under national standards of the Commission on Accreditation of Law Enforcement Agencies (CALEA). CALEA originally was sponsored by LEAA in the 1970s, but was created by a group of law enforcement professional organizations. Since 1984, hundreds of police agencies have been accredited by CALEA. To be accredited an agency must meet high standards for recruiting, training, supervision, management, case work, administration, and accountability—all supported by written policies and actual practices.

Theodore Caplow on Personnel Issues: Theodore Caplow is an organizational sociologist who has examined in great depth the importance of employee morale in organizational assessment. He has concluded

Box 7.4 • Theodore Caplow's High Organizational Morale Indicators

1. There are no cliques, and no groups are fearful of the boss.
2. Although minor infractions do occur, employees know and obey the organization's more important rules and regulations, and the violations that do occur do not impact on the organizational mission (discipline).
3. Employees stay with the organization (low turnover rates)
4. New employees are better qualified than those they replace (rising standards).
5. New employees are rapidly integrated into the informal networks of the organization.
6. Employees accept the goals of the organization (value and goal congruence).
7. Hiring, firing, promotion, and demotion decisions are usually unanimous or consensual.
8. Dismissals and demotions are rare and do not require complex, litigiously elaborate precautions and rules.
9. Supervisors know their subordinates and feel free to share that knowledge with those higher up, although evaluation documents are not taken seriously.
10. Pay and privileges are not major topics of discussion, and the existing distribution of benefits seems acceptable.
11. Organizational ceremonies and events are well attended.
12. Subordinate managers (mid-level managers) do not need to appeal to the top management to maintain their authority.
13. Although conflicts occur, people who enter into them are apologetic and interested in resolving them in a fashion that reunites the organization.
14. Intervention by top management is welcomed when a conflict does occur.

(1983) that organizational morale is high in the workforce when all or most of the 14 features (see Box 7.4) are in evidence.

Morale is satisfaction with the organization and one's place in it. The turnover rate is one of the most obvious clues to gauging employee morale and is a key to organizational efficiency. An astute manager will know actual numbers and percentages of employees departing from the organization and its component units each year, but this information alone is not enough. There are many reasons for turnover. Some of these reasons do not reflect negatively on employee morale. Key questions that each manager should seek to answer for each employee separation are the proportions for:

1. nonorganizational reasons: deaths, serious illness, relocation of other family members, other family priorities, retirement eligibility, etc.

2. disciplinary reasons, to the advantage of the organization; e.g., an employee fired for serious misconduct

3. efficiency or productivity reasons, to the advantage of the organization; e.g.: an employee fired or urged out for poor performance

4. external competitive reasons, other economic activities outside the current career field that draw the employees to seek new career opportunities; e.g., a correctional officer quitting to take a sales job with a retail firm

5. internal competitive reasons, transfers to other organizations engaged in very similar activities; e.g., a municipal police detective applying for and being hired by the FBI or DEA

There is an increasing degree of significance in each of the five reasons. If most employee separations are for the first two reasons, then the manager does not have significant evidence of a morale problem. However, reasons 3 through 5 signal the existence of progressively more serious problems.

Cost-Benefit Analysis

Assessment of decisions can employ **cost-benefit analysis**, a utilitarian concept with its origins in the early nineteenth century (although it was not called that then). Jeremy Bentham spoke of it as his "felicific" calculus or **hedonistic calculus**. In more modern managerial slang, it is spoken of as "running the numbers" or "numbers crunching."

A cost-benefit analysis is a process that identifies, quantifies, and adds together all the positive factors of a decision, activity, or ongoing process to calculate the benefits. Then the analysis identifies, quantifies, and sums up all the negative factors to determine the costs. The two are then compared, and the difference between the two summations reveals if the decision, activity, or process is favorable. The secret to doing cost-benefit analysis correctly is including all the real costs and determining them realistically, as well as properly and accurately calculating the benefits. Fudging the numbers will bias the results and negate the value of doing the analysis.

Cost-benefit analysis is information-based. It must be done systematically. It is the link between the planning and decision-making processes and the budgeting and allocation processes of the criminal justice organization. It is closely integrated into PPBS and ZBB budgeting systems, which will be covered in Chapter 10.

Change in Organizations

One of the principle purposes of evaluation is to effect meaningful, directional change within the work force (changing individuals) and within the whole organization (changing the organization). It is a striving for improvement. Bringing about purposeful, orderly change is a key managerial responsibility—so much so that the "transformational" leadership role (Tichy and Ulrich, 1984) has been identified for special mention.

Justice agency managers have been called upon to effect numerous, major changes in policy, practice, and technology in the years since the LEAA encouraged widespread innovation and reform across the criminal justice system. However, the intervention of the federal government and the infusion of massive amounts of federal funding were only part of the story. The attitude of the criminal justice manager toward change has been critical in bringing about the developments that have been the hallmark of the last generation. Warren Bennis observed that managers can bring about purposeful change by fostering (1966, quoted in Ott, 1989: 584):

1. joint effort: the manager can offer freedom of choice within the change process by sharing information, goals, and situational data

2. a spirit of inquiry: the manager can foster favorable attitudes toward new information and experience, especially by sharing all data

3. relationship-building: the manager can involve the people to be affected by the change by mutual interaction, allowing voluntary participation and allowing all parties equal influence

Freedom of Choice: By interesting those involved in the change and giving them input into the decisionmaking, the personnel become agents of the change by choice. This recalls Mary Parker Follett's advice on giving and taking orders: "One person should not give orders to another person, but both should agree to take their orders from the situation" (Follett, 1926, quoted in Ott, 1989: 259).

New Information and Experience: Many people usually fear change, but also enjoy variety and new experiences. Changes can be packaged as positive attractions rather than fearful episodes. Sending old hands to a computer seminar in a resort city, thus mixing change with pleasure, can make the transition to change pleasant. Identifying the change agents of the organization in a very positive light can encourage participation in the change process.

Involvement: Involvement is akin to freedom of choice—bringing those most involved in the consequences of the change into the initiation of the change. By inviting those who will be impacted most by the changes into the planning process and implementation activities, the criminal justice manager will "co-opt" them, and by doing so make them agents in the change process. Philip Selznick contributed the sociological analysis of co-optation as a managerial device. **Co-optation** is the process whereby the management of an organization absorbs the aims of the workers (Selznick, 1948, quoted in Shafritz and Ott, 1996: 120): "Co-optation is the process of absorbing new elements into the leadership or policy-determining structure of an organization as a means of averting threats to its stability or existence."

Kinds of Change

Problem-solving and innovative decisionmaking produces decisions that are intended to yield organizational changes when implemented. Evaluation and assessment activities identify areas where change is needed to produce a better-performing individual or organization, and later in the change process, to measure the success of the implementation of the intended changes. Change comes in many forms (Bennis, 1966: 81-94).

Natural change involves no deliberation, no goal setting, and exists independently of the existence or absence of hierarchical arrangements. It occurs in three basic patterns: the *straight line* pattern, following a trend in a consistent fashion, either maintaining a steady state, rising, or falling; the *rise-plateau-crash* pattern, in which some feature or technological application rapidly achieves acceptance, stabilizes, and then drops off when a new feature or technology arises to replace it; and the *cyclic* (oscillating) pattern, in which frequencies will rise, then fall, only to rise again, in repetitive cycles. Natural change is not easily managed and is not relevant to this section. It will be discussed again in Chapter 12, however, when "futures" will be discussed.

Planned change ideally occurs with mutual goal-setting, an equalization of power between change agents and those being changed, and deliberateness of process. It is one of the most important reasons for undertaking organizational evaluation. This kind of change is the responsibility of criminal justice managers. Arising from the assessment and appraisal processes of the evaluation function, planned change is undertaken to improve the agency over its prior state.

Indoctrination also occurs with mutual goal-setting, and is deliberate, but the change agent dominates in the power balance.

Coercive change also is deliberate, but lacks mutuality, and has an imbalanced power ratio in favor of the change agent.

Technocratic change does not involve goal-setting (or does not have goal-setting as a prime aspect). It is informationally based and identifies sources of problems with the implicit assumption that their identification will lead to their elimination via some form of actual or social engineering.

Interactional change arises from the normal interaction of people in social relationships. It includes mutual goal-setting and equal power distribution, but no conscious deliberation.

Socialization change is modeled on the hierarchical parent-child and teacher-student relationship, as expressed in training and supervised on-the-job training (SOJT). (This will be discussed in more detail in Chapter 9.)

Emulative change also occurs in hierarchical relationships, wherein subordinates seek to pattern themselves on successful superiors.

Resisting Change

Change may encounter resistance from both personal (individual) and organizational sources (Klofas, Stojkovic, and Kalinich, 1990: 285, Table 12-1). The criminal justice manager needs to accept resistance to change as a normal reaction to new ideas. Such resistance should not be interpreted as disloyalty or distrust of the leader, but it is a managerial problem the manager must work to overcome if positive changes are to be set in place. Therefore, it is important to understand the sources of resistance to change, both rational and emotional, and then to consider strategies that will help overcome them.

Change and Conflict

While change is inevitable, it also often leads us into conflict. Even if we have a near-perfect working situation, natural changes in worker maturity, goal fulfillment, organizational needs, new technologies, and so on will bring about conflict.

Box 7.5 • Resistance to Organizational Change

PERSONAL SOURCES
1. misunderstanding
2. failure to see need
3. fear
4. status and power loss
5. no involvement in change
6. habit
7. vested interest in status quo
8. group norms counter to change
9. threat to existing social network
10. conflict between personal and organizational objectives

ORGANIZATIONAL SOURCES
1. reward system and reward structures
2. rivalry and conflict
3. "sunk costs" — prior investment
4. balance of power shifts
5. organizational climate
6. poor introduction to change
7. past failures with changes
8. structural rigidity
9. conflict between personal and organizational objectives

There are many quite reasonable reasons to resist change that the "transformational leader" must overcome or address (Tichy and Ulrich, quoted in Ott, 1989: 346-347, Table 1).

Source: Lists adapted from Klofas, Stojkovic, and Kalinich, 1990: Table 12-1.

General **conflict theorists** like Ralf Dahrendorf and Austin Turk have shown how change naturally leads into conflict. They begin with four logical "conflict" assumptions:

1. social change occurs everywhere
2. dissent and conflict are everywhere in a society
3. every element contributes to disintegration and change
4. coercion of some by others is everywhere.

Austin Turk's approach to understanding change and conflict is both complex and abstract:

- Each of us has different perceptions and understandings;

- Our disagreements lead to conflicts;
- Each of us promotes one's own concepts;
- Conflict also occurs over scarce resources;
- Alliances with co-believers are forged;
- Conflict becomes institutionalized;
- Political domination and economic exploitation follows from these institutionalized alliances;
- Social power is the key leverage;
- Group membership produces shared experiences and views;
- Human interaction is dynamic and changing, leading to even more conflict.
- "Good" is acceptance of the institutionalized co-beliefs of the dominant coalition.
- "Wrong" is any counterbelief.
- Serious counterbeliefs can be classified as "deviant" or "criminal."

Intervention to manage conflict involves two processes: involvement in the sequence of events (consciousness-raising and interaction management) and structure-altering conditions in the organization (selection and training, context modification). What can be modified?

- working personality
- informal rules
- constituent pressures
- interest competition
- power and status
- organizational policy

Ronald Lynch categorizes the sources of conflict as either emotional or rational, and gives examples for emotional conflict, i.e., defensive attitudes, group loyalty, self-image, face-saving, and interpersonal factors. Conflicts arise from sources that are both emotional and rational—not either/or as Lynch implies (1986: 214)—so we cannot, as Lynch suggests, "distinguish between rational and emotional elements in each major disagreement." He places "values" in the rational category, but excessive attachment to one's values is emotional. A defensive attitude may be perfectly rational, but can lead to a pseudo-paranoid state that clearly is emotional. Group loyalty also is rational; we need our alliances and affinity groups, but overattachment can be excessive. Self-image is a perfectly valid rational concern, but also can become an obsession. Face-saving can become an obsession, but one's reputation and image are rationally valuable attributes for one's career. It is always rational to maintain good interpersonal relations, but balance is the key.

Box 7.6 • Reasons to Resist Organizational Change

Habit and Inertia — The current works have mastered the old ways and are comfortable with them.

"Sunk Costs" — Prior investments in the old ways, old equipment, and previous training all will be lost when the new system is implemented.

Effort and Resources — The old ways were reduced to the most efficient process by trial-and-error and practice; a change will require retraining, learning new ways, acquiring new equipment, and using more resources.

Fear and Anxiety — Change introduces unknowns, and these are as often feared as accepted.

Pride and Traditional Conservative Values — Our sincere convictions about the propriety of the old ways are invalidated when their replacement occurs; the old decisions, policies and procedures are made to seem wrong.

Sense of Lost Power — The veteran members of the organization are made equal with the new people, and this undermines the advantages of seniority.

Self-Interest — How will the change benefits the resister? If there is nothing to gain at a personal level, why should a rational employee support change?

Conflict — Changes evoke conflict.

Suspicion — There are questions about the value of the change to the organization; most veterans in an organization have been through change cycles before and can recall their many failures.

THERE IS A GENUINE AWARENESS THAT SOME CHANGE IS FOLLY:

"I was to learn later in life that we tend to meet any new situation by reorganizing, and a wonderful method it can be for creating the illusion of progress, while producing confusion, inefficiency, and demoralization." Petronius Arbiter, ca. A.D. 60, *The Satyricon*

The folk expression, "Don't fix it if it ain't broke," is another expression of the folly of making some ill-considered changes. In addition, some things simply cannot be changed for the better. As Reinhold Niebuhr said in the "Serenity Prayer," "God grant me the serenity to accept things I cannot change, courage to change the things I can, and wisdom to know the difference."

Excessive group loyalty can lead to cliques and the subversion of the interests of the organization. What Lynch seems to have rediscovered is the ancient Greek adage, "nothing in excess." By focusing on the rational aspects, rather than the sources, of an item in dispute, some change-based conflicts can be resolved. Lynch counsels (1986: 217):

1. Deal in principles, rather than details.
2. Determine criteria against which judgment is to be made.
3. Experiment, not debate with alternatives.
4. Apply rational decision-making processes.

Box 7.7 • Common Features of Organizations That Can Accept Change

1. High complexity in professional training.
2. High decentralization of power
3. Low formalization
4. Low stratification in terms of rewards distribution
5. Emphasis on quality over volume productivity
6. Low emphasis on efficiency vs. product or service quality
7. High job satisfaction levels.

Source: List adapted from Klofas, Stojkovic, and Kalinich, 1990: 287-288.

Kurt Lewin wrote that the process of effecting change involves a three-step procedure (quoted in Ott, 1989: 546-547): (1) **unfreezing:** to "[...] break open the shell of complacency and self-righteousness, it is sometimes necessary to bring about deliberately an emotional stir-up." (p. 547); (2) **moving or changing:** making the change-oriented decisions and beginning the process of implementation; and (3) **refreezing:** allowing the new ways to become established as the replacement habits.

Box 7.8 • Application of Change Strategies

1. modify task structure
2. balance reward-punishment relationships
3. decision centralization and decentralization balance
4. provide achievement emphasis
5. providing training and development emphasis
6. security vs. risk balance
7. favoring openness vs. defensiveness
8. promoting status and morale
9. providing recognition and feedback
10. having organizational competence and flexibility

Source: List adapted from Klofas, Stojkovic, and Kalinich, 1990: 295.

Summary

Evaluation and its related concepts of assessment and appraisal are essential managerial functions. They are needed to pursue good personnel practices and for organizational development, the bringing about of planned change within the criminal justice organization. Evaluation uses

Learning Objectives

Upon finishing this chapter you should be able to do the following:

▶ 1. Distinguish between individual and organizational evaluation.

▶ 2. Discuss the data elements appropriate to an individual evaluation.

▶ 3. Identify sources of managerial information that can be used as criminal justice agency performance measures.

▶ 4. Describe ways of using MBO in both individual and organizational evaluation.

▶ 5. Identify sources of resistance to organizational change.

▶ 6. Identify features of a criminal justice agency that are favorable to change.

IMPORTANT TERMS AND NAMES

- appraisal
- assessment
- CALEA
- coercive change
- conflict theorists
- co-optation
- cost-benefit analysis
- emulative change
- endorser
- evaluator
- hedonistic calculus
- indoctrination
- interactional change

- MBO
- moving or changing
- performance appraisal
- rater
- refreezing
- secret evaluations
- shared evaluations
- socialization change
- "sunk costs"
- technocratic change
- turnover rate
- unfreezing

many tools and sources of data under the control of the manager. These data sources identify what things are going well and what needs to be changed to improve the individual employee or the whole organization. Change encounters resistance, and the wise criminal justice manager needs to understand this resistance in order to overcome it.

References and Supplemental Sources

Bennis, Warren G. (1966). *Changing Organizations*. New York: McGraw-Hill.

Caplow, Theodore (1983). *Managing an Organization*, 2nd ed. New York: Holt, Rinehart, and Winston.

Drucker, Peter F. (1954). *The Practice of Management*. New York: HarperCollins, HarperBusiness.

Follett, Mary Parker (1926). "The Giving of Orders," in *The Scientific Foundations of Business Administration*, Henry C. Metcalf, et al., eds. Baltimore: Williams and Wilkins.

Follett, Mary Parker (1926, 1989). "The Giving of Orders," in *Classic Readings in Organizational Behavior*, edited by J. Steven Ott. Pacific Grove, A: Brooks/Cole.

Klofas, John, Stan Stojkovic, and David Kalinich (1990). *Criminal Justice Organizations: Administration and Management*. Pacific Grove, CA: Brooks/Cole.

Lewin, Kurt (1989). "Group Decision and Social Change," pages 543-548 in *Classic Readings in Organizational Behavior*, edited by J. Steven Ott. Pacific Grove, CA: Brooks/Cole.

Lynch, Ronald G. (1986). *The Police Manager: Professional Leadership Skills*, 3rd ed. New York: Random House.

Massie, Joseph L. (1987). *Essentials of Management*, 4th ed. Englewood Cliffs, NJ: Prentice Hall.

Odiorne, George (1965). *Management by Objectives: A System of Managerial Leadership*. New York: Pitman.

Ott, J. Steven (1989). *Classic Readings in Organizational Behavior*. Pacific Grove, CA: Brooks/Cole.

Selznick, Philip (1948). "Foundations of the Theory of Organization," *American Sociological Review*, 13(1): 25-35.

Selznick, Philip (1991). "Foundations of the Theory of Organization," pages 114-123 in *Classics of Organizational Theory*, 3rd ed., edited by Jay M. Shafritz and J. Steven Ott. Pacific Grove, CA: Brooks/Cole.

Stewart, Debra, and G. David Garson (1983). *Organizational Behavior and Public Management*. New York: Marcel Dekker.

Tichy, Noel M., and David O. Ulrich (1984). "The Leadership Challenge—A Call for the Transformational Leader," *Sloan Management Review*, 26(Fall): 59-68.

Wilson, Orlando W., and Roy C. McLaren (1977). *Police Administration*, 4th ed. New York: McGraw-Hill.

8
Staffing and Personnel Issues

The "S" in both LODESTAR and in POSDCORB stands for "staffing," one of the major managerial responsibilities of a criminal justice official. Staffing involves hiring, fostering career development, protecting the employment rights, disciplining, and promoting agency employees. Most criminal justice staffing actions are covered by civil service rules, but there are some exceptions. In most states, elected criminal justice officials are exempt from some or all of the civil rights laws and regulations, as are many of their personal appointments. This divided approach was one of the recommendations made by Woodrow Wilson in his seminal 1887 article on public administration. Prior to the 1880s, most criminal justice staffing actions were not covered by civil service laws and practices but were in the domain of **patronage appointments**, that is, appointments in whole or in large measure made because of one's affiliation with a victorious political party or candidate.

Historical Developments in Public Personnel Practices

In the United States, the manner in which people have been selected for public service and the ways they have experienced their careers have undergone significant changes since 1789. Frederick C. Mosher (1967: 53-95) proposed that five distinct eras can be defined and delineated by major events in American political history. In this text a similar approach will be taken, but some minor differences between Mosher's typology and the one used here are appropriate.

In this text, "Government by Gentlemen" will be discussed as the **Jeffersonian ideal** (1789-1829). Thomas Jefferson clearly influenced the manner in which both the states and the new federal government selected people for public service positions. People were selected for

Box 8.1 • Frederick C. Mosher's Eras in Civil Service Concepts

Government by Gentlemen, 1789-1829

Government by the Common Man, 1829-1883

Government by the Good, 1883-1906

Government by the Efficient, 1906-1937

Government by Administrators, 1937-1955

government employment based upon Jeffersonian assumptions about *noblisse oblige* (which suggests that a burden of responsibility comes with noble ancestry and privilege) and the concept of **fitness of character** based upon a good family background, educational attainment, social status, and patriotic military or political service during the revolution (Thompson, 1991: 1). In the federal service, another consideration was added: representation in federal hiring among the states approximately proportional to a state's population. Thomas Jefferson's concept of government officials as public servants, with an emphasis on service, was paramount. Most people accepting employment in the state or federal governments did so from a duty to serve rather than as a path to economic reward. Indeed, many already were successful in private careers and enterprises before accepting their government appointments.

"Government by the Common Man" was an expression of **Jacksonian egalitarianism** (1829-1883). From Andrew Jackson's assumption of the presidency in 1829 through the passage of the Pendleton Act in 1883, the prime criterion for being appointed to public service was political loyalty. Jackson saw education and opportunity as being the keys to suitability for public service and equality of performance. He believed that all men were equal in capacity, so anyone properly educated could serve successfully in government if given the chance. Therefore, in his view, political loyalty was an appropriate precondition for selection. Thus, he was committed to a loyalty-based patronage system for selecting men to serve in government. His critics called it a **"spoils system,"** drawing on the expression, "to the victors belong the spoils of war." Jackson was opposed to life-long civil service tenure. Yet his invitation to the "common man" to join and serve in government inadvertently led to the development of government employment as a career choice. The people chosen for patronage appointments were not the wealthy elite gentlemen chosen for government office under the Jeffersonian ideal. For them government employment was a move up. By the standards of the day, it paid well and was far more pleasant work than might otherwise be available to an ordinary laborer. It was very important to such people that they keep their patrons in office as the means of retaining their jobs. There also were positive advantages of a "patronage system" for the public and our two-party political system (Sorauf, 1960: 28). Patronage was useful for:

1.   maintaining an active party organization

2.   promoting intra-party cohesion

3.   attracting voters and supporters

4.   financing the party and candidates

5.   procuring favorable government action

6.   creating party discipline in policymaking

The period of *Reformist Merit Selection* (1883-1930) merges Mosher's "Government by the Good" (1883-1906) and "Government by the Efficient" (1906-1937). The year 1883 marks the passage of the Pendleton Act, the first federal **civil service law**, which held that "appointment or promotion shall be given to the man best fitted to discharge the duties of the position, and such fitness shall be ascertained by open, fair, honest, impartial, competitive examination" (as quoted by Paul P. Van Riper from the 1882 report of U.S. Senate Committee on Civil Service and Retrenchment) (Thompson, 1991: 7; Van Riper, 1958) Although patronage did not go away with the Pendleton Act, this legislation marked the beginning of the decline in patronage selection

Box 8.2 • Theodore Roosevelt: Criminal Justice Manager

Before Theodore Roosevelt, Jr. (1858-1919) became president in 1901, and even before he led Rough Riders against San Juan Hill in Cuba during the Spanish-American War of 1898, he was a member of the National Civil Service Commission (1889-1895) and a vocal advocate of civil service reform (Roosevelt 1897: 135). He was named president of the Police Board for the City of New York in 1895 and undertook the reform of the NYPD, then notoriously corrupt (1897:162). Under his administration hiring standards were raised, the police acquired new crime-fighting techniques, rewarded integrity, efficiency and heroism of its officers, and instituted formal firearms training. The department increased arrests and New York enjoyed a decline in crime (1897: 182-187).

Theodore Roosevelt Jr. as a young adult.

en.wikipedia.org

of public servants. The original civil service law only protected lower-level federal appointees and did not apply to the states. The states copied it, though, and the number of federal employees covered by it expanded over the following decades, until hiring under civil service rules became the primary means of securing government employment at every level.

Applying Woodrow Wilson's political reform ideas (1887) and Frederick Taylor's ideas on efficiency (1911), plus those contributions of other social, governmental, and managerial reformers such as Theodore Roosevelt (1897), civil service rules applied assumptions of merit criteria for screening prospective workers, while also looking into the moral character of prospects. The "rule of three" was pronounced, under which a person would be hired from the top-three scorers on the civil service test. Once on the job, political neutrality was expected. Discharge could occur only for misconduct or poor performance, and never for political reasons. At the federal level, the Congress began giving the executive direction on hiring processes and criteria, giving rise to **Ackerman's question** (Van Riper 1958; 1991: 12). Amos T. Ackerman was President Ulysses S. Grant's Attorney General. Ackerman raised the constitutional question of how much influence the legislative branch should have in the **contracting process** whereby the executive branch selects its preferred work force. Prior to the Pendleton Act, this was exclusively an executive function, but today it is one shared by all three branches.

As Ackerman's question suggests, not everyone was happy with filling public service positions under civil service laws. Even today some criminal justice positions are filled outside of the civil service. Sheriffs, most of whom are elected in partisan campaigns, to this day continue to hire and promote their deputies under a patronage and mixed patronage-civil service selection process. Many state judges, clerks of court, coroners, and prosecutors are still elected, and often the prosecutors and chief clerks of court can appoint and promote their assistants as patronage hires rather than under civil service rules. In the federal courts, judges are chosen by a complex political process of presidential appointment with senatorial advice and consent. Federal prosecutors, known as U.S. Attorneys, are patronage appointees to this day. The chief U.S. marshals also are patronage appointees of the president. Even when civil service rules apply, there are still critics of civil service and some exceptions. Raymond Fosdick, one of the leading police theorists of the early twentieth century, was completely committed to police reform throughout all of his professional life, yet he wrote (1920: 292):

> A far better balance between civil service protection and effective leadership can be achieved than has been reached up to the present. In our endeavors to eliminate the spoils system we have swung too far toward rigidity, and a rational approach

is needed to a compromise which will protect the police force from the politician without robbing the police executive of initiative and leadership.

Fosdick still wanted civil service selection, but with a probationary period and the elimination of promotion solely by examination. Fosdick advocated the use of the Boston promotional system whereby the police commissioner nominated a list of eligible officers for promotion. Civil service tests were administered to all of the nominees to ensure that their intelligence, knowledge, and general capacity were sufficient for promotion. All of those who passed the tests could then be promoted (1920: 294). He also favored police training schools (1920: 293-298) and improved police discipline (1920: 296-297):

> The question of discipline is the final factor in regard to which current civil service procedure needs radical modification. There is no chance for progressive improvement in a police department if the hands of the responsible executive are tied in his dealings with his men. . . . To divide responsibility with a civil service commission, a mayor, a court, or any other authority, is to sow the seed of demoralization and to make real success impossible for any administrator, no matter how able.

Box 8.3 • Features of Civil Service Reform

Sam Souryal (1995) identified these seven key civil service reforms, exemplified in the Pendleton Act of 1883.

1. merit hiring with objective standards.
2. competitive examinations for employee selection.
3. probationary employment preceding tenure.
4. veterans to be given legal preference.
5. freedom from political contribution solicitations.
6. annual reports required of government agencies.
7. creation of the federal Civil Service Commission.

Civil service protections had an unintended consequence for criminal justice employment: the rise of public service unions. This was an era of rapidly expanding industrial union organizing. Observing their success, police unions were organized early in the twentieth century, and were gaining popularity until 1919. In 1918 police officers in Cincinnati went on strike for three days successfully. In that same year in New York union negotiations won pay increases in the face of a strike threat. When the Boston police did the same in 1919, the city declined to negotiate and the police were warned that they would be dismissed for misconduct if they did go on strike (Richardson, 1977: 110-120). They did strike and the city and state retaliated, barring the striking officers from any future public service employment. The strikers were replaced, and the union was broken. Massachusetts and other states passed laws prohibiting public service unions and strikes, making them criminal acts in some cases. Union growth in criminal justice was dealt a major setback from which it would not recover for many decades.

Mosher selected 1937 to delineate the end of government by the efficient. This coincided with Luther Gulick's POSDCORB paper. In criminal justice, though, the year 1930 is a better separation point. In 1930 the Federal Bureau of Investigation began to collect data for the Uniform Crime Reports, and the Wickersham Commission was conducting its hearings into American criminal justice practices. The recommendations of those hearings were to have profound influence on all aspects of criminal justice and included recommendations on improved personnel practices for the entire criminal justice system.

Professionalism and Managerial Emphasis (1930-1973): Applying the ideas of Max Weber (1922) on proper bureaucratic arrangements, Luther Gulick on public administration (1937), the Wickersham Commission reports, and the efforts of then-President Herbert Hoover and others on improving governmental efficiency, in this era public personnel managers continued to apply the ideas of scientific management, while also seeking to apply the best of progressive personnel management practices: intensive formal training and education (e.g., certificate training programs, police academies, masters of public administration degree programs, etc.) and a growing emphasis on what has been called **credentialism**, the emphasis on having the right credentials, transcripts, and documents to demonstrate one's rational–legal competence for a job.

The National Committee on Law Observation and Enforcement, better known as the Wickersham Commission, was established in 1929 by President Herbert Hoover. George W. Wickersham (1858-1936) headed the commission, which was tasked with making recommendations for criminal justice public policy. Although the emphasis was on national alcohol prohibition, the Commission consulted experts in many areas and prepared several reports on their findings, including the final Wickersham report (National Committee on Law Observation and Enforcement, 1931). Primarily written by August Vollmer, the report recommended many managerial reforms. Sam Souryal (1995) has identified six personnel management reforms suggested by the Wickersham Commission.

> 1. Police leaders should be selected for their experience and demonstrated competence.

2. Personnel should be selected who have met intelligence and fitness standards.

3. Adequate salaries should be provided for police and other criminal justice officials.

4. An eight-hour work day, with vacations, sick leave, pensions, and other remuneration and compensation., should be provided

5. Efforts should be undertaken to isolate politics and other corrupting influences from law enforcement.

6. Training should be offered prior to independent employment.

The next major national study of criminal justice was the 1967 U.S. President's Commission on Law Enforcement and Administration of Justice. It released nine Task Force reports plus *The Challenge of Crime in a Free Society*, which called for the creation of the Law Enforcement Assistance Administration (LEAA) to provide federal assistance to state and local criminal justice programs and agencies. Its *Task Force Report: The Police* offered more managerial and personnel reforms. Three recommended personnel reforms were not included in the reform recommendations of earlier eras:

1. state-set minimum training and selection standards

2. minority affirmative action recruitment

3. implementation of career development programs

Many critics of civil service practices have emerged in recent decades, objecting to what the civil service has become. E.S. Savas and Sigmund G. Ginsburg (1973) identify the most commonly noted flaws of the system:

1. There is no scientific evidence to show the entrance examinations really are related to on-the-job performance.

2. The rule-of-three eliminates other, potentially very well qualified applicants.

3. Tenure for life is almost assured, regardless of quality of work output after the probationary period.

4. Dismissal is exceptionally difficult, even with cause.

5. There is little opportunity for job growth within the bureaucracy.

6. Promotions usually come within units, so are not truly open and competitive.

7. Performance may be secondary to examination results in gaining promotions.

8. Salary increases are automatic, and not usually performance-based.

9. Mid-level managers may belong to the same unions as their subordinates, and thus are not as likely to be acting in the interests of the organizational management.

10. Union influence is significant in politics, so the net effect is workers influencing legislators who order about upper-level managers.

While the general thrust of civil service systems and their rules has been to insulate public servants from excessive political influence, not every administration seeks a politically neutral civil service. When President Richard Nixon came to office, he was determined to rid his administration of mid-level managers loyal to the programs and priorities of the Kennedy-Johnson period. This gave rise to the **Malek Manual**, whose rule was "You cannot achieve management, policy or program control unless you have established political control" (Thompson, 1991: 58). Section III-3 is the most devious, suggesting ways of ridding the government of its protected civil servants:

a. elimination:
   a-1. frontal assault
   a-2. transfer technique
   a-3. special assignment technique
b. layering
c. shifting responsibilities and isolation
d. new activities

The **special assignment technique** made the unwelcome worker into a "traveling salesman" for his or her agency, sent to remote locations and kept away from his or her normal duties. Transfers were to undesirable assignments and locations with the intention of convincing the employee to resign or retire. The Malek Manual also contained advice on how to confront bureaucratic countermeasures. Observing how well the Republicans were able to frustrate the aims of the existing civil service, when James Earl Carter became president in 1977, he and the Congress joined in a venture of strengthening and streamlining civil service protections (Campbell, 1978; 1991), leading to the Civil Service Reform Act of 1978. Following that, the National Academy of Public Administration developed its "functional model" (Thompson, 1991: 173-174) with standards for each of the key personnel management responsibilities:

1. recruiting and examining
2. classification
3. merit standards for:
   a. merit protection
   b. merit pay
   c. EEO [equal employment opportunity]

        d. training

        e. performance appraisal

        f. incentive awards

   4. labor-management relations

   5. adverse actions

   6. program evaluation

The Civil Rights Era and Equal Opportunity (1973 - Present): Major victories of the civil rights struggle were achieved between 1954, when the Supreme Court's *Brown v. Board of Education* decision refuted the validity and justice of the doctrine of "separate but equal," and 1964, when the U.S. Congress passed the Civil Rights Act of 1964. But it was not until the Equal Employment Opportunity Act of 1972, as amended in 1973, that civil rights law applied unambiguously to state and local units of government. With the 1973 amendment, all civil rights protections from earlier laws had to apply to public service occupations. The struggle to achieve full civil rights, to do away with unconstitutional bias and prejudice, and to provide true equality of opportunity to all Americans, regardless of race, ethnicity, sex, religion, political preference and ideology, or physical handicap still goes on, but the moral high ground of **equality of opportunity** (an equal distribution of government jobs, promotions, or similar advantages) was established in 1964 and brought to criminal justice agencies in 1973. Oddly enough, it was during the presidency of Richard M. Nixon, a Republican, that the Equal Employment Opportunity Act of 1972 was passed and the federal government took the lead in achieving affirmative action (Yuill, 2006).

Affirmative Action: Today's struggles over civil rights issues involve how far to carry programs to achieve affirmative action. Affirmative action programs precede the initial success of the civil rights struggle by a full decade, though. The first affirmative action program in federal personnel law involves *veterans preference*. **Veterans preference** was part of the civil service reforms of the 1880s. The current federal policies became law in 1944, as the nation, still heavily involved in World War II, was thinking ahead to what would happen when our combat veterans returned home to find their jobs taken by those who had not served in the armed services. In the federal civil service and in many of the states as well, preferential hiring privileges were given to veterans, and an even greater priority was given to hiring those who suffered war wounds.

Discrimination against persons based on sex, race, ethnicity, religious belief, age, and accommodatable disabilities has been outlawed. Affirmative action programs have been created to encourage greater workplace participation by persons previously denied or given only limited access to public service careers.

The Americans with Disabilities Act (ADA) protects the interests of potential public service workers with handicaps that can be overcome with reasonable accommodations. Determining what is a reasonable accommodation is decided situationally, reflecting the demands of the employment and the limitations imposed by the disability. The Equal Employment Opportunity Commission (EEOC) provides a forum for helping resolve questions of reasonableness (Colbridge, 2000: 15).

Frank J. Thompson (1991: 3) identifies five basic values in competition with each other in civil service systems:

1. agency competence

2. individual merit

3. political responsiveness

4. social equity

5. employee rights

Over time, one or another will rise to prominence as the others decline in significance, but all five are retained. Only the priority order shifts.

Scientific Management and Personnel Practices

Frederick Winslow Taylor, in *The Principles of Scientific Management* (1911: 36-37), presented four basic principles on the application of managerial science to the design of work and the selection of workers. These are the essentials of his principles of scientific management:

1. develop a science for each element of a man's work

2. scientifically select and then train, teach, and develop the workman

3. cooperate with the men so as to insure all of the work [is] being done in accordance with the principles of the science

4. divide the work and the responsibility between management and the workmen

From Taylor's first point comes the now common practice of having a detailed job description for each position in an organization. Ideally, the written **job description** lists all the routine and major responsibilities of the position, and is prepared from a careful study of what the worker should be able to do once successfully trained for the position. The *position advertisement* becomes a useful tool in that part of the second principle referring to scientifically selecting the workers. When a vacancy occurs, a criminal justice manager must prepare an advertisement for this job. It is common practice to omit all reference to salary scales. The affirmative action plan probably will require that it include a note to the effect of: "Our agency is an equal opportunity employer." It is up to the manager to select the educational criteria, physical standards (eyesight, height, weight, age, sex, health, and other physical limitations, if any), prior skills or experience, or other preliminary limitations associated with the job. The efficient criminal justice manager will use the advertisement to prescreen the applicant pool, but the screening criteria must be empirically valid and nondiscriminatory. Theodore Caplow made the following recommendations regarding the recruiting process (1983: 118-123):

1. Identify what required qualifications are essential

2. Consider a few candidates, as few as possible

3. Ensure the candidates understand their duties (provide an accurate job description)

    a. Ensure that the hiring manager understands it

    b. Ensure that coworkers and supervisors of the new employee understand it

4. Study the candidates closely

    a. Review their biographies and résumé carefully

    b. Check their official records

    c. Test for their essential aptitudes and abilities

    d. Contact their references

    e. Assess their attitude

5. Be prompt in making the selection

The second of Taylor's principles involves the selection of the right worker for the job and providing that newly selected worker with the proper training needed to master the job. Ideally, the selection criteria should be based upon the job description, to match prospective workers' existing talents, interests, and abilities to the requirements of the job. Taylor knew, however, that having the general aptitude and ability to do a job does not necessarily mean having the specific, detailed knowledge of the way the work is done in a specific agency. The latter requires formal training, **on-the-job training** (OJT), and work experience.

Taylor and other scientific managers knew also that simply having qualified workers did not assure quality work output. That led to his third and fourth principles. The worker had to be supervised and his or her efforts integrated and coordinated with the efforts of others. This was one of the jobs of the manager.

Programs for Affirmative Action

As noted, the first program in modern federal law to seek to achieve an affirmative action purpose was the Veterans Preference Act of 1944, which was meant to help returning veterans, especially those with war wounds, find jobs upon their return from the war. It added points to the civil service tests of returning veterans and additional points to those who were wounded or disabled as a result of their war service. The Equal Pay Act of 1963 required equal pay for equal work, making it unlawful to have different pay scales for men and women or for people of different races or ethnic groups (Stewart and Garson, 1983: 242). The Civil Rights Act of 1964 (Stewart and Garson, 1983: 238) made discrimination based on race, ethnicity, national origin, religion, sex, and political preference unlawful in public accommodation. The Age Discrimination in Employment Act of 1967 (Stewart and Garson, 1983: 244) protects the rights of older workers. Presidential Executive Orders 11246 and 11373 (Stewart and Garson, 1983: 246) created contracting quotas and denied contracts to organizations that discriminate. The Equal Employment Opportunity Act of 1972, with the 1973 amendment that applied it to state and local units of government, prohibited discrimination in hiring and other personnel practices. The Rehabilitation Act of 1973 (Stewart and Garson, 1983: 247) and the Americans with Disabilities Act of 1990 require reasonable accommodations for handicapped people seeking employment as well as those currently employed.

In 1994 the Congress revised the law on veterans' rights and employment preference with the passage of the Uniformed Services Employment and Reemployment Rights Act (USERRA). Like its 1944 predecessor, it guarantees reemployment of veterans who left civilian occupations to perform military service. The federal law does not obligate employers to pay workers for their time in federal military service, but private employers and states can do so. USERRA requires employers to reinstate those taking military leave without loss of seniority or promotional eligibility in the same or similar duties they had prior to military service. Military leave can be for short periods of training, such as weekend training drills (known as inactive duty training (IDT)), or extended periods of activation (mobilization and deployment) lasting many months. The military service can be voluntary or compulsory. One does not need to have been in the military prior to his or her nonmilitary employment, which means that an employee can join the armed services after being hired by a criminal justice agency and seek military leave for initial military training. There are severe civil penalties for supervisors, employers, and organizations that penalize their military members in violation of these reemployment and military leave rights.

The Terminology of Affirmative Action: Affirmative action programs use a variety of abbreviations that everyone involved in criminal justice staffing needs to know:

AA: Affirmative Action

BFOQ: Bona Fide Occupational Qualification

EEO: Equal Employment Opportunity

EEOC: Equal Employment Opportunity Commission

OFCCP: Office of Federal Contract Compliance Programs

Compliance with Civil Rights Laws: The EEOC and the OFCCP have been exerting their influence upon public agencies and local and state units of government by a combination of "carrot and stick." If a public agency or institution does not comply, it can get the stick, that is, be sued in federal courts for denying citizens equal access or opportunity. More often, however, the carrot is offered. Local and state units of government and nongovernmental public service agencies and institutions can qualify for federal funds only if they practice equality of employment opportunity and make strides to effect affirmative action programs. If discrimination is present, a cut-off of federal aid is threatened.

The Role of the Courts: The U.S. Supreme Court has taken the leadership in defining civil rights in recent decades. In a series of decisions, the court has sent confusing and apparently contradictory signals to public service employers. In *Griggs v. Duke Power* (1971), the Court applied statistical evidence to establish the practice of racial exclusion, even when hard evidence of an employer "intentionally engag[ing] in unlawful employment practice" was not demonstrated.

In a 1986 case, the U.S. Supreme Court also allowed to stand a voluntary plan of redress favoring African-American Cleveland firefighters through promotion quotas. The workers' union had disagreed with the city's affirmative action plan, arguing that no clear evidence of discrimination existed in the policies the quota plan replaced, and no victims of deliberate discrimination could be identified. In 1984, the U.S. Supreme Court allowed the seniority plans of Memphis, Tennessee, firefighters to take precedence over affirmative action plans when those seniority plans had been shown to be untainted by racial or other prejudicial exclusions. Historically, the Supreme Court had been opposed to accepting statistical evidence alone, or accepting nonvoluntary affirmative action programs without identifiable victims coming forward to show how they had been harmed by past practices. The Court did not disagree with the Cleveland firefighters union, but saw that in prior history the city had not achieved equal opportunity in hiring and promotions. Some critics of affirmative action have interpreted these rulings as having settled this civil rights issue and that affirmative action programs are needed only where racial or other prejudicial exclusions can be evidenced (Eastland, 1996), but affirmative action plans still govern most civil service employment practices in criminal justice agencies.

Federal courts and political leaders remain divided on whether their goal simply should be providing "equality of opportunity" or achieving the more far-reaching objective of "**equality of result**," which measures success based on results rather than opportunities. Diversity and representativeness in the criminal justice workforce are worthwhile goals that few critics of affirmative action actually oppose (Edelman, Fuller, and Mara-Drita, 2001; Yates, 1994). More often it is the methods used to achieve affirmative action that have troubled its critics (Hammerman, 1988; Livingston, 1979; Loury, 1997; Moore, 2001).

Many proponents of EEO/AA programs see good as determined by "outcome" or "equality of result." This is a consequentialist line of reasoning, although not necessarily utilitarian (fairness in application might not alter the "number" in "the greatest good for greatest number"). Opponents of continuing EEO/AA programs often see good as determined by providing the equality of opportunity, created by the rules themselves, even if the desired outcome—an equal distribution of government jobs, promotions, or similar advantages—is not achieved. If the opportunities are equally accessible, no biased criteria permitted, and only merit, talent, and motivation are used as the selection criteria, then fairness is achieved. This is deontological, nonconsequential reasoning. The critics are especially opposed to the used of quotas for minority hiring in the absence of deliberate discrimination. Quotas are inherently unfair to those categories of people excluded.

Some also make use of the distinction between being **fully qualified** and being the **best qualified**. For example, if seeking the "fully qualified," when minimum passing scores are established, everyone who exceeds the minimum can be viewed as equally qualified for selection or promotion, even though some have passed with higher scores than others. If the "fully qualified" standard is being applied, then this needs to be made clear from the onset.

Unfortunately, subjectivist reasoning can sometimes disguise itself as an ethical argument. "Equality of opportunity" arguments can be used to mask covert racism or sexism. For instance, a black partisan could demand equality of result simply because he or she has a racial bias for his or her own kind—a pattern of pro-minority, anti-majority racism.

Where Will Affirmative Action Take Us Next?

A new civil rights issue was raised and hotly debated in the 1980s, that of **comparable worth**, that is, equal pay for work of equal value. The issue has to do with salary differentials for positions that are similar (i.e., requiring similar credentials), but that have been classified as different. In the past, women working as correctional officers were called "matrons" and were paid less than men who were called "jailers" or "guards," yet all were doing essentially the same duties as correctional custodians. Proponents of comparable worth, including many feminists, see this as an unresolved civil rights question (Gold, 1983; Hill and Kill-ingsworth, 1989; Paul, 1989; Remick, 1984). For the most part, however, criminal justice agencies have not had a recent history of differential pay for similar positions. Examples that have existed in the past, such as the matron-vs.-guard distinction, have generally been eliminated.

More conservative voices claim that affirmative action has gone too far and has evolved into a distasteful form of reverse discrimination against white males. These critics often resist all formal quotas for minority hiring and promotion and oppose using statistical evidence in the absence of hard evidence of actual discrimination (Eastland, 1996).

Sample Personnel Policies

Most criminal justice agencies operate under state personnel laws. As long as an agency complies with those laws, the agency has some discretion to develop personnel benefits packages. The Minnesota Council of Nonprofits has offered some excellent suggestions for nonprofit personnel policies (2007). Their recommendations start with the assumption that the organization is committed "to fair, clearly stated and supportive relationships between the organization and its staff." It is the responsibility of the organization to administer personnel programs that comply with all federal, state, and local laws and personnel regulations.

Employee Classification: Employees are classified as either "regular" or "temporary." Regular employees are those hired without a specific termination date. Temporary employees are those whose position is for a short-term. Full-time employees also are classified as either exempt or nonexempt, according to provisions of the Fair Labor Standards Act (FLSA). Nonexempt employees are protected by the FLSA; exempt employees are not. Full-time employees earning hourly wages, typically working about 2,000 hours per year, and eligible for employee fringe benefits, are covered by the FLSA. Those classified as nonexempt have to be paid at least the minimum wage and extra overtime pay if they work more than the allowable maximum of hours per week, usually 40 hours in a single week (University of Louisville, Human Resources, 2007). Those working rotating shifts and other unusual schedules, averaging 40 hours per week over the work year, also may be excluded from overtime pay. Those on contract to be paid a fixed salary and those classified as managerial employees generally are "exempt" from FLSA and are not covered by its protections. Most civil service hires and entry-level police, corrections, and court officials are nonexempt, while many senior criminal justice managers are exempt. Upon hiring, a new employee should be told his or her status under FLSA.

Affirmative Action: A criminal justice agency is required to provide equal employment opportunity for all persons regardless of race, color, religion, national origin, marital status, political affiliation, disability, sex, or age. Affirmative action programs apply to all personnel practices including, but not limited to, recruiting, hiring, placement, promotion, demotion, transfer, training, compensation, benefits, layoff, recall, and termination.

Recruitment Procedures: A criminal justice agency is expected to recruit, hire, and assign applicants on the basis of the applicant's relative knowledge, skills, and abilities. The decision to employ an applicant should be based on an individual's qualification for the particular position, along with other requisite job skills. Employment qualifications should be specified in the job description. When a position is vacant, the personnel manager or chief executive will generally prepare a job announcement with the position's responsibilities and advertise the position for a reasonable length of time.

Compensation and Benefits: Criminal justice agency employees receive a salary and benefits as established in advance for their position. Agencies can provide salary supplements for education, relevant prior experience, and special skills such as foreign language abilities. At the time of hire, new employees will receive a letter of appointment along with a job description, an enumeration of salary and benefits, and a copy of the agency personnel policies. Larger criminal justice agencies usually provide medical care, disability income, life insurance, and retirement programs for their employees. Often this is governed by state law or local personnel policies.

Work, Leave, and Holiday Schedules: The agency establishes work schedules, and when 24-hour, seven-day-a-week staffing is required, shift assignments may be required. Official holidays as designated by the state or the federal government should be followed when possible, and when employees must work on holidays because of staffing needs, *compensatory leave* days or *overtime pay* usually will be provided.

Anti-Harassment Policy: Workplace harassment is any unwanted attention or action by someone in the workplace that creates or contributes to an intimidating, hostile, or offensive work environment, including sexual harassment. The criminal justice manager must establish and publicize agency procedures for reporting and dealing with this issue. An investigation of each complaint will take place, protecting the rights of all people involved. If there appears to be substance to the complaint, the agency must take steps to resolve the problem. This may include verbal or written reprimand, suspension, or termination. No retaliation can be directed toward an employee who has, in good faith, reported an incident of suspected harassment.

Box 8.4 • Leave Options for Criminal Justice Agencies

Annual Leave (Vacation): Annual leave is provided to all full-time employees, usually based on the length of time employed by the agency. Annual leave often starts with each individual's anniversary date with the agency or by calendar or fiscal year, with proration for partial-year employment. Some agencies will allow leave to be carried over from one year to the next, but in others unused leave will be forfeited.

Special and Compassionate Leave: Special leaves of absence, usually without pay, may be granted to an employee because of highly unusual personal, family, or career situations. Examples include a death or serious, life-threatening illness or injury in their immediate family, such as of a mother, father, sister, brother, spouse, child, grandparent, or grandchild.

Parental Leave: Parental leave assists new parents by permitting leave, usually unpaid, for the birth or adoption of a child.

School Conference and Activities Leave: Some criminal justice agencies will permit employees time off or nonpaid leave to attend school activities when such activities must be scheduled during working hours. In other agencies, vacation leave or compensatory time will be used for such activities.

Sick Leave: Criminal justice agencies will provide leave for health needs, usually paid time off. In some agencies, this sick leave may be accumulated and carried over from one year to the next.

Blood, Organ, and Bone-Marrow Donor Leave: Some criminal justice agencies will give their employees time off to donate blood, organs, or bone marrow. Others will allow their employees to apply sick leave or ordinary leave for such purposes.

Jury Duty Leave: Typically criminal justice system employees will not be seated on juries, but they still will need to answer jury calls. Many criminal justice agencies will pay an employee performing jury duty.

Voting Leave: A few criminal justice agencies will grant their employees brief periods of time off during the working day to vote in elections when voting hours fall within regularly scheduled work time. This is especially appropriate when their agencies require long work shifts that may conflict with voting hours. For example, 10- or 12-hour shifts are required by some police and correctional agencies.

Military Leave: Federal law guarantees that reserve or national guard duty, including extended call-ups, shall be considered as excused leaves of absence, but criminal justice agencies are not obligated to pay service members called to military duty. Employees called up for extended active duty must be allowed a leave of absence to meet their military responsibilities, regardless of the length of their absence. Upon release from active duty, the employee is entitled to be reinstated in the same job formerly held, with the same duties, same level of

Box 8.4 *(continued)*

pay, and same benefits and seniority had the service member not been on active military duty. Typically most employee benefits do not accumulate during military leave. Some criminal justice agencies will allow one of the following options related to their pay:

> The employee may use accumulated vacation time and thereby retain both military pay and the criminal justice agency wages.

> The employee may take unpaid leave form the criminal justice agency and thus will be required to subsist only on military pay.

> A few agencies will continue an employee's criminal justice pay, or make up the difference between the criminal justice pay and military pay during some part of their absence, usually only for a limited time, without requiring the forfeiture of any vacation time.

Substance Abuse: Criminal justice agency employees are in especially sensitive positions regarding unlawful substance abuse. Those needing help with substance abuse problems should be encouraged to seek treatment. The agency will need to determine if such an employee should be placed on leave, suspended, or terminated because of the problem.

Performance Reviews: Newly hired employees should have at least one evaluation during their probationary period. A schedule for periodic personnel reviews should be established by the agency chief executive, and the content of the evaluation should be announced in advance.

Prior Employment References: Criminal justice agencies should have a policy of seeking information on their prospective employees, including prior work locations, job titles, supervisors' names, dates of all prior employment, and reasons given for leaving. The agency also should ask for and contact given references, conduct criminal background investigations, and investigate the applicants' financial and credit information. A criminal justice agency needs to avoid hiring people with serious prior employment problems, histories of criminality and substance abuse, and whose debts and past history of financial difficulty could impact negatively upon their performance.

Termination: A criminal justice employee should tender a resignation in writing well in advance of the effective date of the resignation. The agency should have a policy with regard to the use of or payment for any accrued annual leave. Typically employees are not compensated for any unused sick leave at the time of resignation. "Dismissal for cause" may occur because of serious inappropriate or criminal behavior or a history of unsatisfactory performance. Temporary and long-term layoffs may occur because of fiscal limitations or mission changes. Typically those laid off are given priority when hiring resumes.

Employee Appeals and Grievance Procedures: An employee **appeal procedure** provides a means for employees to resolve their workplace concerns with management. An employee should be able to file a grievance or an appeal to an unfavorable personnel action without risk of retaliation. A grievance or an appeal is appropriate when there is an alleged misapplication of agency personnel policies or violation of employment law. Should there be some substance to the grievance or appeal, the agency should offer a dispute resolution mechanism to resolve the issue. Usually an appeal or grievance initially will be submitted to an immediate supervisor, but if the issue involves that supervisor, an alternative complaint procedure should be in place. Upon investigation, there should be a response to the employee in writing.

Union Membership and Collective Bargaining: Criminal justice employees are allowed to form associations that can represent them in negotiations with their managers. However, some states limit these negotiations, some do not recognize public service unions, and most prohibit one common tactic of labor unions: the strike. Criminal justice worker unions are governed by the labor laws in their states. The South and Southwest have not been supportive of public service organized labor, while the northern, midwestern, and Pacific Coast states typically model their laws and boards after the practices found in the federal National Labor Relations Act of 1935. Where a union is allowed to organize criminal justice system employees, the union organizers usually must win the support of a majority of those they seek to represent. The criminal justice manager and the union then may negotiate the terms and conditions of employment and enter into a contract. When labor disputes arise, the parties will employ a grievance procedure to resolve them. If the matter is not resolved, they then will send the dispute to binding arbitration, where a neutral third party will review the competing claims and render a decision. Where a union exists, criminal justice employees do not have to take part in union activities. However, some states allow closed shops. In a **closed shop**, all covered employees must be members. Some of these states collect union dues from active and passive members alike as a payroll deduction. Other states require public service employment under the rules of an **open shop**, whereby workers do not have to be members but usually acquire the same benefits arising from union negotiations.

Work Products and Files: All supplies, materials, and work products of a criminal justice agency employee remain the property of the agency after resignation, discharge, or layoff of that employee. The employee may retain some personal files, but confidential work files and other documents shall remain with the agency.

Consultant Fees, Honoraria, and Gifts: Criminal justice agency employees are encouraged to participate in a variety of community and professional activities. When such activities are part of an employee's regular duties and responsibilities, consultant fees, honoraria, and gifts should be reported to agency and may be claimed by the agency. To avoid actual conflict of interest, or the appearance thereof, any employee who engages in any compensated activity related to agency programs and activities must have approval from a supervisor or more senior agency manager.

Summary

Staffing and personnel issues are a major responsibility of a criminal justice manager. Staffing involves hiring, fostering career development, protecting the employment rights, disciplining, and promoting agency employees. A knowledge of civil service rules and equal employment opportunity law is essential.

Learning Objectives

Upon finishing this chapter you should be able to do the following:

▶ 1. Identify the key features of the five eras of public service in the United States.

▶ 2. Understand the both the positive and negative aspects of the patronage system for criminal justice hiring.

▶ 3. Identify the seven key civil service reforms exemplified in the Pendleton Act.

▶ 4. Identify key legislation and court rulings bringing about the "civil rights" revolution in criminal justice hiring.

▶ 5. To know the following commonly used abbreviations:
  • AA: Affirmative Action
  • BFOQ: Bona Fide Occupational Qualification
  • EEO: Equal Employment Opportunity
  • EEOC: Equal Employment Opportunity Commission
  • OFCCP: Office of Federal Contract Compliance Programs

IMPORTANT TERMS AND NAMES

- *Ackerman's question*
- *appeal procedure*
- *best qualified*
- *civil service law*
- *closed shop*
- *comparable worth*
- *contracting process*
- *credentialism*
- *employee classification*
- *equality of opportunity*
- *equality of result*
- *exempt*
- *fitness of character*
- *fully qualified*

- *Jacksonian egalitarianism*
- *Jeffersonian ideal*
- *job description*
- *Malek Manual*
- noblisse oblige
- *non-exempt*
- *on-the-job training (OJT)*
- open shop
- *patronage appointments*
- *special assignment technique*
- *spoils system*
- *staffing*
- *veterans preference*
- *workplace harassment*

References and Supplemental Sources

Age Discrimination in Employment Act of 1967.

Americans with Disabilities Act of 1990.

Brown v. Board of Education of Topeka, 347 U.S. 483 (1954).

Campbell, Alan K. (1978). *Civil Service Reform*. U.S. House Committee on Post Office and Civil Service. Washington, DC: U.S. Government Printing Office.

Campbell, Alan K. (1991). "Testimony on Civil Service Reform and Organization," pages 82-104 in *Classics of Public Personnel Policy*, 2nd ed., edited by Frank J. Thompson. Pacific Grove, CA: Brooks/Cole.

Caplow, Theodore (1983). *Managing an Organization*, 2nd ed. New York: Holt, Rinehart, and Winston.

Civil Rights Act of 1964.

Civil Service Reform Act of 1978.

Colbridge, Thomas D. (2000). "Prohibited Discrimination under the Americans with Disabilities Act," *FBI Law Enforcement Bulletin*, 69(12): 14-21.

Eastland, Terry (1996). *Ending Affirmative Action: The Case for Colorblind Justice*. New York: Basic Books.

Edelman, Lauren B., Sally Riggs Fuller, and Iona Mara-Drita (2001). "Diversity Rhetoric and the Managerialization of Law," *American Journal of Sociology*, 106(6): 1589-1641.

Equal Employment Opportunity Act of 1972, as amended in 1973. (Note: The amendment applied the 1972 act to state and local units of government.)

Equal Pay Act of 1963.

Fair Labor Standards Act of 1938, as amended in 1974.

Firefighters v. City of Cleveland, 478 U.S. 501 (1986).

Firefighters v. Stotts, 467 U.S. 561 (1984).

Gold, Michael Evan (1983). *A Dialogue on Comparable Worth*. Ithaca, NY: ILR Press/ Cornell University.

Griggs vs. Duke Power, 401 U.S. 424 (1971).

Gulick, Luther (1937). "Notes on the Theory of Organization," *Papers on the Science of Administration*, edited by Luther Gulick and Lyndall Urwick. New York: Institute of Public Administration.

Hill, M. Anne, and Mark R. Killingsworth (1989). *Comparable Worth: Analyses and Evidence*. Ithaca, NY: ILR Press/Cornell University.

Hammerman, Herbert (1988). "Affirmative-Action Stalemate: A Second Perspective," *Public Interest*, 93(Fall): 130-134.

Livingston, John C. (1979). *Fair Game? Inequality and Affirmative Action*. San Francisco: W.H. Freeman and Company.

Loury, Glenn C. (1997). "How to Mend Affirmative Action," *Public Interest*, 127 (Spring): 33-43.

Minnesota Council of Nonprofits (2007). "Sample Personnel Policies," *How to Start a Nonprofit: Templates and Samples*. Available at http://www.mncn.org/info/ template_hr.htm

Moore, Eric William (2001). "Emerging Legal Constraints on Affirmative Action in Police Agencies and How to Adapt to Them," *Journal of Criminal Justice*, 29(1): 11-19.

Mosher, Frederick C. (1967). *Democracy and the Public Service*. New York: Oxford University Press.

National Commission on Law Observance and Enforcement [Wickersham Commission] (1931). *Report on the Enforcement of the Prohibition Laws of the United States*. Available at http://www.druglibrary.org/schaffer/library/studies/wick/wick3.html

National Labor Relations Act of 1935.

Paul, Ellen Frankel (1989). *Equity and Gender: The Comparable Worth Debate*. New Brunswick, NJ: Transaction.

Rehabilitation Act of 1973.

Remick, Helen (1984). *Comparable Worth and Wage Discrimination*. Philadelphia: Temple University Press.

Roosevelt, Theodore (1897). *American Ideals and Other Essays Social and Political*. New York: The Knickerbocker Press, G.P. Putnam's Sons.

Savas, E. S., and Sigmund G. Ginsburg (1973). "The Civil Service: A Meritless System?" *The Public Interest*, 32(Summer): 70-85.

Sorauf, Frank J. (1960). "The Silent Revolution in Patronage," *Public Administration Review,* 20(1): 28-34.

Souryal, Sam S. (1995). *Police Organization and Administration*, 2nd ed. Cincinnati: Anderson.

Stewart, Debra, and G. David Garson (1983). *Organizational Behavior and Public Management*. New York: Marcel Dekker.

Taylor, Frederick W. (1911). *Principles of Scientific Management*. New York: Norton Library, Harper and Row.

Thompson, Frank J. (1991). *Classics of Public Personnel Policy*, 2nd ed. Pacific Grove, CA: Brooks/Cole.

U.S. President's Commission on Law Enforcement and Administration of Justice (1967). *The Challenge of Crime in a Free Society*. Washington, DC: U.S. Government Printing Office.

U. S. President's Commission on Law Enforcement and Administration of Justice (1967). *Task Force Report: The Police*. Washington, DC: U.S. Government Printing Office.

Uniformed Services Employment and Reemployment Rights Act of 1994.

University of Louisville, Human Resources (2007) "What Does It Mean to be an 'Exempt' or 'Nonexempt' Employee?" University of Louisville, Louisville, Kentucky. Available at http://louisville.edu/hr/payroll/faq/what-does-it-mean-to-be-an-exempt-or-nonexempt-employee.html

Van Riper, Paul P. (1958). *History of the United States Civil Service*. New York: Harper and Row.

Van Riper, Paul P. (1991). "Americanizing a Foreign Invention: The Pendleton Act of 1883," pp. 6-16 in *Classics of Public Personnel Policy*, 2nd ed., edited by Frank J. Thompson. Pacific Grove, CA: Brooks/Cole.

Veterans Preference Act of 1944.

Weber, Max (1922). *Economy and Society*, 2 volumes, edited by Guenther Roth and Claus Wittich. Berkeley, CA: University of California Press.

Wilson, Woodrow (1887). "The Study of Administration," *Political Science Quarterly*, 2(2): 197-222.

Yates, Steven (1994). *Civil Wrongs: What Went Wrong with Affirmative Action?* San Francisco: ICS Press.

Yuill, Kevin L. (2006). *Richard Nixon and the Rise of Affirmative Action: The Pursuit of Equality in an Era of Limits*. Lanham, MD: Rowman and Littlefield.

9

Training and Education for Criminal Justice

The "T" in LODESTAR stands for "training." Although there was no "T" in POSDCORB, Luther Gulick (1937) was aware of the importance of training as part of the staffing function. Frederick Taylor (1911) also stressed the importance of training new employees, making it a component of one of his four principles. Neither man, however, gave much attention to continuing education and in-service training, both of which occupy much of the time and a considerable part of the budgets of criminal justice agencies. Clearly the training function has grown in importance since the 1911-1937 period between Taylor's and Gulick's major articles on staffing. In large measure due to "failure-to-train" lawsuits (Ross, 2000: 330-331), providing personnel with current, correct, and comprehensive training is a major managerial responsibility.

A History of Criminal Justice Training and Education

In 1900 the police academy was virtually nonexistent. Many states permitted the election or appointment of prosecutors and judges who had not attended law school. Few correctional officers received any training at all. Most people undertaking employment in criminal justice agencies were expected to learn on the job, with the talents and skills they had prior to being hired, appointed, or elected. In just one century this has changed dramatically.

Buffalo had a police training program in 1871, but it was discontinued soon after. In 1886 Cincinnati established a program of police instruction that endured (Richardson, 1977: 12). Few other cities followed in the nineteenth century, but more police academies were established early in the twentieth century. Most police were trained on the street, under the mentorship of a veteran partner. No training curriculum was established, and police officers often went on duty first—and were issued a uniform, gun, and badge with little or no guidance on how to use them. In 1895 New York began to require pistol practice for its police (Roosevelt, 1897: 185).

Leonhard Fuld wrote *Police Administration* (1909), the first textbook on how to be a police manager. With an audience of prospective police managers, it offered his experience-based prescriptions on how to run a police agency. Coming in the era of social reform, the book was reform-oriented, and Fuld was both critical of existing personnel practices and an advocate for civil service improvements. He supported police training, the lateral entry of highly qualified, university-educated non-police managers in to police executive positions (in opposition to selecting police managers from the ranks), and was a strong advocate of improved line supervision by police sergeants and mid-management captains as the keys to better policing.

However, criminal justice education, other than in law, was virtually nonexistent in the nineteenth century, and Fuld's book had a very limited potential audience. As the "new ideas" man of American law enforcement practice, August Vollmer sought to change that. Under Vollmer's influence, San Jose State College offered the first college degree program in law enforcement studies (Walker, 1977: 136), the forerunner to today's criminal justice and criminology degree programs.

Vollmer and his supporters also sought improved police training for officers and police managers already hired. In that time few cities and no states required any formal police recruit training. Police academies were established in a few of the more progressive cities, but their curricula were ill-defined. Promotion in most police agencies was from the ranks, and little or no supervisory or managerial instruction was available. The pro-education reformers within the American police establishment sought to change all of this. They lobbied for recruit training academies, mid-career supervision courses, and managerial education.

Judges, prosecutors, and defense attorneys were allowed to hold offices and practice law without law degrees in the first half of the nineteenth century, but by the 1880s many states were requiring at least passage of a state bar examination. The practice of "reading law" in an apprenticeship with a veteran lawyer has lasted, and seven states still permitted it at the start of the twenty-first century (MacDonald, 2003).

Previously we have discussed the contributions of Frederick Taylor and the application of his four principles of scientific management (1911: 36-37) to the design of work and the selection of workers. The second of these was to "scientifically select and then train, teach, and develop the workman." A formal training plan, based on the job description, was a necessary feature. The **training plan** first recognizes the skills and education the new worker should bring to the job, and then outlines the on-the-job and specialized occupational training program that the criminal justice agency will require and provide for the new employee. This will specify the general kinds of training to be given, who will provide the required training to the new employee, or how it will be acquired. The roles of the supervisor, a training academy, or a specialized workshop or course will be included.

Corrections training applied Taylor's principles, but many correctional agencies had lagged behind other parts of the criminal justice system in setting appropriately demanding entry requirement and training requirements until the middle of the twentieth century (Johnson, Wolfe, and Jones, 2008). The President's Commission on Law Enforcement and Administration of Justice (1967) recommended both formal training and higher educational standards for correctional officers in its *Task Force Report: Corrections*. With the development of the **rehabilitative ideal** in corrections, which focuses on effecting change in the character, attitudes, and behavior of convicted offenders, it became necessary for correctional institutions and programs to employ college-educated teachers, social workers, counselors, and correctional psychologists. These were not programs that could be managed by high school graduates or those with even less education. By the time the reports of the National Advisory Commission on Criminal Justice Standards and Goals were published (1973), the federal government was calling upon the states to undertake studies of what education and training should be required for criminal justice occupations, work with colleges and universities to provide appropriate educational programs for criminal justice professionals, develop curricula, and coordinate their offerings with criminal justice managers and federal recommendations to ensure that their programs would be relevant. Knowledge and skill requirements for criminal justice hiring, initial, and in-service training were recommended, and incentives for upgrading the training and education of existing employees suggested. Evaluation of training and educational efforts was advised (1973: 168-169). To help the states pay for these new programs, LEAA grants were authorized for new training centers and programs, for the creation of new criminal justice educational programs in colleges, and tuition assistance through the Law Enforcement Education Program (LEEP).

The Law Enforcement Education Program (LEEP) was a short-lived program that paid the tuition of full-time criminal justice system employees to attend college-level criminal justice programs. In the 1970s tens of thousands of service police, correctional, juvenile justice, and other criminal justice employees were able to attend college and earn associate's, bachelor's, and even master's degrees in criminal justice or other related academic disciplines. The funding ended with the budget cuts imposed by the Carter administration, but criminal justice employees already in criminal justice educational programs were eligible to finish their degrees, so that LEEP funds continued to flow into the early 1980s. Many thought that the decade-long effort to improve the educational level of criminal justice practitioners would collapse with the end of LEEP support for criminal justice education, but that did not prove to be the case. Fewer in-service criminal justice practitioners were in college classrooms after 1980, but the appeal of criminal justice education was attracting pre-service students thinking about criminal justice careers. Most of the college criminal justice programs created at community colleges, four-year colleges, and universities continue to offer their courses to another generation of students.

College Education for Criminal Justice

The results of LEEP raised some important criminal justice policy questions. How much education is necessary to qualify one for a criminal justice occupation? Does one need a high school diploma, an associate of arts (AA) or associate of applied sciences (AAS) degree, a bachelor of science (BS) or bachelor of arts (BA) degree, or even more formal education to perform well in a criminal justice occupation? The debate has continued since the 1970s. Certainly more education, especially that which is focused on one's career choice, is a good thing to have (Mayo, 2006; 2008), But the jury is still out on the question of its necessity.

Professional degrees are needed for some public service occupations: An assistant district attorney or a judge will be expected to have a law degree. Several states require social workers working in corrections to have a master of social work (MSW). A senior planner might be required to have a graduate degree in an academic discipline related to planning. Many of those holding line positions in criminal justice agencies should have some post–high school education, and certainly supervisors and managers would benefit from college. Other criminal justice organization positions easily can be filled by persons with much less education. Skilled laborers, janitorial staffs, receptionists, security guards, and many others can perform quite well with a high school diploma, and perhaps even less.

It is obvious that the position itself determines the education prerequisites. A criminal justice manager must make a realistic assessment of the requirements of the job and must be aware of what each level of education is likely to provide toward meeting those requirements. What can a high school graduate reasonably be expected to do? What knowledge, skills, and talents can be associated with the diploma? What about a specialized AAS or any other two-year college degree? Or a generalist BA or BS coupled with a major in a traditional liberal arts academic discipline in a technical field or applied science? Or should one acquire a bachelor degree in criminal justice or criminology? Which is better? In most cases a master's degree is not needed as an entry-level credential for most people in law enforcement, corrections, or court administration, but would be an asset in correctional and juvenile justice counseling occupations, especially if the degree is in social work, counseling, or applied psychology. The master of public administration (MPA) is an excellent and valuable credential for a person already in a criminal justice field preparing to advance into a managerial position, or already holding one and seeking to rise further.

What should the education of a criminal justice professional include? The appropriate education for someone in public service has been an open question for more than 2,000 years. Plato expressed his opinions on this matter in *The Republic*, citing the ideas of Socrates, an advocate of what we now refer to as the "liberal arts education" ideal:

> Our best guardians will be a select band, those who are of the right temper and thoroughly trained; fierce to foes but gentle to friends. ... The known are friends, the unknown foes—knowledge begets gentleness.
>
> So our guardians must be trained to knowledge; we must educate them. Music and gymnastics, our national intellectual and physical training, must be taught. Literature comes first . . .

On this issue, too, there is some debate. What are the purposes of a liberal arts education? Would not a professional preparatory education be superior? Training, both at entry and in-service, will provide for the technical skills needed on the job, so technical and professional curricula will be duplicated if also taken in college. A broader education in the liberal arts, as suggested by Plato 2,400 years ago, therefore, has greater advantages. The technical and professional skills of this decade will some day be as obsolete as those acquired in the 1970s and 1980s are now, but the skills learned in the liberal arts will endure. In criminal justice occupations, excellent communications skills, the ability to comprehend a foreign language (especially Spanish), and the skills to deal with mathematical applications will be far more important by the time one is in mid-career in the 2020s than will be having mastered the crime scene technologies, correctional procedures, or court administrative practices of today.

While even 20 years ago a majority of the surveyed police departments informally gave preference to college-educated applicants, the overwhelming majority of police agencies formally require only a high school diploma or its general educational development (GED) test equivalent. Only 13.7 percent of surveyed law enforcement agencies in a Police Executive Research Forum (PERF) study (Carter, Sapp, and Stephens, 1989: xvii) had a formal college entry requirement, and those that did usually a required a two-year AA/AAS degree or 60 hours of college education. A slight majority (54.1%) reported their hiring efforts

Box 9.1 • Three Ways to Train

ADVANTAGES	DISADVANTAGES
On-the-Job (OJT)	
It is the least expensive means of training.	Supervisors may not be good trainers.
It is done under existing supervisors, thus better acquainting trainees and the supervisors for whom they will work.	Supervisors may not be acquainted with the most progressive and innovative methods in the field.
The trainee is available for work while training.	It can be hard to find sufficient training time in a busy work environment.
There is a totally realistic setting that replicates actual work situations and environment.	Training continually is interrupted by the actual work of the agency.
There is time flexibility, with continuous training opportunities provided over an extended duration.	The work and training pace may be too fast for a new worker.
	Generally it takes longer than formal training.
	Unapproved practices, rather than formally approved policies, may be taught or shown.
In-House	
It acquaints new employees with additional organizational staff members, rather than just the immediate supervisors.	It is provided in a less realistic environment.
It can provide training on and familiarization with activities conducted in other departments of the agency beyond the immediate workplace.	In-house trainers usually have other responsibilities in the organization and rarely are totally qualified as trainers.
It is usually quicker than OJT.	It takes trainers away from their other, principle duties.
Time is provided exclusively for training.	The trainee is not available for productive labor while in training.
Trainers are well acquainted with agency requirements, peculiarities, eccentricities, and unique situations.	In-house trainers may not be acquainted with the most progressive and innovative methods in the field.

Box 9.1 *(continued)*

ADVANTAGES	DISADVANTAGES
Contracted-Out	
Presumably the trainers are totally professional and experienced in their subject areas.	It is the most expensive means of training.
It can provide training on and familiarization with activities conducted beyond the immediate workplace and in similar agencies, ideally including the most progressive and innovative methods in the field.	Trainers may not be knowledgeable of agency requirements, peculiarities eccentricities, and unique situations.
It offers the most efficient use of agency labor and time: only the trainees participate, thus it does not obligate the time and effort of supervisors or in-house trainers.	Scheduling inflexibility is common; programs are offered when the training contractor is ready and available, not necessarily when the agency needs the training.
Time is provided exclusively for training.	Workers often are sent "away" from agency when in training and are not available for productive labor while in training.
It is usually quicker than OJT.	

were oriented toward recruiting college students, but only 6.6 percent targeted college students as their primary or exclusive applicant pool (Carter, Sapp, and Stephens, 1989: xix).

Given the education that a potential criminal justice agency employee brings to the job, what training is necessary to make that employee into a fully functioning staff member? How should criminal justice training be acquired? Three major approaches can be used: (1) *on-the-job training (OJT)* under normal supervisors, (2) *in-house training* with staff providing trainers, and (3) *contracted-out training programs* using specialists. There are distinct advantages and disadvantages to each that a criminal justice manager needs to consider (see Box 9.1).

Selecting the approach to be taken to training is a major managerial responsibility. Time, cost, instructional requirements, and available qualified instructors are all factors to be considered. So is litigation. **"Failure to train" liability lawsuits**, which allege that there was a "deliberate indifference" to proper training, are a real risk to criminal justice agencies, and both police and corrections agencies have found themselves in court to answer for their training failures (Ross, 2000:

330-331). The absence of training in key performance areas—and incorrect or inadequate training in those areas—often will be cited to demonstrate an agency's negligence in such lawsuits.

Continuing In-Service Training and Education

Formal training should not end with the conclusion of the formal probationary period. Ideally, it will continue as long as the employee works for the agency. However, the character of the training and education will change as the employee proceeds up the organizational ladder. Some of that training and education will be self-acquired, as advancement-oriented individuals seek to better themselves with further training courses and participation in college degree–granting programs.

Continuing Education Seminars: Some post-hire education is provided by the agencies directly or the professional organizations affiliated with them. The American Bar Association has a long record of providing training seminars for practicing member attorneys, in and out of public practice. The American Correctional Association actively supports continuing education of its membership. The International Association of Chiefs of Police provides many seminars and training sessions for police managers and specialists.

This is true even in areas where high educational criteria are the norm for entry. Judges in some states are required to take courses on judgeship before taking the bench, but now some are even engaging in advanced study of the judiciary (Green, 1987) to help them grow in their key roles.

College Education: During the golden years of the LEAA, criminal justice professionals had federal funding for college courses through the LEEP program. Thousands of police, courts, corrections, and other justice-system employees either returned to college or began college programs for the first time. Average police educational attainment advanced substantially, so that a majority of police officers were college-educated, usually in fields and majors related to their work, by the end of the program in the early 1980s.

Graduate Studies: In 1950 there were virtually no graduate programs specifically in criminal justice or criminology. Criminal justice courses often were offered in sociology, political science, and public administration graduate programs. Since the 1970s an increasing number of universities have been offering graduate-level criminal justice programs. Doctoral programs now exist at some of America's finest universities.

There now is an Association of Doctoral Programs in Criminology and Criminal Justice (2008), whose members are the universities offer-

Box 9.2 • The Association of Doctoral Programs in Criminology and Criminal Justice 2008 North American Institutional Members

American University

Arizona State University — West Campus

California State University — Fresno and University of California Joint Program

Florida International University

Florida State University

George Mason University

Indiana University

John Jay College of Criminal Justice

Michigan State University

North Dakota State University

Northeastern University

Old Dominion University

Pennsylvania State University

Prairie View A&M University

Rutgers University — Newark

Sam Houston State University

Simon Fraser University

State University of New York at Albany

Temple University

Texas Southern University

University of Pennsylvania

University of Texas — Dallas

University of Arkansas — Little Rock

University of California — Irvine

University of Central Florida

University of Cincinnati

University of Delaware

University of Florida

University of Illinois at Chicago

University of Maryland

University of Missouri — St. Louis

University of Montreal

University of Nebraska — Omaha

University of North Dakota

University of South Carolina

University of South Florida

University of Southern Mississippi

Washington State University

ing a doctoral program in criminal justice and criminology. The members meet in conjunction with the American Society of Criminology, conduct annual surveys of doctoral programs activities, and promote the advanced study of crime and criminal justice.

There are a number of institutes and centers providing graduate-level courses for in-service criminal justice managers. Police managers enroll in various police institutes—among the oldest and best are the FBI Academy and its University of Virginia graduate program at Quantico, Virginia, the Southern Police Institute of the University of Louisville, and the Traffic Institute of Northwestern University. The federal government sponsors the John B. Pickett Fellowships in Criminal Justice Policy and Management at the John F. Kennedy School of Government at Harvard University for a select few, leading to the MPA degree (NIJ, 1993; 1995). The University of Virginia offers a master of laws in collaboration with the Appellate Judges Conference of the American Bar Association to sitting judges via a summer program (Green, 1987). The federal government has a Federal Executive Institute for its upper-level managers (including those in criminal justice) who are competing for "super-grade" status in the federal government. These and other programs provide advanced in-service educational opportunities to criminal justice professionals.

Fitting into the Organization

Chris Argyris and Immaturity-Maturity Theory: In his book, *Personality and Organization* (1957), Chris Argyris sought to examine the worker as part of a dynamic "system" of personal and organizational growth and development. The "systems theory" and "systems analysis" arose as an attempt to reconcile the extremes of the individual-oriented human relations focus with the needs of the organization, the exclusive concern of the scientific management advocates. The point raised by the systems advocates is that the individual finds identity and satisfaction as part of a social entity, and that can be his or her work group if the work environment promotes integration of one's identity with the organizational goals.

Taking ideas already popularized in educational psychology, also known as developmental psychology, especially the work of Jean Piaget in France on the development of intellectual maturity and reasoning in

---

Box 9.3 • Chris Argyris and Immaturity—Maturity Theory

1. FROM: Passive (order taking),
   TO: Active (offering suggestions and ideas).

2. FROM: Dependent — waits for instruction,
   TO: Independent — works from one's own initiative.

3. FROM: Limited (self-restricted) behavior,
   TO: Diversified Behavior (will try experiments).

4. FROM: Shallow Interest (ignores policies and politics),
   TO: Deeper Interest (concerned with office politics and issues).

5. FROM: Limited Time Perspective (here and now),
   TO: Long-Term Perspective (past and future).

6. FROM: Subordinate,
   TO: Superior (Seniority).

7. FROM: Not Self-Aware (a weak sense of one's workplace identity),
   TO: Self-Aware (a well defined sense of one's place in the agency).

children, Argyris used a similar developmental approach to describe the progressive maturity of an employee. Argyris saw this process as gradual, continuous, and approximately sequential.

Occupational Socialization

"**Occupational socialization** is the process by which a person acquires the values, attitudes, and behaviors of an ongoing occupational social system" (Klofas, Stojkovic, and Kalinich, 1990: 150). It is described as a continuous process, both intentional and unintentional, both legal and illegitimate, and typically stable and persistent. Often informal occupational socialization will have more influence on a new criminal justice employee than his or her formal training.

The role of personality also needs to be considered. For decades there has been a suspicion that some occupations attract different personality types. As for the police personality question (Klofas, Stojkovic, and Kalinich, 1990: 151-152), the evidence is not completely clear. We are aware, though, that those who wish to become police are somehow different from those who want to become social workers, librarians, teachers, ministers, or accountants.

There is much stronger evidence that the job contributes to the creation of an officer's **working personality**. This concept was contributed to the study of policing by sociologist Jerome Skolnick (1966: 42), and applied socialization concepts used earlier by Howard S. Becker and Anselm L. Straus (1956). Socialization into the "fraternal organization" of policing, lawyering, or judging is another explanation. There are three stages to the process: the anticipatory stage, the formal stage, and the informal stage.

The *anticipatory stage* involves what the potential applicant perceives the organization to be like. It is the image the agency projects to outsiders. For most criminal justice occupations, this is created by the mass communications media, especially entertainment programs on television.

The *formal stage* (training) includes both entry-level and in-service training. Herbert Kaufman examines the role of post-entry training in preparing men to become forest rangers (Thompson, 1960; 1991: 212-214), a specialized form of law enforcement. Kaufman states that post-entry training creates the capacity—by which he means the skills, knowledge, and factual premises—to facilitate adherence to the work norms of the organization. The training will not necessarily the develop the will to do so, however.

The *informal stage* (peer-group and coworkers' influences) is also critical. This was addressed in the article, "Banana Time: Job Satisfaction and Informal Interaction," written by Donald F. Roy in 1959. In this article he asked which has more influence on workers: the formal policies and the managers, or the informal work groups and their "play"?

Factors influencing socialization include an "organizational culture" as discussed by Shafritz and Ott (1992: 482), "...a strong organizational culture literally controls organizational behavior." The formal rules and authority systems do not control the worker as much as the cultural norms, values, beliefs, and assumptions of the coworkers—the organizational culture. This can be defined in terms of six features identified by Edgar H. Schein (1985; 1992: 492):

1. observed behavioral regularities

2. social and productivity norms

3. dominant values (and ideologies) expressed

4. philosophy

5. informal rules and "the ropes"

6. the social climate and layout of the workspace

Symbolic Management: Schein goes further, discussing the levels of culture that include what he refers to as artifacts, values, and basic underlying assumptions. These features are all symbolic measures that a manager can manipulate. **Symbolic management** includes the interpretations given events in an organization, often more important than the events themselves. Because ambiguity and uncertainty are common to most organizations, they preclude rational problem-solving and decisionmaking. Thus, symbolic meanings and ritual actions gain weight beyond their "rational" content. The symbols of the organization, such as logos, flags, lapel pins, and so on, are important to the management of the organization (Shafritz and Ott, 1992: 484-485).

To study and comprehend workplace socialization, the organizational observer needs to examine (Klofas, Stojkovic, and Kalinich, 1990: 154, Figure 7-1):

- organizational factors
- attributes of the person
- interpersonal factors
- role building process
    - (1) role expectations—preconceived notions
    - (2) role senders—communication put out about the role
    - (3) received role—messages received on the role
    - (4) role behavior—the actions of the receiver

Police Socialization

Police socialization now begins with a police academy. There are four variations of police academy training, when considered on two variables: a *residential* versus *commuter* program, and a *collegiate* versus a *paramilitary* curriculum. **Residential academies** once were very common, but they are costly to manage, and fewer cities and states now provide full residential academies. More often, there are **commuter academies**, at which cadets commute to the academy from home or from temporary lodgings provided for them off-campus.

A **paramilitary curriculum** is structured similarly to a professional military force; a **collegiate curriculum** has more of the atmosphere of a college. The manner in which a police cadet is trained initially will vary in intensity of the formal socialization process. A paramilitary curriculum presented in a residential setting is the most intense. These often require the cadet to wear uniforms at all or most times, require military drill and daily physical fitness training, and are modeled on military boot camps and basic training programs. The cadets are boarded in barracks or dormitories at the academy, and have meals together. A commuter program with a collegiate curriculum is the least intense. In some of these, uniforms are not required. Most training is given in a classroom setting, study is done individually, and the cadet is not removed from daily contact with family and friends. In between, in terms of socialization intensity, are the other two options: the paramilitary, commuter academy and the residential, collegiate academy.

When police cadets finish their academy experience, they are often assigned to a "field training officer" (FTO), a veteran officer selected to serve as a mentor to the new officer. The FTO concept differs from the old OJT approach of attaching a new officer to a veteran in that the FTOs are given training to become trainers, and usually do their work from a curriculum of skills they are expected to teach to the new officers and then observe them perform. The old veteran simply had the new officer "tag along" as the veteran officer performed his or her duties.

Socialization in the Courts

Kenneth Peak discusses the training of judges and court administrators, observing that "judges now must train to take the bench" (1988: 177). There is a National Judicial College in Reno, Nevada, and an advanced judicial institute at the College of William and Mary. The National Center for State Courts' Institute of Court Management was created in 1970 to train court administrators, not all of whom are actually judges. The center continues to provide seminars and online learning for judges (National Center for State Courts, 2008). Court clerks generally learn on the job, but increasingly more state-run court administration offices provide formal training. Many assistant clerks of court are hired from the graduates of paralegal studies programs offered at community colleges, training institutes, and colleges and universities.

Box 9.4 • The Fable of the Moth, the Screen, the Light Bulb, and the Pressure Cooker

Once upon a time there was a moth who was irresistibly attracted to a glowing light bulb in the night. But each time the moth attempted to reach this object of desire, the moth encountered a fine mesh screen barring the way. After much effort the moth finally found a way past the screen and joyfully embraced the glowing orb. To the moth's shock and surprise, the embrace was a very painful and traumatic experience. Letting go of the hot bulb, wings burned by the heat, the moth dropped into a pot sitting below the bulb. Before the moth could escape, a tight lid was placed on the pot and the poor moth discovered that it was now in a pressure cooker. The moth's infatuation with the light bulb was over, but it was trapped in a place where it was very unhappy indeed. The moth endured but was never again the same.

The *Moth* represents the characteristics of potential police applicants. The work traditionally attracts Euro-Americans more so than other races and ethnicities, and males disproportionately, people from lower middle class, laboring, blue-collar families, people who are generally idealistic, seeking job security, but also interested in glamour, excitement, outdoor work, and variety. The alleged attraction of authoritarian, coercive personalities to police work does not appear to be true.

The *Screens* are those factors used to select police recruits and eliminate police "wannabes." Some of the things keeping some "moths" from law enforcement include: (1) educational requirements, generally only a high school diploma; (2) residence, usually police must live in the same political jurisdiction or a closely adjacent one; (3) testing, including written examinations and oral interviews, usually conforming civil service standards, sometimes including psychological testing; (4) age, usually falling within the 21-to-35 range; (5) character and prior record, a felony conviction usually will disqualify one, but minor traffic violations and minor offenses (misdemeanors) usually do not. Most departments require a background investigation. Drug use and drug testing seems to be finding a place in police screening, with court decisions generally supporting testing. Some debate is now ongoing about whether individuals with a past drug-use history should be hired. Many agencies will hire former users who no longer experiment with controlled substances.

The *Lightbulb* stands for those factors drawing people to police work. The features of police careers that draw such people include the image of glamour, excitement, outdoor work, and variety associated with police work. It also offers modest benefits, about on par with entry skilled blue-collar trades, and more job security than is associated with most such trades. The media have given police work most of its "glamour" image; the reality of the job is quite a bit duller. Many more people are not moths, but are like the butterflies who find the light bulb to be of little interest or appeal.

Box 9.4 *(continued)*

> The *Pressure Cooker* is what happens to the people entering into police careers. Peer socialization, traumatic on-the-job experiences, job stress, the overt hostility of some segments of the public, bad press, the temptations of corruption, and exposure to the cynicism of more veteran peers all contribute to the development of the police officer's "working personality" (Skolnick, 1966).

Socialization in Corrections

The attractions of a career in correction include steady pay and job security. Applicants for positions as correctional officers rarely have much advance knowledge of the job's features prior to their application (Peak, 1998: 250). Some images of correctional work may have been acquired from popular culture, especially film and television (Freeman, 2000: 38-51). One of the virtues of a college criminal justice education is that students considering a corrections career have a more realistic image of what to expect in their future work.

Since the influence of the LEAA, there has been an increase in the use of academy training for custodial correctional officers. Often training is initiated after employment has begun, especially for local jailers. High rates of turnover are common in custodial corrections, and much of the work force is inexperienced as a result. Better educated custodial correctional officers often experience higher levels of job dissatisfaction than their less well educated peers, especially if they do not rise rapidly into managerial or administrative positions (Peak, 1998: 251). Fortunately, promotion is rapid in correctional work, and those with more education and good leadership and communications skills can expect to advance quickly. The use of the field training officer (FTO) concept is infrequent in this field, and many correctional FTOs are poorly prepared for their roles as mentors for new correctional officers. Informal socialization includes experiences of mistrust and lack of confidence in their peers and manager. The inmates also play a role in new guard training and socialization.

Probation and parole officers are more commonly college-educated and often are recruited from police departments and custodial corrections units. So they enter their careers with greater experience and maturity. The very nature of probation and parole supervision within the larger community allows officers greater independence and autonomy. A laissez-faire management style often is employed by probation and parole managers (Peak, 1998: 267). Therefore, organizational socialization factors are less intensive than in custodial correctional settings.

General Socialization Strategies

Media images are very important in producing the initial perceptions of new police and corrections officers. Changing those media messages is beyond the capacity of criminal justice managers, but is a function that criminal justice educators can undertake (Freeman, 2000). More appropriate recruitment and selection standards also can help modify the socialization experience into one that is both more realistic and more favorable. New employees must lose their misconceptions about the job, learn what is really involved in their employment, and come to accept their work roles in harmony with the rules and needs of the organization. These are the concepts of unfreezing, remolding, and refreezing that Kurt Lewin identified as the steps in the change process a new worker will undergo (Souryal, 1995: 128-129). A criminal justice manager can use these concepts to the advantage of the agency but needs to pay close attention to:

- job qualifications of new officers
- psychological assessment of recruits
- training of both new officers and veteran officers
- using workplace socialization to a managerial advantage

This can be done by developing and employing most of six socialization strategies:

1. collective socialization strategy (training in and as a group)
2. individual socialization strategy (apprenticeship)
3. sequential socialization strategy (training stages)
4. serial socialization strategy (veterans train rookies)
5. divestiture socialization strategy (stripping away an old identity)
6. investiture socialization strategy (accepting and establishing a new identity).

Summary

Developing appropriate standards for training and education are two major requirements of the modern criminal justice manager. To a degree, recruiting better educated officers will help. Once new employees are chosen, they need to be given initial training, and as they advance in their careers they need to acquire additional in-service education. A mix of OJT, in-house, and contracted-out training should be considered by the criminal justice manager to provide training. Career advancement will be helped by further higher education. Formal education and training are only a part of the process. The job itself helps share the working personality of the staff, and peer-based organizational socialization also is important in the development of a criminal justice employee.

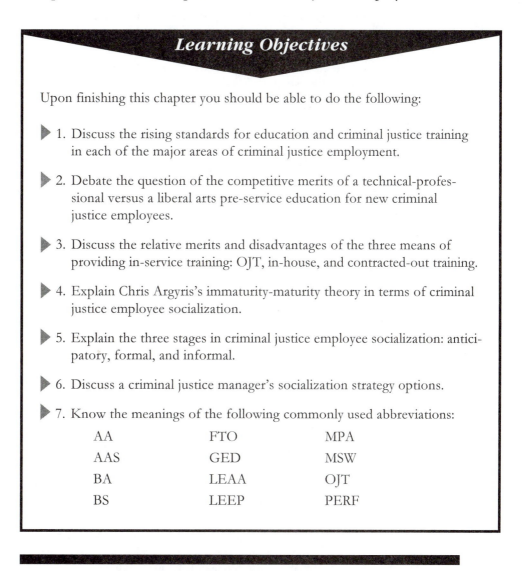

Learning Objectives

Upon finishing this chapter you should be able to do the following:

▶ 1. Discuss the rising standards for education and criminal justice training in each of the major areas of criminal justice employment.

▶ 2. Debate the question of the competitive merits of a technical-professional versus a liberal arts pre-service education for new criminal justice employees.

▶ 3. Discuss the relative merits and disadvantages of the three means of providing in-service training: OJT, in-house, and contracted-out training.

▶ 4. Explain Chris Argyris's immaturity-maturity theory in terms of criminal justice employee socialization.

▶ 5. Explain the three stages in criminal justice employee socialization: anticipatory, formal, and informal.

▶ 6. Discuss a criminal justice manager's socialization strategy options.

▶ 7. Know the meanings of the following commonly used abbreviations:

AA	FTO	MPA
AAS	GED	MSW
BA	LEAA	OJT
BS	LEEP	PERF

IMPORTANT TERMS AND NAMES

- collegiate curriculum
- commuter academies
- "failure to train" liability lawsuits
- occupational socialization
- paramilitary curriculum

- rehabilitative ideal
- residential academies
- symbolic management
- training plan
- working personality

References and Supplemental Sources

Argyris, Chris (1957). *Personality and Organization.* New York: Harper and Row.

Association of Doctoral Programs in Criminology and Criminal Justice(2008). *ADPCCJ.* College of Criminal Justice, Sam Houston State University. Available at http://www. adpccj.org/

Becker, Howard S., and Anselm L. Straus (1956). "Careers, Personality and Adult Socialization," *American Journal of Sociology,* 62(3): 253-263.

Carter, David L., Allen D. Sapp, and Darrel W. Stephens (1989). "The State of Police Education: Policy Directions for the 21st Century." Washington, DC: Police Executive Research Forum.

Fuld, Leonhard Felix (1909). *Police Administration: A Critical Study of Police Organizations in the United States.* New York: Putnam

Green, Lois M. (1987). "From Courtroom to Classroom," *UVA Alumni News,* (January/February): 24-25.

Gulick, Luther (1937). "Notes on the Theory of Organization," *Papers on the Science of Administration,* edited by Luther Gulick and Lyndall Urwick. New York: Institute of Public Administration.

Johnson, Herbert A., Nancy Travis Wolfe, and Mark Jones (2008). *History of Criminal Justice,* 4th ed. Newark, NJ: LexisNexis Matthew Bender

Kaufman, Herbert (1960). *The Forest Ranger.* Baltimore: John Hopkins University Press.

Kaufman, Herbert (1991). "Developing the Will and Capacity to Conform," pages 212-214 in *Classics of Public Personnel Policy,* 2nd ed., edited by Frank J. Thompson. Pacific Grove, CA: Brooks/Cole.

Klofas, John, Stan Stojkovic, and David Kalinich (1990). *Criminal Justice Organizations: Administration and Management.* Pacific Grove, CA: Brooks/Cole.

MacDonald, G. Jeffrey (2003). "The Self-Made Lawyer," *Christian Science Monitor On-Line* (June 3, 2003). Available at http://www.csmonitor.com/2003/0603/p13s01-lecs.html

Mayo, Louis (2006). "College Education and Policing," *Police Chief,* 73(8). Available at http://policechiefmagazine.org/magazine/index.cfm?fuseaction=display_arch&article_id=955&issue_id=82006

Mayo, Louis (2008). "Support for College Degree Requirements: The Big Picture," *Police Chief On Line.* Available at http://www.policechiefonline.com/magazine/index.cfm?fuseaction=display&article_id=959&issue_id=82006

National Center for State Courts (2008). *Welcome to the National Center for State Courts* Available at http://www.ncsconline.org/

National Institute of Justice (1993). *John B. Pickett Fellowships in Criminal Justice Policy and Management.* Washington, DC: NIJ.

National Institute of Justice (1995). *John B. Pickett Fellowships in Criminal Justice Policy and Management.* Washington, DC: NIJ.

Ott, J. Steven (1989). *Classic Readings in Organizational Behavior.* Pacific Grove, CA: Brooks/Cole.

Peak, Kenneth J. (1998). *Justice Administration: Police, Courts, and Corrections Management*, 2nd ed. Upper Saddle River, NJ: Prentice Hall.

Roosevelt, Theodore (1897). *American Ideals and Other Essays Social and Political.* New York: The Knickerbocker Press, G.P. Putnam's Sons.

Ross, Darrell L. (2000). "Correctional Administration and Section 1983 Liability Issues," pp. 317-342 in *Handbook of Criminal Justice Administration*, edited by M. A. DuPont-Morales, Michael Hooper, and Judy H. Schmidt. New York: Marcel Dekker.

Roy, Donald F. (1989). "Banana Time," pages 163-182 in *Classic Readings in Organizational Behavior*, edited by J. Steven Ott. Pacific Grove, CA: Brooks/Cole.

Schein, Edgar H. (1992). "Defining Organizational Culture," pages 490- 502 in *Classics of Organizational Theory*, 3rd ed., edited by Jay M. Shafritz and J. Steven Ott (1992). Pacific Grove, CA: Brooks/Cole.

Shafritz, Jay M., and J. Steven Ott (1992). *Classics of Organizational Theory*, 3rd ed. Pacific Grove, CA: Brooks/Cole.

Sherman, Lawrence W., and the National Advisory Commission on Higher Education for Police Officers (1978). *The Quality of Police Education.* San Francisco: Jossey-Bass.

Skolnick, Jerome H. (1966). *Justice without Trial: Law Enforcement in Democratic Society.* New York: John Wiley and Sons.

Walker, Samuel (1977). *A Critical History of Police Reform.* Lexington, MA: Lexington Books.

Taylor, Frederick W. (1911). *Principles of Scientific Management.* New York: Norton Library, Harper and Row.

U.S. President's Commission on Law Enforcement and Administration of Justice (1967a). *The Challenge of Crime in a Free Society.* Washington, DC: U.S. Government Printing Office.

U. S. President's Commission on Law Enforcement and Administration of Justice (1967b). *Task Force Report: Corrections.* Washington, DC: U.S. Government Printing Office.

U.S. President's Commission on Law Enforcement and Administration of Justice (1967c). *Task Force Report: The Police.* Washington, DC: U.S. Government Printing Office.

10
Allocating Key Organizational Resources

In LODESTAR, the "A" stands for "allocating." A manager is called upon to manage not just the staff of the organization but also vital organizational resources, such as *time, funds, equipment,* and *facilities*. This is the **allocation function** of the manager, assigning these key assets to individuals and units within the organization in a manner most closely suited to advancing the mission, goals, and objectives of the organization. There is a great deal of competition—even open conflict—within an organization for the scarce resources of each organization. As Douglas Yates Jr. points out, the personal resources of the manager are required to discourage or control this kind of conflict, those personal resources being (Yates, 1985; 1989: 500-501):

- personal managerial authority
- coercive power and force
- persuasion
- rewards
- personal style
- bargaining techniques
- negotiating and mediating skills
- coalition-building approaches
- allocation strategies for the benefits, material rewards, and punishments

Time Allocation

After people and money, time is the next most precious resource a manager has to work with. In some ways, it is the most valuable, for lost time never truly can be replaced. Often a task that should have been done

193

Box 10.1 • Advantages and Disadvantages of Shift Rotation

ADVANTAGES	DISADVANTAGES
Rotating Shifts	
Skills are balanced on every shift. Because all crews take equal turns at covering the undesirable shifts (weekends and nights), there is no incentive for all of the senior, more skilled workers to pool together on a single crew.	Employees prefer fixed shifts. About 90 percent of all shift workers prefer fixed shifts to rotating shifts.
All workers are given equal exposure to day shift. As crews rotate through their turn on day shift, they are exposed to managers, engineers, vendors, and company support personnel.	Unbalanced workloads are difficult to manage with rotating shifts. If the work to be done on different shifts differs greatly, there may be a problem with essentially identical crews being assigned to the work.
Training assets can be consolidated. Because all employees rotate through day shifts, there is no need to duplicate training efforts on all shifts.	It is generally more difficult for the body to adjust to rotating shifts. Slowing down the rotation rate can mitigate this.
Product uniformity goes up. As result of equal training, equal exposure to support and management, and equal skills, all crews will perform in a much more uniform manner.	
Fixed Shifts	
On a fixed shift schedule, each crew comes into work at about the same time every day they are scheduled to work. Some variations include a rotation between days off during the week and varying shift lengths.	
Employees prefer fixed shifts. The reasons for this vary. Senior people want to get (and stay) on day shift. Junior employees like the idea of eventually being able to get to a favorite shift. And most people simply want the stability of always knowing when they do not have to be at work—allowing them to better plan their family and social lives.	Recruiting new employees becomes more difficult. After a brief training period, new hires are generally assigned to the least desirable shifts. Often it is many years before they can get to the shift they want.
Unbalanced workloads can be more easily matched. If the workload is lighter on the night shift or if it requires different skills, it is a simple manner to create a crew that matches that specific condition.	Different shifts become different companies. As the disparities between the crews (skills, seniority, morale, etc.) grow, the crews themselves will become more independent of each other. This can affect productivity, safety, quality, attrition, and other performance measures.

Source: Adapted from Shiftwork Solutions (2005). See http://www.shift-work.com/shiftwork-search.htm

at one point in history does not have the same consequences if done later. The folk adage about the foolishness of "closing the barn door after the horses have gone" illustrates the point. Timing can be critical.

Many criminal justice agencies need to conduct operations 24 hours a day, seven days a week, including all holidays. This adds to the time-management demands a criminal justice manager must meet. Reflecting their 24-hour-a-day operations, many criminal justice agencies employ shifts, and essentially become three suborganizations with entirely different staffs on duty at different times of the day. Whatever these shift teams are called—be they midnight, daylight, and twilight, or first, second, and third—a criminal justice manager faces additional challenges with continuous operations (Shiftwork Solutions, 2003). Some agencies will have **rotating shifts**, and others will have **fixed shifts**.

If shift rotation is the option the manager selects, a **rotation plan** will have to be developed that shows how the shifts will change. There are many options to consider in shift rotation. There is a debate in the research literature about the merits of shifting forward or shifting back, slow or quick rotations, partial rotations (some staff on fixed shifts, others rotating), and even oscillating shifts in which one shift is fixed and the other two swap work hours (Shiftwork Solutions, 2005).

Time Management Tools

A number of techniques for time management have been developed. Among them are the **Gantt chart**, developed by Henry L. Gantt (1861-1919), a contemporary and colleague of Frederick Taylor (Massie, 1987: 17, 24), and prolific author of books and articles on management in the early decades of the twentieth century (1903; 1916; 1919) The Gantt chart is a form of bar chart in which each task is given a horizontal line scaled to reflect how long that task should require. Time thus is depicted graphically (Massie, 1987: 149). There were earlier attempts to manage time graphically, including the **"harmonogram"** of Karol Adamiecki (March, 1975).

Karol Adamiecki (1866-1933) was a Polish engineer and 1925 co-founder of the Polish Institute of Scientific Management. He is credited with developing the prototype of the Gantt chart. Adamiecki called it a "harmonograf," and others called it a "harmonogram."

en.wikipedia.org

Reading and Using a Gantt Chart

Regardless of the contribution of Adamiecki, it was Henry Gantt who introduced his version of the chart to American managers. The chart is a scheduling tool that illustrates time in a linear graphic format. Today a Gantt chart can be developed using Microsoft Project, Microsoft Excel, or specialized software expressly written to produce Gantt charts such as SmartDraw® and Match-Ware.® However, in Gantt's day, one would be prepared on graph paper.

The horizontal axis represents time, and the vertical axis lists the key components of the project. Equally spaced horizontal bars in the chart represent time units (the hours or days or weeks or months) needed to complete each component of the project. The criminal justice manager using a Gantt chart will break down the project into discretely defined pieces and list them in approximate chronological order on the left margin (vertical axis) of the chart.

Henry Gantt was an American engineer who developed the Gantt chart as a graphic device to aid in scheduling and monitoring the progress of complex projects.

A quick examination of Figure 10.1 will reveal that the plan assumes a total of 49 weeks of work, but the program only runs from mid-January to the end of August, about 32 weeks. The value of a Gantt chart is that it illustrates what tasks can be undertaken concurrently, and also indicates which participants are involved in implementing the plan at any moment. For example, on February 15, the plan will require the efforts of the Chief of Police, the City Manager, the City Council, the contractor hired to help design the plan, the staff of the Vollmer City Police Department (VCPD) Training Division, the VCPD supervisors, and the VCPD Personnel Director.

A more careful consideration of the plan will reveal that some tasks must be concluded successfully before other tasks can be initiated. For example, the training cannot proceed until the training plan and lesson modules are completed and the community-oriented policing (COP) cadre are chosen. This interdependency of tasks can be discovered using a simple Gantt chart, but such interdependence and the consequences of delays in much more complex projects are not as easy to identify using a Gantt chart. This led to the development of other graphic representation tools for time management, including Critical Path Method (CPM) and Program Evaluation and Review Technique (PERT).

Figure 10.1 • Sample Gantt Chart for Community-Oriented Policing (COP) Program

Vollmer City Police Department (VCPD) Community-Oriented Policing (COP) Initiative

Event	Participants	Task	Start	End	Weeks	Jan	Feb	Mar	Apr	May	Jun	Jul	Aug
1	Contractor	prepares draft of community concerns survey, briefs Chief and conducts survey	1/15	1/29	2	[---							
2	Contractor and Chief	analyze input from community surveys to design VCPD COP plan	2/1	2/8	1		[-]						
3	Chief and community leaders	meet to create neighborhood partnerships and secure more community input for COP	2/14	2/28	2		[-]						
4	VCPD Training Division and Contractor	prepare training plan and develop lesson modules for the VCPD trial COP program	2/8	3/10	4		[----	--]					
5	Chief and City Manager and City Council	approve and fund the implementation of VCPD trial COP program	2/15	2/15	1		[]						
6	VCPD supervisors and Personnel Director	recruit, interview and select COP cadre within VCPD	2/15	3/12	4		[---	--]					
7	Contractor, VCPD managers and key city leaders	conduct the VCPD COP training program for new cadre on site	3/16	3/31	2			[---]					
8	VCPD PIO and Chief	prepare press released and hold press conferences on new trial COP program	3/16	3/31	2			[---]					
9	VCPD Operations Division & Chief	open COP-neighborhood kiosks around Vollmer City	4/1	4/8	1				[-]				
10	Chief, Operations Division, and new COP cadre	initiate trial COP program and deploy staff to kiosks	4/1	7/31	13				[------	------	------	---]	
11	Chief , COP cadre and Operations Division	collect data on VCPD trial COP program efforts and kiosk activities	4/15	8/15	15					[--	------	------	--]
12	Chief and City Manager	evaluate trial COP program and kiosk activities data to revise program as needed	8/16	8/30	2								[---]

Network Analysis with CPM and PERT

Network analysis was the next graphic time management approach to be developed. It provided a better way to illustrate the more complex interdependency of tasks in large-scale projects. In the 1950s, two very similar versions were developed, essentially parallel developments: the **Critical Path Method (CPM)** and the **Program Evaluation and Review Technique (PERT)**. Today CPM and PERT have been blended into a common technique, the one illustrated in the **PERT chart** in Figure 10.2. Various criminal justice and public service applications have been offered (Clayton, 1980; Sylvia, Sylvia, and Gunn, 1997).

Network analysis uses the concepts of *events* and *activities*. An **event** typically is the accomplishment of a task, and an **activity** is the doing of a task. Events will occur at a moment in time, while activities require time to be accomplished (they have duration). CPM/PERT recognizes that some events must be accomplished prior to the beginning of some activities.

The CPM/PERT technique allows a manager to represent this interaction of events and activities graphically, recognizing that there are **leader events** and **follower events**. They are linked together with **activity arrows**, which are connected into **pathways**. The pathway that actually determines how long a project will take is designated the **critical path**.

Some of the leader events must be done on schedule in order to avoid delaying a complex task. Others can be delayed for various durations without upsetting the project time table. The amount of time in which an event can occur without producing a delay on subsequent events is its **float time**. Some float time can be expended with absolutely no consequences on subsequent events (**free float**), while other float time consumes later available float time (**interfering float**). A manager can schedule work most efficiently by computing each of these and setting work-event completion times to reflect these floats. The PERT chart also allows a criminal justice manager to calculate the consequences of any delays in events on the final completion of a project, or on intermediate activities and events. The basic principle is that any change that adds to any activity on the critical path will produce a corresponding delay in the time needed to complete the entire project.

Today computer programs can do all the complex calculations of float times and all the intermediate computations required to prepare a PERT chart. Complex tasks, involving hundreds of people and performing hundreds of interrelated activities, can be coordinated via such a chart, with the optimum use of time. Learning how to compute CPM/PERT equations is not necessary in this day and age, but learning how to read a PERT chart is a basic skill a criminal justice manager will need to acquire.

Figure 10.2 • PERT Chart for Opening a Victim/Witness Service Center

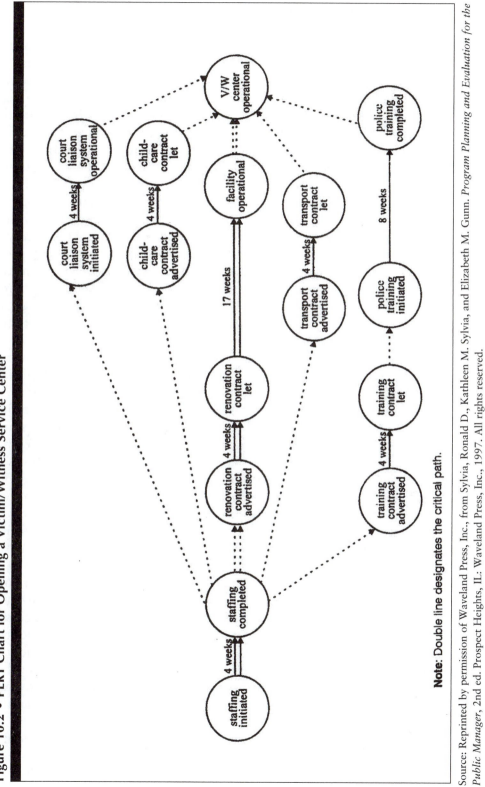

Note: Double line designates the critical path.

Source: Reprinted by permission of Waveland Press, Inc., from Sylvia, Ronald D., Kathleen M. Sylvia, and Elizabeth M. Gunn. *Program Planning and Evaluation for the Public Manager*, 2nd ed. Prospect Heights, IL: Waveland Press, Inc., 1997. All rights reserved.

Allocating Equipment and Facilities

The facilities and equipment of an organization are part of the physical environment of the organization. They create the capacities of and restraints on the organization. Reflecting the importance of equipment and facilities, the **capital budget** of an organization often is kept separate from the **operational budget**. Unfortunately, it is often the capital budget that gets cut, leaving the organizational aspects lacking their essential physical environment support base. The **physical plant** of an organization is important to the overall ability of the organization to perform its mission.

Even before Charles Babbage, whose contributions on the applications of advanced technologies to improved management were mentioned in Chapter 3, leaders in business, industry, and public service saw the advantages that equipment and facilities can provide to advancing organizational objectives. Since the 1980s, the computer has become the instrument of influence, as the telephone was some 70 years earlier and the telegraph before that. In law enforcement, the automobile changed the nature of police patrol from the 1930s foot-patrol approach to the fully motorized police of the 1960s.

Facilities and equipment can also be used as incentives or rewards for performance. The "best office" can be assigned to the best worker as a reward. New desks and furnishings can be used to uplift morale. A take-home car is a major perk for some employees, and especially fitting for those who have to be available "on call." Similarly, facilities and equipment can be used to improve agency morale. Paint and new carpet can make a sterile workplace cozy. An agency that lacks the resources to have their offices refurbished can allocate a day to improvements, with the agency buying only the paints and materials to make the improvements. Such an exercise can improve agency morale and commitment to the agency. The labor donated by the workers to make improvements in the facilities becomes a basis for greater personal involvement, an emotional investment in the place.

Facilities and equipment can promote positive change in an organization. When outdated ways are yielding a performance deficit or there is an attitude problem toward the work, new equipment and facilities can provide a means to overcome these problems. For example, the acquisition of advanced probationer monitoring devices can enhance the overall productivity of a probation office, reduce the labors of probation officers, better keep track of probationers, and improve the overall mission of probation services in the community. New equipment and new or rehabilitated facilities also can improve agency morale.

Facilities and equipment can improve performance. Better equipment and facilities can result in improved work quality when properly employed, but often agencies will become slaves to their equipment and

Box 10.2 • Allocation of "Plum" Assignments

The Vanderbilt County Sheriff's Department has both four-wheel, rough-terrain vehicles and several power boats to provide patrol and protective services in and around the Fosdick Mountain resort areas, many of which can be accessed only by rough forest trails, and on Lake Peel, a popular summer vacation area in the county. The nearby Vollmer City Police Department has neither boats nor rough-terrain vehicles, but is provided a mobile crime scene lab vehicle that goes out to felony crime scenes to support evidence-gathering. The Vanderbilt County Sheriff has learned that assigning deputies to lake patrol duty in the late Spring through the Fall is considered a **plum assignment** and has made selection for lake duty a reward for excellent performance by his deputies. The Chief of Police in Vollmer City has nothing to compare with lake duty, but does assign new police cruisers to those officers with accident-free driving records as a reward for their good safety records. Getting one of the oldest police cars is a subtle but clearly noticed acknowledgment that the officer has not been careful with his or her previous police vehicle. The Chief also is considering rewarding his most community-oriented officers (i.e., those with the fewest complaints filed against them by the public and those receiving the most favorable letters from the public) by offering them assignments to the proposed COP kiosks and other community-oriented-policing assignments.

facilities. Old technologies retard them; new technologies overwhelm them. Sometimes people rely excessively upon technological solutions, often ignoring older, simpler, and more reliable methods. When "the computer is down," all work stops in some offices. People become overly dependent upon technology. It is a managerial responsibility to see that they do not.

A criminal justice manager is responsible for the allocation of the equipment and facilities available to his or her agency. The manager can further allocate equipment and facilities, either by formulae or on a case-by-case basis, to support agency operations. The equipment and facilities at the disposal of each agency reflects each agency's mission, size, and circumstances. A fictionalized example based on real examples is provided in Box 10.2.

Assignments to preferred duties and provision of better equipment, better offices, new furniture, and so on, are perquisites (**perks**) that a manager can use as rewards and incentives. This aspect of the allocation function is an important managerial power. In some cases it has to be diluted by union agreements and seniority systems. But when such limitations are absent or do not specifically apply, then such allocations are the rewards that can enhance the power, authority, and esteem of the manager wisely distributing them.

The capital facilities given to an agency are valuable public assets for which the agency manager must provide care and maintenance. While no one expects the warden of the Alexander Maconochie Correctional Center to actually make repairs to buildings and equipment at the prison, it is expected that he will ensure that his middle managers will see to having it done. The police vehicles of the Vollmer City Police Department need routine oil changes and occasional repairs. The chief is not the one who will be changing out oil and replacing oil filters, but it is the chief who is responsible for seeing that it is done. So an additional allocational duty of a criminal justice manager is providing the funds, time, and the personnel to attend to these important maintenance functions.

Fiscal Management and Funding Sources in Public Service

Appropriated Funds: A legislative body can allocate an agency either a total sum ("cap") or dictate detailed expenditures by category ("line items"). Agencies either can submit budget proposals to their legislatures, or respond to allocations given to them. It is common for both to occur at the same time. For example, an agency proposes a budget to its legislative body; the legislature provides some part of it; the agency rebudgets with the funds provided. Money voted to an agency or program by a legislative body, or allocated to it under legal rules, usually from tax collections, fines, forfeitures, or user fees, is known as its **appropriation**.

Tax Revenues: Most appropriations for government agencies come from taxes levied against income, property, services, or commercial transactions. Taxes collected for public purposes are not especially popular in the United States, and many jurisdictions seek other ways of funding essential public services.

Fines and Forfeitures: Fines and forfeitures are funding sources readily available to criminal justice agencies. Under federal or state law or via local ordinances, agencies can be authorized to collect fines and seize property that can be sold to raise additional revenues. In compliance with laws or regulations, these fines and forfeiture revenues either are retained by the agency to continue its operations, or are turned over to the government treasury or fiscal agency. Some court assessments known as **court costs** are not "fines" in a legal sense but are actually **user fees**. Agencies must follow laws, rules, and guidelines for the expenditure of such funds, with a general rule being that these funds may be used only for purposes approved in advance by the funding jurisdiction. The actual expenditures are subject to periodic audit.

User Fees: User fees are funds collected by government agencies for the services or goods they provide to the public or other agencies. In compliance with the laws or regulations that set such fees, the fees either are retained by the agency to fund continuing operations, or are turned over directly to the treasury or fiscal agency of the government. Licenses of all kinds are considered to be user fees, although many are used to raise revenues well beyond the actual cost of services or goods provided.

Nonappropriated Funds: The revenues and resources coming from other than tax appropriations—including earnings, gifts, grants, and other lawful conversions to cash of agency services and products—fall within the category of nonappropriated funds. Among the many sources of such funds will be employee association dues and club fees, agency fundraisers, fees for and profits from vending machines installed in agency buildings, profits from logo item sales, donated frequent flyer credits, interest on agency deposits from other sources, and any other income not derived from tax revenues or other legislated sources such as user fees, fines, and forfeiture. The rules governing expenditures of such funds may differ from those associated with appropriations, and often an agency manager will have far greater latitude in spending these funds. They are commonly used for social events and gifts within the work force, or to purchase items that cannot be acquired with appropriated funds. However, when legislation or rules require that nonappropriated funds be returned to the treasury, or reported in the budget and managed in the same fashion, then these will be treated as if they were appropriated funds.

Other Budget Terms

A variety of additional terms are used in relation to budgeting in government service. A contemporary criminal justice manager is quite likely to encounter most of terms that follow.

Capital Budget: Those line items in an agency budget that pay for long-lasting agency assets, such as its buildings and durable goods—that is, those items of equipment that will last for many years—often are treated separately from other categories of funds. These are referred to as the **capital budget**.

Operational Budget: In contrast to the capital budget, those expenditures that will be consumed in the ordinary operations of the agency are classified as parts of its **operational budget**. Usually salaries; consumables such as gasoline, electricity, water, and other utilities; short-lived equipment; office supplies; postage; and other expendable items fall within this category.

Personnel Budget: Those agency expenditures having to do with staffing often are identified and separated into a **personnel budget** or staffing budget category. Such items as salaries, training costs, medical insurance, withholding taxes, Federal Insurance Contributions Act (FICA) tax, and agency contributions to retirement plans are all typical personnel items in a budget.

Expendables: Those items that are consumed ("expended") or rendered to be of no further value by their use are classified as **expendables**. In policing, bullets and paper clips are typical expendables. In any office, copier paper, envelopes, pens, and pencils are typical expendables. In standard accounting practice, the issue of the item to an "end user" will terminate its audit record. As soon as it is placed in the hands of an appropriate user, it is considered expended, even if it has yet to be consumed.

Accountables: Those items of agency property that have greater value and that can endure after initial usage are classified as **accountables**. Uniforms, weapons, and some kinds of equipment (such as office machines, computers, scanners, telephones, office furniture, recording equipment, etc.) eventually will wear out or become obsolete, but for some time they will be inventoried and their users will be held accountable for them. The audit train of an accountable item only ends when it is turned in and sold as scrap or is property disposed of. For example, when old weapons no longer are considered safely serviceable, they will be destroyed and a witnessed destruction certificate will be put on file to document their disposal.

Supplemental Appropriations: Legislatures and local legislative bodies can authorize additional funds to an agency in the middle of a budgetary term to meet unplanned needs or urgent requirements. These are called **supplemental appropriations**.

Encumbered Funds: **Encumbered funds** are funds against which obligations already have been made, although not yet paid.

Sequestering: Withholding or canceling a previously approved (appropriated) government expenditure or obligation occasionally becomes necessary. **Sequestering** may be ordered by either the executive or the legislative branch of government, and can be conditional or absolute.

Diversions: Under legislation, regulation, or executive orders, funds can be redirected from one agency or budget category to another. For example, due to a drop in fuel prices, a surplus that develops in the Vollmer City Police Department "fuels" line item can be diverted to cover the increased expenditures in the local courts caused by an unexpected postal rate increase. A **diversion** often takes the form of supplemental appropriation for the beneficiary.

"Bill-Payers" and "Beneficiaries": The **bill-payers** are the agencies giving up funds under such diversions. The **beneficiaries** are the agencies or programs gaining funds under such diversions. As another example, the Vollmer City Police Department becomes the bill-payer when it is instructed to reallocate $1.5 million in operating funds to the Vollmer City Fire and Rescue Department (the beneficiary) to cover its operational shortfall due to a massive chemical spill.

Return on Investment (ROI): In economics, the **return on investment (ROI)** is the mathematical calculation of the ratio of the difference between the realized gain of an investment minus the cost of that investment to the cost of the investment:

$$ROI = [gain - cost] / cost$$

In a criminal justice application, the Vanderbilt County Courts have been paying $1.8 million in overtime salaries to clear a backlog of paperwork. The chief clerk secures an appropriation of $800,000 to purchase new computers and software and to hire a contractor to help install the new system and train the existing clerical staff. In the first year of the program, overtime salaries are cut in half to $900,000, and most of the backlog is caught up. ROI = [$1,800,000 - $900,000] - $800,000]/$800,000 = 12.5%. In this illustration, the new equipment, software, and training produce a savings of $100,000 in the first year and reduce overtime demands on the staff. Most ROIs are not this profitable as quickly, but new cost-cutting technologies and methods do repay their initial costs over time.

Value-Added Contributions (VACs): An expenditure for new equipment or training can add to the productivity of the organization or the work output of the newly trained staff. These expenditures are referred to as **value-added contributions (VACs)**. In some cases this can be measured by making before-and-after comparisons, but more often this is not possible. If a new technology or new training strategy makes the agency more efficient, often work output will increase, but new tasks that had not been considered before also will be undertaken. Some VACs are either hypothetical or defy actual calculation, such as improved skills and confidence, better worker relations, or personal workplace fulfillment. Some VACs are simply estimated. Some can be identified via surveys of those involved (i.e., managers, workers, and clients). Often it is difficult to assign a definite dollar amount to a savings on such a theoretical abstraction, but some do try (Whetten, 1989). Even if they defy accurate measurement, these value-added contributions are real consequences of some agency expenditures.

Subscriptions: Subscriptions are rarely used now, but once governments actively served as collection agencies for "subscriptions" for public services or projects. For example, when several civic groups in Vollmer City wished to build a monument to commemorate the city's hero and namesake, August Vollmer, the city council voted to appropriate no public funds for the purpose. Instead, it instructed the city treasurer to collect donations and hold them until sufficient funds were donated to build the monument. Many employees of the police department took part in the fund-raising efforts when off duty, and the money was "subscribed" in just eight months. In many states, there are items on tax return forms that permit and encourage the taxpayer to donate to various state-approved endeavors. These are contemporary subscriptions to which you can contribute when you file your state tax return. By doing so, you give up some part of your tax refund, which then is held by the state for use by this state-sponsored fund.

Check-Offs: Check-offs are provisions of the tax-collection process that allow small sums of tax dollars to go to specific purposes. These are modified subscriptions. Two contemporary check-offs with which you might be familiar are the federal and state election campaign withholdings, both collected when a taxpayer voluntarily elects to designate a small part of their tax payment to these funds. Some states make extensive use of both tax check-offs and subscriptions, wherein you transfer a small part of your state tax return to some state-endorsed public fund or activity.

Pass-Thrus: When an agency serves to transfer funds from one source to another, with little or no direct benefit to itself, it is understood to be passing such funds through as a convenience to both the spending and receiving parties. Police and sheriff's departments and other criminal justice agencies occasionally allow their officers to take private employment for which the agency functions as an employment agency. Officers are hired out to private parties who pay the agency and then see that the officers are paid overtime rates for their services. These sources of income and expenditure are classic **pass-thrus**.

Sunk Costs: The **sunk costs** are the historical expenditures of an organization that cannot be effectively recovered by cessation of their use, and that cannot be liquidated for their original value because the actual and book value has declined or depreciated substantially. **Book values** are market-based or depreciation-based assessments of the value of property or equipment belonging to the organization. The "book" referred to is the ledger of the organization wherein the property is listed as an asset.

Depreciation: Depreciation is the process whereby an asset declines in value over its useful life. It can be calculated as either "straight-line" or by some "accelerated" formula. Some assets will depreciate to zero value, while others will retain a salvage value (a term described below).

Surplus Properties: **Surplus properties** are assets of the organization that no longer are needed for current and anticipated organizational operations. When laws and regulations permit, these surplus properties may be sold off and the funds received will be returned to the treasury or added to the selling agency's budget. Police departments routinely sell off high-mileage police cars, and all criminal justice agencies have old computers and other outdated technologies that can be sold, often only as scrap. Occasionally real estate becomes surplus and unused land and buildings will be offered up for sale.

Salvage Value: **Salvage value**, also known as scrap value, is the price that can be anticipated when an organizational asset is disposed of at the end of its useful life. Rarely is aged surplus property of much value, and the return is a very small fraction of the original expense. However, there are other advantages to disposing of surplus property for its salvage value, one of the most obvious being freeing up storage space and reducing the labor of maintaining inventories of obsolete and broken equipment.

Budgeting Approaches

Budgeting is an important aspect of fiscal management. It is a specific subarea of organizational planning. There are four commonly used approaches to budgeting:

1. Traditional, Line-Item, and Incremental Budgets
2. Program Planning and Budgeting System (PPBS) and Performance Budgets
3. Zero-Based Budgeting (ZBB)
4. Pay-As-You-Go (PayGo) Budgets

Line-item budgeting (or **incremental budgeting**) is the traditional approach to preparing a budget. Usually this method uses expenditure from past budget periods to project expenses for the coming period, usually done by "line-item":

- salaries
- copiers
- vehicles
- stationery
- uniforms
- gasoline

It is the easiest form of budgeting to do, the most reliable in a static organizational environment, and the easiest to modify if there are cost increases in any particular areas. If postage rates rise, the amount of the increase will be added to the prior year's postage expenses. If gasoline costs drop, a savings will be reflected in the new budget. If new people are hired, their salaries will be added to the existing personnel line. In this way, the budget is modified up or down with "incremental" adjustments from the prior budget term.

The **Program Planning and Budgeting System (PPBS)** and the closely related **performance budgeting** both are related to management by objectives (MBO). Just like in other MBO applications, the manager preparing or revising the budget first considers the agency mission, and then its needs, goals, objectives, and conducts a search for alternative ways to accomplish the objectives. When a good alternative is found, then a program is designed or modified and its budget prepared.

A large organization often will prepare separate subunit budgets, using either the same PPBS approach or by requiring subunits to use traditional line-item budgets for their components. For example, a large correctional institution may use PPBS overall, but its central kitchen may be given a line-item budget for its budget planning.

Another aspect of PPBS performance budgeting is that the actual work done is recognized in the budget allocation for operations. A jailer will be given a fixed amount for each inmate for each day that inmate is held. If the number of inmates in custody rises, automatically the funds available will rise in direct proportion. If the number in custody declines, the total amount available will decline. The amount per person remains constant, but the available funds will increase or decrease to match the jail population. PPBS commonly is used in preparing a budget for a new program or activity. It is heavily used in grant development. It is performance- and program-oriented. (Schick, 1966: 243-258).

The **PayGo (pay-as-you-go) budgeting** process involves matching expenditures to revenues. Some criminal justice agencies and activities actually raise revenues. In a PayGo budgeting plan, the more revenues collected, the more will be available for agency operations, or equipment or facilities. The approach approximates the private, for-profit approaches of business. Top-end expenditure levels may be set by the legislation or regulations governing the process, but actual expenditures or obligation of funds cannot occur above the level of funds actually taken in by the agency or the government setting the PayGo terms. Revenue sharing between police agencies and the courts will occur by the allocation of fines and court costs. Parking ticket collections can be set aside for supporting the ordinance enforcement costs. Profits from correctional industries can be used to initiate new correctional activities. The PayGo process often is used when severe financial restrictions are being encountered, especially in governments having strict balanced-budget rules.

Zero-based budgeting (ZBB) is related to MBO, using a "from-the-ground-up" approach to build a budget. An agency's activities are subdivided into its components, and programs are then prioritized. Then each program is divided into its component activities, and these are prioritized, using a task-oriented approach. Within each program, a PPBS or line budget is prepared. If full funding cannot be provided, the lowest-priority activities and programs are cut. Funds are allocated to the most effective aspects of the organizational activities. In this way, every activity and program is reassessed for its importance in each budgetary term. ZBB often is used when agencies are facing severe financial and program reductions.

Summary

A contemporary criminal justice manager is responsible for the allocation of money, time, equipment, and facilities within the organization in support of the organizational mission. This function is supported by complex time management and budgetary systems. There may be a time when you, as a junior manager, will be responsible for allocation functions within your unit. Knowing that such resources exist and knowing how to recognize them will help you acquire the actual knowledge you will need to schedule and budget, allocate scarce resources, and best use facilities that have been entrusted to you.

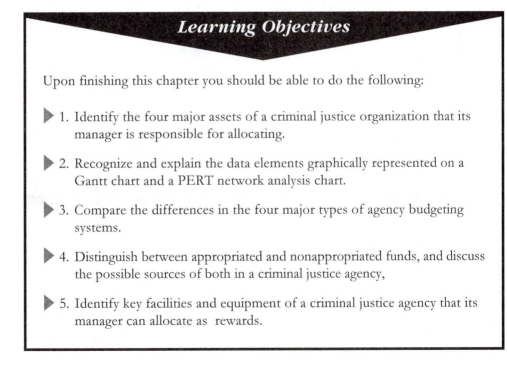

Learning Objectives

Upon finishing this chapter you should be able to do the following:

▶ 1. Identify the four major assets of a criminal justice organization that its manager is responsible for allocating.

▶ 2. Recognize and explain the data elements graphically represented on a Gantt chart and a PERT network analysis chart.

▶ 3. Compare the differences in the four major types of agency budgeting systems.

▶ 4. Distinguish between appropriated and nonappropriated funds, and discuss the possible sources of both in a criminal justice agency,

▶ 5. Identify key facilities and equipment of a criminal justice agency that its manager can allocate as rewards.

IMPORTANT TERMS AND NAMES

- accountables
- activity
- activity arrows
- allocation function
- appropriation
- beneficiaries
- bill-payers
- book values
- capital budget
- check-offs
- court costs
- critical path
- Critical Path Method (CPM)
- depreciation
- diversion
- encumbered funds
- event
- expendables
- fines and forfeitures
- fixed shifts
- float time
- follower events
- free float
- Gantt chart
- harmonogram
- incremental budgeting
- interfering float
- leader events
- line-item budgeting
- network analysis
- operational budget
- pass-thrus
- pathways
- PayGo/pay-as-you-go budgeting
- performance budgeting
- perk
- personnel budget
- physical plant
- plum assignment
- Program Evaluation Review Technique (PERT)
- PERT Chart
- Program Planning Budgeting System (PPBS)
- return on investment (ROI)
- rotating shifts
- rotation plan
- salvage value
- sequestering
- subscriptions
- sunk costs
- supplemental appropriation
- surplus properties
- user fees
- value-added contributions (VACs)
- zero-based budgeting (ZBB)

References and Supplemental Sources

Caldiera, Greg A., and Andrew T. Cowart (1980). "Budgets, Institutions And Change: Criminal Justice Policy in America," *American Journal of Political Science*, 24(3): 413-438.

Clayton, Ross (1980). "Techniques of Network Analysis for Managers," in *Managing Public Systems: Analytic Techniques for Public Administration*, edited by Michael J. White, Ross Clayton, Robert Myrtle, Gilbert Siegel, and Aaron Rose. North Scituate, MA: Duxbury.

Fox, Vernon (1983). "Fiscal Management," in *Correctional Institutions*, pages 264-280. Englewood Cliffs, NJ: Prentice Hall.

Gantt, Henry L. (1903). "A Graphical Daily Balance in Manufacture," *Transactions of the American Society of Mechanical Engineers*, 24: 1322-1336.

Gantt, Henry L. (1916, 1973). *Work, Wages, and Profits*, 2nd ed., New York: Engineering Magazine Co., 1916 original. 1973 reprint, Easton, MD: Hive.

Gantt, Henry L. (1919, 1973). Organizing for Work, New York: Harcourt, Brace, and Howe, 1919 original. 1973 reprint, Easton, MD: Hive.

Lynch, Ronald G. (1986). *The Police Manager: Professional Leadership Skills*, 3rd ed. New York: Random House.

Marsh, Edward R. (1975). "The Harmonogram of Karol Adamiecki," *The Academy of Management Journal*, 18(2): 358–364.

Massie, Joseph L. (1987). *Essentials of Management*, 4th ed. Englewood Cliffs, NJ: Prentice Hall.

Schick, Allen (1966). "The Road to PPBS, The Stages of Budget Reform," *Public Administration Review*, 26(December): 243-258.

Shane, Jon M. (2005). "Activity-Based Budgeting: Creating a Nexus Between Workload and Costs," *FBI Law Enforcement Bulletin*, 74(6): 11-23.

Shiftwork Solutions (2003). "Fixed Shift Schedules or Rotating Shift Schedules" *Shiftwork Solutions LLC*. Available at http://www.shift-work.com/law.htm

Shiftwork Solutions (2005). "Fixed Shift Schedules or Rotating Shift Schedules?" *Shiftwork Solutions LLC*. Available at http://www.shift-work.com/shiftwork-search.htm

Sylvia, Ronald D., Kathleen M. Sylvia, and Elizabeth M. Gunn (1997). *Program Planning and Evaluation for the Public Manager*, 2nd ed. Prospect Heights, IL: Waveland Press.

Taylor, Frederick Winslow (1911; 1967). *The Principles of Scientific Management*. New York: Norton Library, Harper and Row.

Tucker, Harvey J. (1982). "Incremental Budgeting: Myth or Model?" *Western Political Quarterly*, 35(3): 327-338.

Whetten, David A. (1989). "What Constitutes a Theoretical Contribution?" *Academy of Management Review*, 14(4): 490-495.

Yates, Douglas, Jr. (1985). *The Politics of Management*. San Francisco: Jossey-Bass.

Yates, Douglas, Jr. (1989). "Identifying and Using Political Resources," pages 500-509 in *Classic Readings in Organizational Behavior*, edited by J. Steven Ott. Pacific Grove, CA: Brooks/Cole.

11
Reporting for Criminal Justice:
Information Management and Organizational Communications

In both POSDCORB and LODESTAR the "R" represents the "reporting" functions of the criminal justice manager. In Luther Gulick's time (1937), most reporting was done orally or in writing on paper. The earliest applications of electronically assisted communications were in use then. The telephone had been in use since the 1880s, the two-way radio was in use in police operations, and intercom systems existed within some correctional units. However, other than the telephone, these criminal justice applications were quite limited in their impact on managerial communications. In contemporary times, that reporting function has been expanded via the use of additional communications media such as television (including cable channels), fax machines, voice mail, e-mail, and other computer-based communications, such as blogs, podcasting, instant messaging, and the use of Internet sites like Facebook (Abram and Pearlman, 2008; Sahlin and Botello, 2007) and YouTube (Fahs, 2007; Miller, 2007). If anything, the modern criminal justice manager is facing a severe communication overload—too much information coming from too many sources of information.

Trained in psychology and in the principles of scientific management, Mary Parker Follett nevertheless clearly foreshadowed the human relations school. In 1926, in her frequently reprinted article (1989), "The Giving of Orders," she advocated coordination as the key to successful management. Arguing against authoritarian commands, she observed that, "One might say that the strength of favorable response to an order is in inverse ratio to the distance the order travels. Production efficiency is always in danger of being affected whenever the long-distance order is substituted for the face-to-face suggestion that we want

213

so much as the joint study of the problem." As mentioned earlier in this text, she wisely observed that "orders will not take the place of training…. One person should not give orders to another person, but both should agree to take their orders from the situation."

Follett advocated a three-part process to giving instructions: (1) they should not be orders, but the law of the situation; (2) one should recognize that situations are always evolving, so that rigid orders are quite out of place most of the time; and (3) orders should be circular (reciprocal) in character, not linear (unidirectional) behavior.

Reporting Obligations

The contemporary criminal justice manager has reporting obligations to superiors, to the public, to the press, to peers, and to subordinates. Precisely what those reporting requirements are varies according to the information possessed by the manager, laws, confidentiality regulations, security classification rules, and policies of the agency. As a general principle, more information is better than less information, but there are clear exceptions to this principle. Modern criminal justice managers have numerous means of communicating the information they possess, including direct communication in spoken and written messages, broadcast methods such as e-mails and organizational memos, and formal reports. Managers also are called upon to address the mass communications media, including newspapers, radio, and television, especially in crisis situations and when dealing with major criminal cases.

Communication Styles

Communication styles vary with the individual manager. Some criminal justice managers are excellent communicators and enjoy the opportunity to convey their ideas by various means. Others are reluctant communicators and uncomfortable expressing themselves. Some prefer to write messages rather than speak in public, or vice-versa. The type of manager will predict the preferred method of communication. Type-A managers who employ Theory-X strategies generally prefer direct orders and explicit directions. Type-B managers generally prefer dialog and discussion.

How does a criminal justice manager best convey ideas? Recall that Mary Parker Follett advocated, "not the face-to-face suggestion…so much as the joint study of the problem." Follett favored circular or reciprocal communications. She advised against order-giving. Even the Type-A, Theory-X manager (the authoritarian order giver) cannot be sure his or her orders will be followed. The Type-B, Theory-Y manager faces an even more difficult problem because this style lacks the clarity of direct orders.

Communicative Behavior: Four basic patterns of managerial communication have been described: (1) *controlling:* the manager dominates discussions, gives direction, and does not listen much to subordinates or peers; (2) *relinquishing:* the manager gives up most of his or her influence, allows others to dominate exchanges; (3) *defending:* the manager withdraws from exchanges passively, or withdraws altogether, is not involved in the discussions, and avoids the issues that are raised; (4) *developing:* the manager encourages and participates in reciprocal exchanges of ideas, acknowledges and uses other's ideas, shares thoughts, and remains involved in the process throughout.

Communications Audiences

A criminal justice manager has obligations to report to superiors, to the public, to the press, to peers, and to subordinates. The reporting obligations differ according to the audience. Within the organization, formal communications should follow the chain of command (Klofas, Stojkovic, and Kalinich, 1990: 56-57) and often must conform to rigid rules and procedures regarding issues such as the number of copies and their distribution, who must be informed, in what sequence, and so on.

The communications process involves organizing a thought, referred to as **encoding**. The message then is "transmitted" through some communications medium, known as the "channel." Those receiving that message then "decode" that message into their own thoughts (Klofas, Stojkovic, and Kalinich, 1990: 54). Both the encoding and decoding processes involve the science of **semantics**, the study of meaning in communication. Both the coder and decoder of the message apply their interpretations to the words used. Ronald Lynch (1986) notes that there are two elements to communication: (1) what is said or written in a given exchange, and (2) the prior history of interactions among the principles sharing the communication.

Moreover, there are many forms of communication. How do we communicate?

- spoken words
- written words
- tonal qualities merged with spoken words
- body language
- symbolic and other nonverbal means

Some managers want to see everything; others are experts at triage: dealing with crisis issues at once, dumping hopeless cases in the trash, putting less critical items into a delayed suspense file or system, and so on. As the "communications load" ((Klofas, Stojkovic, and Kalinich, 1990: 60) rises, the importance of informal channels rises.

Communications networks are constructed within organizations to facilitate formal communications. But rarely do these function well. Hence, supplemental, informal networks spring up, and these are sometimes referred to as **back channels**. A phone rings, you pick up the receiver, and a friendly voice from another unit in the organization says, "The warden will be sending your division head a memo on the widget works project later today. Your division will get the lead assignment but will have only three days to carry it out. I thought you might like to know." In virtually all large organizations, informal communications supplement formal ones.

Reporting and Communications Problems

There are a number of communications problems that various management authors have identified. Gossip and rumors are troublesome, and serve to supplement back-channel communications. Communications problems are common to most organizations. Joseph Massie cites several types of communication problems (1987: 113):

1. Technical transmission problems
   - noise
   - redundancy

2. Semantic problems (proper meanings)
   - past communication experiences
   - communications environment (context)
   - facts-versus-opinions problems
   - abstractness of symbols
   - complexity

3. "The effectiveness problem"—the balance of effects and results
   - levels through which information must be transmitted
   - the size of organization
   - acceptance of message (psychological dimensions)

Line loss is the condition of informational loss as a message passes from one person or hierarchical level to another. Anyone who has played the parlor game of whispering a message to one person, then that one whispers it to another, and so on, until all have heard it, knows how much the message will have changed. Stewart and Dixon (1983: 107), citing a report by William Conboy (1976), noted one managerial study that revealed the scope of the problem. At a meeting of a board of directors, 100 percent of them received the message correctly. However, as it was passed to their vice presidents, just 67 percent correctly acquired the information. General supervisors got it right 56 percent of the time. Plant managers received it correctly only 40 percent of the time, and foremen only 30 percent. As a result, only 20 percent of the workers received the message correctly.

Andrew J. DuBrin (1978) identified eight common communications barriers (Klofas, Stojkovic, and Kalinich 1990: 54): (1) preconceived ideas; (2) denial of contrary information; (3) use of personalized meaning; (4) lack of motivation or interest (MEGO: "my eyes glaze over"); (5) noncredibility of the source; (6) lack of communications skills; (7) poor organizational climate; and (8) use of complex channels.

Massie named three communications barriers (1987: 117): (1) distortion, (2) filtering, and (3) overload. **Distortion** is similar to line loss, but it reflects interpretational biases of the listener. The listener received the message but interprets it to fit his or her preconceptions. This approximates DuBrin's preconceived ideas, as does use of personalized meanings.

Filtering also is similar to line loss. The listener retains that part of the message that fits his or her own interests without retaining those parts that do not. It is similar to DuBrin's denial of contrary information.

Overload is one of the most common communication problems facing the contemporary manager. Load is a measure of the rate and complexity of the communications being processed. Overloads easily occur in an organization. Too much paper passes through the channels, and important items are smothered among the routine items. Load crises are related to (1) organizational instability (rigid, traditional, hierarchical bureaucracies are considered stable in this context); (2) the individual capacity to manage message inputs and output; (3) reading speed, and the ability to communicate in print or orally, memory, etc.; and (4) the individual and systemic desire for information.

Jargon: Some communication problems arise from **jargon**, which is an overuse of technical and professional language and obscure vocabulary. In public service agencies, there also is a vast overuse of abbreviations, slang, and almost incomprehensible terminology. Within the closed work group, such usages may not be a problem, but people from outside the organization listening to such terms may not comprehend.

Optimum Legibility Formula: Learning how to avoid the difficulties and problems of poor communications requires effort and practice.

Box 11.1 • Jargon: "Mary Had a Little Lamb" — The Police Report

The subject, a female Caucasian, hereinafter known as Mary, surname unknown, has been frequently observed in the close company of an immature member of the Bovidae family...whose remarkable flocculent albino surface resembles frozen precipitation in the form of hexagonal snow crystals. It appears that regardless of Mary's migratory habits, the woolly juvenile maintained pursuance. Such pursuit of the subject led the unfledged species of the genus, Ovis, to the subject's institute of learning—in absolute violation of Section 63.55 of the Municipal Code. The subject's academic peers subsequently engaged in exultation, jubilation, frolic, and general rejoicing at the incongruous apparition of a callow member of the Hollow Horn Ruminant family at a place of academia (*The Legal Guide to Mother Goose*, "translated" by Don Sandburg, 1978).

"Mary Had a Little Lamb"
Mary had a little lamb
With fleece as white as snow,
And everywhere that Mary went
The lamb was sure to go.
It followed her to school one day.
That was quite against the rule.
It made the children laugh and play
To see a lamb at school.

B.R.S. Silverman gave guidance on how to communicate more clearly in an article, "The Optimum Legibility Formula" (1980: 581-583). According to the **optimum legibility formula,** one should:

1. Write the complete message down as quickly as possible.

2. Determine the purpose of the message by listing a few potential sentence subjects it implies or states.

3. Attempt to answer the six basic journalistic questions: who, what, when, where, why, and how.

4. Rearrange the sentences in priority order.

5. Place verbs immediately after their subjects.

6. Eliminate all linking verbs.

7. Use one verb per sentence.

Nonverbal Communication

David Givens (1984) is a linguistic anthropologist who publicized his studies of nonverbal communications in the 1980s. His research included a critique of judges in their courtrooms (Klahn, 1981). "In the courtroom, judges don't have to say a word to make their feelings perfectly clear—and perhaps unfairly influence juror's decisions." He added, "Unlike Justice, the blindfolded lady weighing the evidence on her scale, courtroom participants consider more than what they hear. What they see, especially in the judge, makes an impression on jurors and others in courtrooms, says anthropologist David Givens." Givens was quoted further as saying, "If a judge's opinion is clear, people will try to follow his lead"... "if his opinion is clear non-verbally, the same things happen."

Givens's point is that we communicate in unspoken and unwritten ways, some of which we may not even realize. Our faces, our postures, our gestures, our movements, how we occupy space, touching and avoiding touching, and symbolic emblems we display all add to our communication messages.

Facial Expressions and Eye Contact: Faces can reveal pleasure, tension, hostility, or fear. There is eye contact when people want to exchange ideas, and eye contact is broken when there is disinterest. To stare is to express exaggerated interest. A smile can be genuine or false, and there are ways to tell which is which. A real smile is revealed in the muscles that orbit the eyes (Tavris, 2003: 87-88). Paul Ekman's *Emotions Revealed* (2003) discusses such clues.

Basic Body Language: Basic body language includes kinesics, gestures, and posture. **Kinesics** is the interpretation of body language, such as facial expressions and gestures, or nonverbal behavior related to movement, either of any part of the body, or of the body as a whole. Posture will reveal if a person is tense or relaxed. Other gestures and indicators of body language can be decoded as well. Some, like **illustrators**, are quite obvious. They include pointing, waving someone forward, nodding one's head to indicate yes or no, or raising one's hand to answer a question or to get a speaker's attention. **Affect displays** are facial expressions that send a message rather than just reveal a state of mind. Common examples are a frown, a smile, blushing, sticking out one's tongue, and the like. **Regulators** are gestures such as nodding in agreement as someone else speaks, making encouraging or discouraging facial signals as someone is speaking, answering a question, looking upward or out a window when bored with the topic, and so on. **Adapters** are mannerisms that are not meant as communication but can be translated by a perceptive observer (Ekman and Friesen, 1969).

Space and Territory: The manipulation of space and territory, known as **spatial distribution**, can communicate feelings as well. Commonly used expressions such as "you're crowding me," "he's in my face," "she's stand-offish," "he's distant," and "I need my space" all reflect a subtle awareness of this fact. Deference can be revealed in a person's posture and use of space. For instance, because of military training, most veterans shift to a "position of attention" in the presence of those feared or respected but remain relaxed amid equals and inferiors, and those who are not found threatening.

Environment: Messages can be found in the arrangement of furniture. Do you have to talk to a manager "across a desk," or does your supervisor have a pair of overstuffed chairs in which both parties sit during a conversation? If the director's office is buffered by a secretary's desk or an anteroom to filter out access, this communicates a wish to be left alone. An easily accessible ground-floor office and an open door suggest a willingness to communicate.

Touch (Tactile Communication): Messages are sent through the rules of touching (**tactile communication**)—whom one may and will touch, the kinds of touching, and even the duration of physical contact. Friends shake hands, but usually rivals do not. Putting an arm over a friend's shoulder or patting a buddy on the back is acceptable behavior with close associates, but not with strangers or those with whom one does not have close personal relations. There are stricter rules about contact between males and females (Henley, 1977), and a mistake can lead to a complaint of sexual harassment. The rules of etiquette vary by culture and subculture. For example, East European friends kiss in situations in which few Americans would. When a person puts an arm around your shoulder, is it a friendly gesture or a control posture? Who can do this to whom?

Emblems: **Emblems** include various graphic symbols and hand or body gestures. The 1960s peace sign, the "A-OK" popularized by pilots and astronauts, the Vulcan salute copied from "Star Trek," the "New York salute" (or "flipping the bird"), and so on—each communicates a message.

Nonverbal Speech Cues (Paralanguage)

When people speak, it is not just the word but also the other nonverbal vocal cues that help them convey what they are thinking.

Tonal Cues: Tonal cues are factors such as vocal pitch and whine, which augment and alter the meaning of the words a person speaks. The words "I could kill you" can be spoken jokingly, neutrally and unemotionally, or threateningly. It is the tone of voice that conveys whether the speaker is being humorous, factual, or threatening.

Pace of Speech: People speak more rapidly when tense, and slower when more relaxed.

Volume: People may engage in shouting at someone whom they feel is inferior or stupid. Raising one's voice is generally an indicator of anger.

Silence and Pauses: The so-called "pregnant pause," when all conversation ceases after some remark, also is communication. The delay while a person considers a question, the time lag in returning a call, or the failure to reply at all ("If he really wants to speak to me, he can call back.") reveals disinterest. Placing a subordinate's memo or report aside as it is turned in has the meaning that "this is not as important to me as it is to you."

All of this is communication. The methods used, consciously or unconsciously, by one person to convey an idea to another are not limited to the vocabulary employed. An astute criminal justice manager learns to use these added features of communication to convey additional meaning to his or her words.

Using False Signals: All of these same cues can be used to send **false messages.** Imagine a police officer who is quiet, passive, and a model of courtesy until he needs to make an arrest. Then he turns livid, speaks with a violent rasp to his voice, and stands with fists clenched. His posture is very threatening, but it could be an act to intimidate the person he was planning to arrest.

The Language Itself: The Choice of Words

Samuel I. Hayakawa: Samuel Hayakawa (1906-1992) was a distinguished university professor of English, president of San Francisco State University, and former United States Senator from California from 1977 to 1983. His major contribution to English is his book, *Language in Thought and Action*, published in five editions since 1949 (a revision of his 1941 *Language in Action*). He was greatly influenced by Alfred H. S. Korzybski (1879–1950), a Polish-American philosopher who developed the theory of general semantics. Korzybski thought that knowledge is limited by the structure of the human nervous systems and the structure of language. Humans experience life through linguistic "abstractions," yet our linguistic understandings can deceive us. Hayakawa expanded on Korzybski's concepts on the study of semantics, which he defined as "the study of human interaction through communication"

en.wikipedia.org

Samuel I. Hayakawa was a major language theorist and a leading expert on semantics. He advocated English as the national language, even though he was of Japanese ancestry. After serving as a university professor and college president, he was a U.S. Senator from California between 1977 and 1983.

(1972: ix). Hayakawa founded the organization, U.S. English, which sought to make English the official language of the United States.

Hayakawa taught that words are symbols. As he would say, "The word is not the thing...The symbol is not the thing symbolized....The map is not the territory." Hayakawa (1972: 34-42) divides communications into three categories of statements: reports, inferences, and judgments.

We must forever be aware of the ease of confusing facts and inferences. What one actually knows and what one may sincerely believe are quite different. A **fact** is first-hand, empirical observation, while an **inference** is an assumption or a probability statement.

Of even greater risk is assuming that judgments actually convey any information about the topic under consideration. They are statements that tell only the speaker's personal opinion or prejudices about the topic under discussion. Thus, they tell the listener very little about the topic but much about the speaker.

Box 11.2 • Hayakawa's Classification of Statements

Reports are statements that can be independently verified or disproved.

Inferences are statements of the unknown made on the basis of what is known, the essence of all theory.

Judgments are expressions of approval or disapproval, usually opinions about something that tell more about the speaker than about the subject under discussion.

Semantic Problems with the Spoken Word

Hayakawa coined the phrases *snarl words* and *purr words*. **Snarl words** are unfavorable adjectives and nouns used in conjunction with persons or things that we dislike (e.g., "incompetent," "flip-flopper," "terrorist"). **Purr words** are favorable adjectives and nouns about things we like (e.g., "bright," "beautiful," "witty," "sweet"). Police occasionally are spoken of as "Nazis," "Gestapo," and "Fascists" when used to express displeasure with their actions. Words like "hero," "leader," "champion," or "star" are used to characterize those whom we like (Hayakawa, 1972: 40-41).

The "one-word, one-meaning fallacy" (Hayakawa, 1972: 54) is the mistake of taking a word to mean one thing when it can mean another. In your mind, think of a "cat," and jot down the following information about "your cat," the one you were thinking about: the sex, long or short hair, color or fur pattern, age group (a kitten, young adult, old adult), frisky versus taciturn. Or did your describe a piece of construction equipment, also a "CAT." Or maybe you still remember the abbreviation for "cable access television" broadcasting (CAT). The same words have multiple meanings according to their context and the "history" of the user and listener.

"Words with built-in judgments" (1972: 68-71) are terms that convey information but also subtly reveal one's prejudice for or against the person or thing identified. Less obvious than snarl and purr words, their use still will identify people or concepts that are disliked: a man who has been convicted of a minor criminal offense is "a criminal"; a disliked woman who has been involved in a casual sexual affair is a "tramp" or a "slut"; a businessman who is doing too well for our taste is "a shark" or "a white-collar criminal." On the other hand, someone liked or sympathized with might be "a man who made a mistake," a "liberated woman," or "a successful entrepreneur." Racial and ethnic appellations obviously convey prejudice. The so-called "N word" has become an infamous term in our public vocabularies, too value-loaded to be used even in a neutral academic context such as this passage. Such a word offends, and each such word suggests prejudice in the person using it, even if that is not the case.

"The language of social control" (1972: 88-91) permits language to be used to give directions without the obvious force of orders. When we speak of the future as fact we can see how language directs us to act: for example, "There will be a test in the next class." Sometimes the direction is more subtle. A manager may express a vague hope that something will be done in anticipation that it will be taken as an order without having the officiousness of making it one: for example, "Will someone find me the case report?" may sound like a question, but it is a direction to a junior subordinate to find and bring back the case report.

Written Communications

Most governmental communication involves a great deal of paperwork. The quantity of paperwork in most criminal justice administrative jobs can be frightening. The "action occupation" of police work is overwhelmed by the reports required for each request for assistance, investigation, search, arrest, booking, release from custody, and so on.

A routine investigation leading to an arrest, booking, and custody will involve (1) a case or incident report, (2) one or more follow-up reports, (3) an arrest report or record, usually with one or more sets of fingerprint cards, each requiring basic information on the suspect and the charge, (4) an arrest warrant issued by a magistrate, but containing service-execution information supplied by the police, (5) an inventory of personal effects taken from the suspect in custody, (6) a "mittimus" to record the transfer of the prisoner out of police custody, and (7) a request for paid overtime to get all of the paperwork done. In addition, each police officer is advised to keep a police notebook of his or her activities, summarizing all of the above.

As modern bureaucracies, all criminal justice agencies must keep and rely upon files. Documentation is required within every agency in the criminal justice system in order to produce records on every legal action and procedure. The courts must keep records of all judicial proceedings. Prosecutors must keep extensive case files. Correctional units must keep files on all inmates and all correctional operations. Probation and parole offices must keep extensive records on client caseloads. Felony criminal cases require transcripts that have to be available if there are appeals. Appeals are filed with extensive "briefs" of the case law and legal arguments behind the appeal. With extensive files in their possession, criminal justice managers have to ensure that these are stored in an orderly manner, are classified and categorized, and can be retrieved when needed.

Document Classification and Protecting Sensitive Information

In an open society it is often too easy to ignore the fact that some knowledge and information is not public but is instead **proprietary information** (i.e., privately owned information). Governments freely give away great quantities of knowledge and information (or try to), but in some cases their goal is to shelter critical, sensitive knowledge from the general public.

In this computer age, access to information has expanded greatly. Everyone with access to a computer has at his or her fingertips more information than exists at any major library. Even so, there are those who want more: they want to see the proprietary information of corporations, the defense secrets of the nation, or the financial information of private individuals. Using a computer it is possible to "hack" into computer systems to steal these data.

Protecting information is the purpose of **information security (INFOSEC)**. Part of the security effort of a criminal justice manager is defining what information needs protection and why. Often referred to as **document security**, many managers employ systems that are the same or similar to those used by the Department of Defense to protect their documents and data banks. These systems rely upon **document classification**, the terminology of which usually matches the security clearances and access controls of the Department of Defense.

"For Official Use Only" (FOUO) is used to identify information that is "sensitive" and could violate basic privacy rights of persons named in the documents, or could result in interference in an investigation or a case. Records and documents containing a name, birth date, and social security number together are typical FOUO materials, as are medical records. Releasing the addresses and telephone numbers of witnesses and crime victims can result in persons being harassed by offenders or the media. Access requires employment or affiliation with the organization possessing the information, and typically that involves a simple background check.

"**Confidential**" is used to identify information that would be prejudicial to the interests of the agency or its clients. What is meant by "prejudicial" is deliberately vague. The practical definition is based on the harm that may be done when the information falls into the hands of an unauthorized user. In law enforcement, it might include leaks of evidence that might help a suspect better evade detection or prepare a better alibi. Access again usually requires employment or affiliation with the organization possessing the information, as well as a simple background check.

"**Secret**" is used when unauthorized disclosure could bring about real and substantial "damage" to the state, the United States, its allies, or the organization. Real damage can be measured in major dollar losses, injuries, and deaths. The planning of a police raid to capture dangerous criminals would be so classified as secret. Authorized access requires a more thorough background investigation and a clear "need to know" about the information, operation, or activity that has been classified "secret."

"**Top Secret**" is used when "grave damage" would be expected to result from the unauthorized disclosure of such information. "Grave damage" is not specifically defined but is assessed by the worst-case scenario that can be projected from such information being released to an enemy. Imagine a domestic Al Qaeda terrorist cell gaining access to names, addresses, and identifying information of all of the FBI and state and city anti-terrorist agents and investigators working in your state. Access to "top secret" information requires a comprehensive, thorough background investigation and a clearly defined need to know.

"**Top Secret with Special Access**" implies caveats and compartments, which define access and will require additional authorization based on "need to know" criteria. A **caveat** is a broad categorization of who may or may not see the data. "NOFORN" (no foreign nationals may see the information) and various "EYES ONLY" notations naming those groups that may see the information are examples. Assigning **compartments** involves identifying the units within a government agency that may be allowed to see the raw data or the finished product. Prior to September 11, 2001, "9/11," the CIA often "overcompartmentalized data" so that the FBI did not know what the CIA knew, and the FBI frequently denied access to state and local police and even the Defense Intelligence Agency (DIA) about criminals and ongoing investigations.

In the federal government the National Security Agency is tasked with interagency **operational security (OPSEC)** training. An Interagency OPSEC Support Staff (IOSS) exists to train and coordinate OPSEC efforts of the National Security Agency (NSA), FBI, CIA, General Service Administration (GSA), and Department of Defense (DOD), among others. A state or local OPSEC plan or standard operating procedure (SOP) should be developed for criminal justice agencies of the states or localities wherever sensitive information is generated, kept, or used. Initially it may seem that localities and states do not need to be concerned with such matters and will not be dealing with secret and top-secret matters, but in the aftermath of 9/11 and with the continuing threat of terrorist threats to the United States, this is naïve. A terrorist cell or violent criminal gang could be active anywhere in the country, and there are targets at risk in every county and city in the country. Most terrorist cases will be handled by federal authorities, but many gang-related cases remain under local jurisdiction. Court administrators and correctional managers will find themselves dealing with such individuals in their facilities.

The criminal justice manager finding his or her agency involved with such cases or handling sensitive information about dangerous groups or individuals must develop its own information security (INFOSEC) plan. According to G.F. Jelen (1994), the plan needs to accomplish five aims (quoted in Ortmeier, 2005: 180):

1. Identifying and assessing the value of the information the agency routinely handles, the criminal justice manager must determine what data in the agency needs to be protected.

2. Identifying the potential threat, the criminal justice manager needs to know who this information should be kept from and why.

3. Identifying organizational vulnerabilities is another criminal justice managerial responsibility. The agency needs to be aware of how protected data can get out.

4. Assessing the impact of the threat versus the costs of the protection systems used is another managerial priority. The criminal justice manager needs to calculate the cost to the agency if its data were leaked and also compute the costs of each additional level or layer of information security. The manager needs to assess the "return on investment" (ROI) and "value-added contribution" (VAC) of the new security procedures.

5. Designing countermeasures is the final step in developing an agency information security plan. A countermeasure is a response to a known or suspected disclosure of sensitive information. Countermeasures can include changing access codes, passwords, or encryptions immediately if they have been compromised; changing the timing or the details of the plans that have been revealed; or changing features of protective procedures that have been exposed.

State and local government agencies engaging in coordinated security operations working in cooperation with the U.S. government typically use the hierarchical security classification system of the Department of Defense. However, they may employ their own systems for internal security.

Criminal justice agencies are obligated to release some information to the press and the public under the Freedom of Information Act and state "**sunshine laws**" (federal and state laws requiring regulatory authorities' meetings, decisions, and records to be made available to the public), so the criminal justice manager needs to conform agency INFOSEC practices to meet the requirements of the law. Often they are authorized or obligated to protect unclassified information as well, such as private personnel information kept in their files. The INFOSEC plan needs to address these legal requirements. Criminal justice employees can be obliged to sign security, confidentiality, or secrecy agreements that will bar them from disclosing any protected information they acquire from their employment. Any failure to comply can result in lawsuits and payment of damages.

Computer and Communications Security (COMSEC)

A contemporary criminal justice manager must be aware of the communications security measures that can be employed, and also should know what the most common threats to communication and computer are. The following topics should be considered.

Encryption and **ciphers** (algorithms for performing encryption and decryption) are used to protect classified information and limit access. Passwords, access codes, key-card systems, and secure safes and vaults for confidential storage of information all can use encryptions. *Cryptography (cryptology)* is the science of both encryption and code-breaking.

Cryptographic security is a managerial responsibility that includes protecting encryption codes and machines as well as other security devices. It includes *line security*, the security equipment, procedures, and practices needed to protect the organization's own internal communications systems. Increasingly more criminal justice agencies are relying upon various forms of *space-radio communications*, such as cellular and wireless phones, fixed and mobile radio systems, satellite radio systems, microwave transmissions, and many other communications systems using the open "air-waves" method of sending communications. *Transmissions security* must be considered when using such equipment. Any such transmission can be heard by unintended listeners who are willing to acquire the equipment and apply the effort to listen in. Related to this is *emanations security*, which tries to protect or disguise the electromagnetic signature of the communications equipment in use.

Computer and Internet Security: The threat to computer data cannot be underestimated. **Firewalls** and anti-virus protections, usually achieved through commercial software, should be installed to help protect computers. Even with these protections, weaknesses common to most computer systems include unintentionally sending out passwords on wireless networks and other methods of losing passwords. When protecting sensitive communications or stored documents, access codes must be limited to as few users as possible and should be changed frequently to avoid compromise. Computer crimes can target criminal justice agencies just as easily as commercial businesses and private individuals (Britz, 2004; Schmalleger and Pittaro, 2008; Taylor et al., 2006). These include online computer frauds, identity thefts, hacking into data and resultant data thefts, data alterations, computer attacks such as contriving to overload web sites, and the insertion of **malware** (malicious software), such as virus and worm programs.

Information Sharing and Communication Networks

It is nonetheless possible to over-restrict access to criminal justice information. Limiting access and "overcompartmentalization" can keep data from other component agencies of the criminal justice system who will need it. Often it is learned that one police agency has released a suspect sought by another, or that a correctional unit is holding a person who is suspected in an earlier case and cannot be found, or that the police have in custody a person who is under probation or parole supervision but neither the police not the community corrections officers are aware of their common interest in the person. To help overcome such common, self-imposed limitations on information sharing, a criminal justice manager must determine in advance what kinds of information should be shared with other criminal justice agencies and what information it will want from them in exchange. The result will be the establishment of interagency communications networks. Larger agencies also should establish coherent information-sharing plans for internal use.

Numerous management writers refer to the several variations in communications networks. Joseph Massie (115-116) describes direct, star, circular, radial, and serial patterns. Klofas, Stojkovic, and Kalinich (1990: 62-65) illustrate similar wheel-and-spoke, chain, circle, and all-channel (star) networks. Souryal (1985: 58) describes networks as vertical, horizontal, diagonal, and circular. Stewart and Garson (1983: 110) apply similar models taken from an article by Alex Bavelas and Dermat Barrell (1951: 370-371). There are both formal and informal communications networks in most organizations (Klofas, Stojkovic, and Kalinich 1990: 67-69). In the informal network, there is a **linking pin** (also called a "lynch pin" or "linchpin"), that is, a person who is the central cohesive element and key to keeping communications open and flowing. When the linking pin functions informally, the information often is considered office gossip, and such networks are known collectively as the "**grapevine**" (Massie, 1987: 115). The reliability of the grapevine is difficult to ascertain, and a wise manager will independently verify the information before acting on it.

Face-to-Face Communicating: Giving a Formal Briefing

The formal staff meeting briefing often is used as the means of achieving face-to-face communications, but it can fail when certain rules are not followed. There are some practical communication rules that a manager should employ to make best use of a formal briefing opportunity. A common form of briefing will be an agency's routine staff briefing.

Speaking to a group often results in confusion as to whom an assignment or responsibility has been given. The chair or staff person tasked should restate new decisions and missions: for example, "So I'll send X to support Y for today and tomorrow." or "It's agreed then, that

Box 11.3 • Features of a Well-Prepared Staff Meeting

1. There should be an agenda announced in advance, but it need not be followed slavishly.

2. No staff member should brief the whole group on any topic that does not require knowledge by the chief manager and at least two others. An item, even if very important, that involves only the boss or only one staff member—or just other staff, not to include the boss—ought be discussed directly between affected parties.

3. Petty informational items ought to be kept to a minimum, but items that may seem petty, but will affect internal functions and routines, should be addressed. Any change of routines affecting most staff should be included. Examples would be conveying that the copier is down; important visitors will be visiting in the afternoon; three secretaries are out with flu, producing a typing backlog; the cafeteria will be closed tomorrow for a special function; or the new phone system goes online next Tuesday.

4. Decision items should be previewed in an advance memo. If this is not done, then decisions should be deferred until all parties involved can have the time to research and reconsider the impact of the decisions being sought.

Bill and Tom will assist Frank on the XYZ Project." Other methods involve sending the participants in the meeting a "memorandum for record" to summarize the decisions made and tasks allocated. The taking and circulating of meeting "minutes" serves a similar function. In each of these examples, any receiver of the communication has a duty to respond with corrections or clarifications.

Box 11.4 • Components of Information Management Systems

1. Reporting systems = input systems
2. Records keeping systems = storage systems
3. Data retrieval systems = output systems
4. Data analysis =
      process systems
      management summaries
      consolidated reports
5. Transmission systems

Information Storage and Retrieval Systems

A massive amount of criminal justice information is generated by the various components of the criminal justice system. With the addition of various kinds of electronic media to the great quantity of written and printed material, a criminal justice manager must have a system in place to store and retrieve information.

The police generate incident and investigative reports, arrest records, inventories of property seized and evidence collected, and much more. Police managers are responsible for the collection and storage of this information, much of which is sensitive and not available to the public. Other police data are made public regularly, in the format of the Uniform Crime Reports, prepared by local police agencies around the nation and compiled for the public by the Federal Bureau of Investigation. Police managers have a duty to inform the public via the news media about major criminal cases under investigation, but it is part of their managerial responsibility to be cautious and selective about what information to reveal and what information to make public.

Prosecutors also have access to great quantities of criminal case information that is highly sensitive. Information given to grand juries is held under a seal of secrecy and may be disclosed only in the furtherance of criminal due process. A prosecutor can reveal indictments, presentments, and "no bills" of a grand jury to the public. Prosecutors also compile summary statistics on cases reviewed, dismissed, nolleprosequed, plea bargained, brought to trial, or producing convictions or acquittals. By their rules of ethics they are obligated to avoid generating prejudicial pretrial publicity. In court their cases are fully public and available to the news media, except in some cases involving juvenile defendants and witnesses.

The courts compile and publish their performance records, transcripts of the trial proceedings in major cases, sentence data, appeal records, and similar public reports.

Correctional agencies and community correctional units are limited in what information they can reveal about those in custody or under supervision, but keep extensive files on the people under their control. They do publish and share data on the numbers of people they manage and people under sentence of death, parole data, recidivism statistics, and similar information about the offenders in their care.

Agencies have stored some of their data in print form in traditional files; on microfilm; on microfiche; on electromagnetic data cards; on reel-to-reel magnetic tapes; on 8-inch, 5.25-inch, and 2.5-inch computer disks; on beta-cassettes; on 8mm and 16mm film; on VHS cassettes; on audio cassettes; on servers; on hard drives; on zip drives; on CDs; on DVDs; and other storage devices. Some of these storage media no longer are supported by equipment maintained in the agency. If data no longer can be retrieved, they no longer can be used. In an age when "cold cases" now can be solved using technologies that did not exist when the crime occurred, when courts allow appeals of convictions rendered decades earlier, or when researchers want long-term recidivism data to evaluate correctional programs, this loss of access to stored data can be critical. Therefore, it becomes necessary that criminal justice agencies have means of accessing old data. Options include transferring data to new storage formats, making print copies for archives, and keeping older data-retrieval technologies available and serviceable for decades to come.

Making Use of Criminal Justice Data: Reporting Revisited

Having good data is almost meaningless if the criminal justice manager is not using the data that is available to support other managerial functions. Formal analysis of routine information is a key managerial responsibility. Knowing how to use the data the agency already has in its storage can enhance agency performance and identify better ways to manage the organization. Numerous aids can be employed to make data analysis easier for the criminal justice manager:

- spatial distribution graphics
- temporal distribution reports

- individual performance summaries
- unit performance summaries
- client-characteristics summaries
- case characteristics summaries
- case flow reports (offense or offender-based reports)
- financial summaries

Agency data also can be used to undertake special research projects. Such data will be needed for an internal research or auditing unit. Outside evaluation teams, accreditation committees, and commissions also will need to have access to appropriate information. If management consultants are to be employed for some purpose, they too need key data.

Summary

Ultimately, the information generated by a criminal justice agency will be needed by its political superiors to help them plan and make policy. Moreover, criminal justice information needs to be provided selectively to the general public. Each criminal justice agency head and every senior manager must be held accountable to the public, and proper reporting of police, prosecutorial, judicial, and correctional data in accurately analyzed formats will help the criminal justice manager meet that mandate.

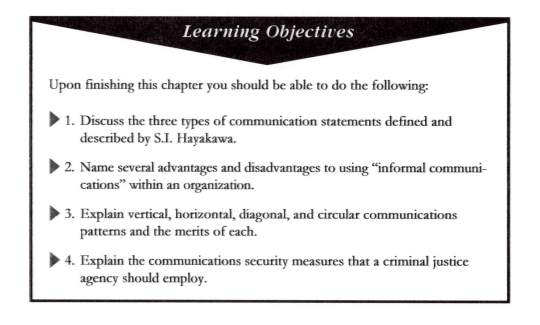

Learning Objectives

Upon finishing this chapter you should be able to do the following:

▶ 1. Discuss the three types of communication statements defined and described by S.I. Hayakawa.

▶ 2. Name several advantages and disadvantages to using "informal communications" within an organization.

▶ 3. Explain vertical, horizontal, diagonal, and circular communications patterns and the merits of each.

▶ 4. Explain the communications security measures that a criminal justice agency should employ.

IMPORTANT TERMS AND NAMES

- adapters
- affect displays
- back channels
- caveat
- ciphers
- communication overload
- compartments
- distortion
- document classification
- document security
- emblems
- encoding
- encryption
- fact
- false messages
- filtering
- firewalls
- Mary Parker Follett
- for official use only (FOUO)
- grapevine
- illustrators

- inference
- information security (INFOSEC)
- jargon
- judgments
- kinesics
- line loss
- linking pin
- malware
- operational security (OPSEC)
- optimum legibility formula
- overload
- pace of speech
- proprietary information
- purr words
- regulators
- semantics
- snarl words
- spatial distribution
- sunshine laws
- tactile communication
- tonal cues

References and Supplemental Sources

Abram, Carolyn, and Leah Pearlman (2008). *Facebook for Dummies*. New York: For Dummies, Wiley.

Bavelas, Alex, and Dermat Barrell (1951). "An Experimental Approach to Organization Communication," *Personnel* (March): 370-371.

Birdwhistell, Ray L. (1970). *Kinesics and Context: Essays on Body Motion Communication*. Philadelphia: University of Pennsylvania Press.

Britz, Marjie (2004). *Computer Forensics and Cyber Crime: An Introduction*. Upper Saddle River, NJ: Pearson/Prentice Hall.

Conboy, William A. (1976). *Working Together: Communications in a Healthy Organization*. Columbus, OH: Charles E. Merrill.

DuBrin, Andrew J. (1978). *Fundamentals of Organizational Behavior*. New York: Pergamon Press.

Ekman, Paul (2003). *Emotions Revealed*. New York: Time Books, Henry Holt and Company.

Ekman, Paul, and W. Friesen (1969). "The Repertoire of Non-Verbal Behavior: Categories, Origins, Usage, and Coding," *Semiotica*, 1: 49-98.

Fahs, Chad (2007). *How to Do Everything with YouTube*. New York: McGraw-Hill.

Follett, Mary Parker (1926). "The Giving of Orders," in *The Scientific Foundations of Business Administration*, edited Henry C. Metcalf, et al. Baltimore, MD: Williams and Wilkins.

Follett, Mary Parker (1926, 1989). "The Giving of Orders," in *Classic Readings in Organizational Behavior*, edited by J. Steven Ott. Pacific Grove, CA: Brooks/Cole.

Hayakawa, Samuel Ichiye (1972). *Language in Thought and Action*, 3rd ed. New York, Harcourt Brace Jovanovich.

Henley, Nancy M. (1977). *Body Politics: Power, Sex, and Nonverbal Communication*. New York: Simon & Schuster.

Givens, David B. (1984). "What Is Nonverbal Communication?" and "What Body Language Can Tell You That Words Cannot," *Nonverbal Q & A*, American Anthropological Association. Available at http://www.geocities.com/marvin_hecht/givens.html

Jelen, G.F. (1994). "OPSEC for the Private Sector," *Security Management*, 38(10): 67-68.

Klahn, Jim (1981). "Body Talk," *The Charlotte Observer* (June 7, 1981): D-1.

Klofas, John, Stan Stojkovic, and David Kalinich (1990). *Criminal Justice Organizations: Administration and Management*. Pacific Grove, CA: Brooks/Cole.

Lynch, Ronald G. (1986). *The Police Manager: Professional Leadership Skills*, 3rd ed. New York: Random House.

Lynch, Ronald G., and Scott Lynch (2005). *The Police Manager*. Newark, NJ: Lexis-Nexis Matthew Bender.

Massie, Joseph L. (1987). *Essentials of Management*, 4th ed. Englewood Cliffs, NJ: Prentice Hall.

Miller, Michael (2007). *YouTube 4 You*. New York: Macmillan Computer.

Ortmeier, P.J. (2005). *Security Management*, 2nd ed. Upper Saddle River, NJ: Pearson/Prentice Hall.

Sahlin, Doug, and Chris Botello (2007). *YouTube for Dummies*. Indianapolis: Wiley.

Sandburg, Don (1978). *The Legal Guide to Mother Goose*. Los Angeles: Price/Stern/Sloan.

Schmalleger, Frank, and Michael Pittaro, eds. (2008). *Crimes of the Internet*. Upper Saddle River, NJ: Pearson/Prentice Hall.

Sewell, James D. (2007). "Working with the Media in Times of Crisis," *Crime and Justice International*, 23(98): 32-35.

Silverman, B.R.S. (1980). "The Optimum Legibility Formula: A Written Communications System," *Personnel Journal*, 56(July): 581-583.

Souryal, Sam S. (1985). *Police Organization and Administration*. Cincinnati: Pilgrimage/Anderson.

Stewart, Debra, and G. David Garson (1983). *Organizational Behavior and Public Management*. New York: Marcel Dekker.

Tavris, Carol (2003). "A Polite Smile or the Real McCoy?" *Scientific American*, 288(6): 87-88.

Taylor, Robert W., Tory J. Caeti, D. Kall Liper, Eric J. Fritsch, and John Liederbach (2006). *Digital Crime and Digital Terrorism*. Upper Saddle River, NJ: Pearson/Prentice Hall.

12
Future Issues in Criminal Justice Management

What does the future hold for tomorrow's criminal justice managers? While we cannot be certain, forecasts can prepare us for what we may experience in years to come. Forecasting is one of the planning tools mentioned in Chapter 6. Forecasts typically look to the past and consider contemporary developments to predict the future. A criminal justice manager in the twenty-first century can expect to face many of the same issues that challenged managers in the past.

An entire new discipline appeared in the 1960s called **futuristics**, the prediction of the future based on the scholarly study of existing conditions. **Futurologists** (also called **futurists**) in criminal justice have offered numerous insights into what may be in store for your career as a criminal justice manager some decades ahead.

Two organizations have been leaders in the study of the future: the World Futures Studies Federation (WFSF), founded in 1967 in Oslo, Norway, and the World Future Society (WFS), founded in the United States in 1966. The WFS publishes two journals, *Futures Research Quarterly* and *The Futurist*. The *Journal of Futures Studies*, published by the Graduate Institute of Futures Studies of Tamkang University in Taipei, Taiwan, is another scholarly outlet for such studies. Many futurists have looked ahead to the risks that we face from crime and terror. None, though, is more distinguished than Wendell Bell (2000), one of the founders of futurology, and the author of one of its major works, *Foundations of Futures Studies* (1996; 1997).

The Society of Police Futurists International is a nongovernmental organization dedicated to applying futuristics to policing. In 1991, William Tafoya, then with the FBI, cofounded the Society of Police Futurists International. He has lectured and consulted on various futuristic threats, including cybercrime in its infancy. Another leading futurist in criminal justice, studying for more than a quarter century, is Gene Stephens. In a recent report (2005), he summarized some of the predictions that he and others see ahead for American law enforcement, including such things as the expanded use of nonlethal force, customization of police and criminal justice services to meet specific public needs, greater demands on first responders, cybercrime, and terrorist incidents including the threat of bioterrorism.

One of the leading futurists looking at the court system is Sohail Inayatullah (1990; 1992). Having worked on a judiciary improvement project with the Hawaiian courts, Inayatullah writes of futures for judicial bureaucracies (Inayatullah and Monma, 1989). The project initiated a problem-oriented planning process, and considered options for the future, including some low-probability issues such as the rights of robots, sentencing offenders using natural brain drugs, and even the secession of Hawaii from the United States.

Many others also are looking ahead. Georgette Bennett sought to predict future crime trends in her 1987 book, *Crimewarps* (revised in 1989). Her predictions relied heavily on demographic trends and foresaw the problems of cybercrime. Another future-looking expert on demographic trends and crime is Alfred Blumstein whose work (1995; Blumstein and Rosenfeld, 1998; Blumstein and Wallman, 2000; 2006) was recognized with the 2007 Stockholm Prize in Criminology for his predictive work on human rights, age-based crime trends, and studies of incarceration rates in American correctional institutions among other subjects. His advanced statistical analyses have produced complex predictions on the productivity of deterrence, the growth of prison populations, and the problems and future of drug-enforcement policies. He developed the statistical concept of "lambda" as a reliable predictive measurement of an individual's offending frequency within a possible life-long criminal career. Roslyn Muraskin and Albert Roberts have compiled a collection of essays, *Visions for Change* (2009), that addresses future issues for the twenty-first century. The authors look at recent developments and future directions in technological applications, forensic sciences, globalization, victimology, drug policy, cybercrimes, juvenile justice issues, media matters, gender issues, and all of the components of the justice system.

These leading futurists and others have looked ahead to the future of criminal justice. Others have undertaken efforts to direct that change into improved futures. These kinds of managers are change agents in the pattern of such great criminal justice reformers of the past as Cesare Beccaria, Jeremy Bentham, Zebulon Brockway, Dorothea Dix, August Vollmer, Orlando W. Wilson, Bruce Smith, Arthur Vanderbilt, Katharine Bement Davis, Mary Belle Harris, and George Beto. Future criminal justice managers need to recognize three distinctive patterns of change: (1) straight-line change, (2) rise-plateau-crash change, and (3) cyclic change.

Natural Patterns in Change

Straight-Line Change: Change often will follow a trend in a consistent fashion, either steady-state, rising, or falling. In criminal justice, **straight-line change** patterns have existed involving: training requirements, entry educational requirements, and in-service educational achievements, all rising gradually over the decades.

Rise-Plateau-Crash Change: In criminal justice, specific technologies have appeared, become popular (rising), then become commonplace (the plateau), only to be replaced by new technologies and thus vanish (the crash). This **rise-plateau-crash change** has been evident especially in the applications of communications technologies (the call box, one-way radio, two-way radio, and in-car computer) and in suspect and offender identification (the Bertillon system, inked fingerprints, scanner prints, and DNA identification). Correctional innovations also have followed this pattern (the Pennsylvania silent penitentiary movement, the Auburn congregate system, the rehabilitation movement, correctional boot camps, and, more recently, three-strikes legislation and career-offender long-term incarceration programs. Media attention to spectacular criminal cases also follows this pattern (Marsh, 1991).

Cyclic Change: The most predictable events undergo **cyclic change** or follow an **oscillating change pattern**, in which frequencies of some feature will rise, then fall, only to rise again. This cyclic change is obvious in the long-term history of criminal justice; consider issues such as brutality complaints, corruption scandals , and the bias against minorities.

Issues Criminal Justice Managers Will Face in the Future

Brutality and Excessive Force Issues: Police and correctional officers are obliged to use force in the performance of their duties. Several hundred people are killed each year by police and correctional officers, far more than are lawfully executed. This use of force, whether *deadly force* or *nonlethal force*, can be used wrongfully. When serious abuse of force occurs, there will be protests, lawsuits, and changes made in criminal justice training standards to present future abuses. Criminal justice managers also are looking to new nonlethal force devices to reduce the number of police-caused homicides and to reduce cases of excessive force. The *crisis-planner* manager will respond in reaction to such cases; the manager who is a *purposeful planner* will anticipate such problems and prepare for them before they occur.

In 1985, a change in case law (*Garner v. Tennessee*) altered the standards by which police could use deadly force. Even before the U.S.

Supreme Court made its ruling, though, the IACP (1981) was anticipating what the future would bring to police deadly force practices. Police managers were preparing to apply more restrictive shooting standards. When the court rendered its decision, these managers' agencies were prepared to accept the new standards. These progressive police managers used a process like that described by Kurt Lewin (1890-1947), who wrote that the process of effecting change involves a three-step procedure (Lewin, 1989: 546-547; Souryal, 1995: 128-129):

> *Unfreezing:* to "[...] break open the shell of complacency and self-righteousness, it is sometimes necessary to bring about deliberately an emotional stir-up."

> *Moving or Changing:* make the change-oriented decisions and begin the process of implementation.

> *Refreezing:* allow the new ways to become established as the replacement habits.

By the time the court decision was made, most progressive police departments already were training their officers in the procedures recommended by the IACP that were to be expressed in the court ruling. Old procedures, especially the outdated "fleeing felon" rule, already had been discredited (unfreezing). When the new standard was promulgated, police all over the country were anticipating it (changing), and most were ready to apply it (refreeze).

General Ethical Failures and Shortcomings: Periodically new scandals arise in which various criminal justice officials engage in corrupt or immoral activities. There are seven recurring ethical problems facing all those who take on responsibilities in the name of justice: (1) wrongful pursuit of personal gain, (2) favoritism and bias, (3) abuses of power, (4) a flawed personal life, (5) deceitfulness, (6) denial of due process to those involved with criminal justice, and (7) neglect of duties (Kania and Dial, 2008: 169).

Box 12.1 • Seven Recurring Ethical Problems in Criminal Justice

1. Wrongful Pursuit of Personal Gain
2. Favoritism and Bias
3. Abuse of Power
4. Flawed Personal Life
5. Deceitfulness
6. Denial of Due Process
7. Neglect of Duties

Personal Gain: The criminal justice manager must avoid unlawful personal gain from the position, and similarly must be aware that such misconduct is prevented, detected, investigated, and punished when it occurs within the organization. The criminal justice manager must enforce the prohibitions, both in law and in ethical guidelines, against using public service for personal enrichment, profit, pleasure, or benefits not specifically authorized by law, the work contract, or the rules. Included in this category are the rules against:

- taking bribes and extorting pay-offs
- accepting gratuities and unauthorized benefits
- receiving excessive compensation and benefits
- using the office to promote personal aims
- harboring and advancing excessive ambition (Kania and Dial, 2008: 170)

Favoritism and Bias: Because it is unethical to use one's office to aid those whom we like or to interfere with those whom we dislike, a criminal justice manager must be attentive to this perpetual threat to agency integrity. These biases often arise from divided and mixed loyalties, holding one's obligation to the public interest below that of oneself (egoism), family (paternalism, nepotism), friends, personal associates, co-workers and peers (peer bias), one's political party and programs (patronage, ideological bias), or church and spiritual faith (theological bias). Included in this category are rules against:

- political and ideological patronage
- racial, ethnic, and religious bias (favorable and unfavorable)
- nepotism and other family favoritism
- overt and covert discrimination (racial, ethnic, sexual, political, etc.) (Kania and Dial, 2008: 170)

The Abuse of Power: The prohibitions against public officials using their offices to place their values, desires, needs, or preferences above those of the public they serve, and over the rules and laws they must uphold, are sometimes broken, leading to abuses of power. Criminal justice managers must be alert to such abuses. These need not involve personal material gain. These violations include such activities as:

- authoritarianism, coercion, and harassment
- arranging or condoning unjustified arrests
- seeking to deny opportunities for reasonable bail
- denial of liberty by lengthy detention prior to trial (Kania and Dial, 2008: 170)

The Flawed Personal Life: Criminal justice managers must maintain socially respectable private lives and also must enforce the prohibitions against personal activities outside the workplace that serve to bring discredit upon the public servant and the servant's agency or profession among their employees and subordinates. These include private violations of the criminal law and moral violations that are not necessarily illegal but are generally frowned upon by the public. These include:

- criminal wrongdoing by criminal justice officials

- financial improprieties and tax evasion by criminal justice officials

- sexual misconduct, deviance, or unconventionality by criminal justice officials

- civil illegality (tax, regulatory, and civil law violations)

- questionable associations and membership in controversial organizations

- private prejudicial expressions and actions (Kania and Dial, 2008: 171)

Deceitfulness: Deceitfulness includes violations that run counter to the expectation that our public officials will be honest and forthright with the public on matters involving their work. Criminal justice managers must set an example for honesty and truthfulness for their agencies to emulate. When they do not, managers must take action to root out dishonesty and restore truthfulness within their agencies. The rules against deceitfulness include the rules against:

- overt lying, duplicity, loop-holing, and evasions

- covering up misdeeds

- unwarranted secrecy in the conduct of the public business

- fraud, trickery, and hypocrisy (Kania and Dial, 2008: 171)

The Denial of Due Process: Due process comprises the rules for procedural correctness in dealing with all administrative matters, both within the justice system and in all public service bureaucratic activities. Criminal justice agents are required to follow the policies set out for them, and should not invent personal solutions to the situations they encounter. Criminal justice managers have the responsibility to train staff, monitor their conduct, and take disciplinary action when due process is not followed properly. Citizens have the right to expect that their cases will be dealt with fairly, in accordance with the rules for such cases. Failures include:

- ignoring the civil rights and constitutional guarantees

- not following the rules and procedures

- failing to comply with internal bureaucratic rules
- ignoring regulatory and statutory guarantees
  (Kania and Dial, 2008: 171)

Neglect of Duties: All criminal justice occupations and positions have associated duties and obligations that must be fulfilled. A criminal justice official who does not fulfill these duties is violating that mandate, and sometimes even will be violating laws against:

- malfeasance
- nonfeasance
- misfeasance
- disobeying lawful orders
- abuse of discretion
- failing to comply with regulations and standing orders
  (Kania and Dial, 2008: 172)

Box 12.2 • Neglect of One's Duties

Both the law and ethical standards obligate public office holders to be faithful to their lawful duties. Three common failures are:

nonfeasance—the failure to perform one's duty by oversight or omission, usually inadvertent (willful nonfeasance typically will be considered malfeasance)

misfeasance—the wrongful performance of one's duties, usually in the form of making mistakes, not following procedures correctly, or other unintentional blunders

malfeasance—the intentional performance of an official act or use of one's official powers to achieve an end that is circumstantially illegal, harmful, and/or unjustified

Actual ethical failures in practice have often overlapped two or more of these categories. A criminal justice manager must anticipate that each and every one of these failures will occur. They may be reduced, minimized, or mitigated, but the wise criminal justice manager must be aware and prepared for these failings to recur.

Ethnic, Race, and Community Relations: Implicit in the discussion of the failures above, under the categories of bias, abuses of power, and due process especially, are the seeds of public dissatisfaction with the performance of criminal justice agencies. These result in poor criminal justice–community relations. In the 1950s, progressive leaders in criminal justice began the effort to reeducate criminal justice agencies, especially the police, in better community relations efforts. Many programs were developed and experiments attempted. Community-oriented policing and other programs have been tried to improve the image of the police and the justice system, yet problems in race and ethic relations continue to recur.

Sometimes it is not the criminal justice agency that is the source of the problem. Some members of racial and ethic groups engage in behaviors that clash with the customs and laws of the United States. The criminal justice system must maintain a balancing act in trying to enforce the law and also trying to respect the customs and behaviors of such groups. To add to the problems managers will face, leaders of these groups will occasionally seek to confront the laws of the United States and hope to create an us-versus-them conflict. A good criminal justice manager will stay ahead of the conflict, anticipating the reasonable and lawful demands of minority groups, striving to meet those by training agency employees, hiring people able to communicate effectively with minority groups, and creating programs to achieve cooperation and harmony.

When examples of bias, prejudice, or injustice occur, the criminal justice manager has an obligation to address these promptly and judiciously. To suppose that good relations existing today will last indefinitely is naïve. Communities are forever in flux. Good relationships with adults of the minority communities will not guarantee good relationships with their offspring, and new groups will enter into the community or the client population. The future-oriented criminal justice manager must prepare for new challenges.

Applying New Technologies to Criminal Justice: What will the new technologies of 2025 and 2050 be? Certainly we cannot do more than guess, but if we have learned from the past and present, we can be sure that new technologies will emerge that will apply to criminal justice.

Existing technologies certainly will be improved upon. Communications, computers, video, transportation, criminalistics, nonlethal weapons, and emergency medical technologies have been improving so dramatically in the past 35 years that criminal justice practice is far different from what it was when the LEAA was helping agencies acquire their first computer systems, upgrade their telecommunications, and add nonlethal controls to supplement the use of firearms.

Foresighted criminal justice managers will stay informed about new technologies and think of ways that they can be applied to criminal justice roles. More than one hundred years ago, August Vollmer and his peers applied the new inventions of their age to police applications, including the patrol car, the police radio, fingerprint identification, and ballistics. In the 1960s, progressive criminal justice managers were exploring ways to use computers to enhance criminal justice operations. Using the unique features of DNA for identification was a new idea just two decades ago. The criminal justice managers who conceived of using it to solve crimes were highly original thinkers (Wambaugh, 1989). What new technology might you apply to criminal justice if you come to hold a managerial position? You might be the change agent who brings about a major improvement in criminal justice practices in the future.

Media Attention: A criminal justice manager cannot necessarily predict when a major case within his or her jurisdiction will grab the attention of the mass communications media (Mannion, 1993). When "the big one" hits, the prudent criminal justice manager will have a plan in place to handle the media onslaught. Otherwise there is a great risk of conflict between the media and the agency (Mozee, 1987). There are 12 lessons that a criminal justice manager can learn from the past to anticipate the future:

1. A major disaster or crisis can happen anywhere, anytime. Even the smallest criminal justice agency in the smallest of communities must be prepared to face this reality (Mannion, 1993).

2. The criminal justice manager must prepare for two aspects of the crisis: the major crime or disaster case itself, and the media onslaught that will follow it (Mannion, 1993).

3. The media will be invasive and lack respect for the people involved. For them, the story always takes precedence (Skolnick and McCoy, 1985: 114; Wilson and Fuqua, 1975: 124). The criminal justice manager must be prepared to thwart the media's desires to invade the crime scene and exploit morbid curiosity, while still giving the media opportunities to get key visuals to support their stories (Mozee, 1987: 143).

4. Such a case invariably will have a long-term impact on relationships among and within the criminal justice agency, the community, and the news media (Mannion, 1992).

5. The media are a criminal justice agency's most direct link with the public, and can be helpful to the police, the prosecutor, the courts, or corrections if the right lessons are learned and the proper steps are taken to prepare for such a catastrophic event (Garner 1987: 15-16; Graber, 1980; Skolnick and McCoy, 1985: 132).

6. The media will cooperate with criminal justice agencies when given useful information, sensible direction, and assistance (Jones, 1987; Mannion, 1993; Skolnick and McCoy, 1985: 132).

7. The media will not go away, but if ignored by official sources, it will seek out less well-informed and less reliable ones to get a story (Jones 1987: 164).

8. Criminal justice agencies need to know the variety and informational requirements of the news and entertainment media organizations and freelancers that now exist (Mannion, 1993).

9. The criminal justice manager must have advanced knowledge about how various media organizations operate and their technology and facility requirements (Garner, 1987: 110-113), organization, and ethics.

10. The criminal justice manager must be aware of the capabilities, possible consequences, and hazards of instantaneous live broadcasting (Jones, 1987: 160).

11. Criminal justice agencies need knowledge of the objectives, rivalries, ideologies, and hidden agendas of media organizations (Mozee, 1987: 144-145; Sherizen, 1978).

12. The "media" are not limited to the traditional local and national news-gathering organizations. Criminal justice agencies should expect movie producers, book writers, tabloid newspapers, and television and radio talk shows to join the "feeding frenzy" at the crime scene, and all will likely claim full First Amendment rights and freedoms (Mannion, 1993).

Educational and Training Standards: When criminal justice managers were recruiting staff a century or more ago, a high school diploma was considered an advanced educational standard. By the beginning of this century, this has become a minimal standard for most criminal justice occupations. A law degree was not even required to practice law when Abraham Lincoln hung out his shingle as an attorney. Today no one in the United States can practice law without a legal education and having passed the bar examination. A century ago, most police departments and correctional agencies provided no training to their employees. Now in-service training is an essential part of personnel practices in most agencies.

What will the future bring in criminal justice education in the next several decades? What initial training will be required? How much more in-service training will be provided? Straight-line change predicts that all of these will increase gradually over time.

Criminal justice managers will have to revise their recruiting requirements and budget for more training to prepare for the future. Higher entry educational standards and specific educational curricula may need to be specified. In-service training will have to prepare their agencies to deal with each of the future challenges anticipated above. Flexibility and intellectual agility will be needed to deal with these and any other challenges not anticipated in the preceding pages.

Summary: Using the Future for the Better

Criminal justice needs to be future-oriented. The past is behind us and cannot be redone. We may try to correct past errors and injustices, but they never will go away completely. Some old wounds will last forever. However, the future holds out hope to our society, to the justice system, and to criminal justice agencies. There can be progress. Old mistakes need not be repeated. New technologies can be added. Ineffectual methods can be improved upon. Our objectives can be better met. Moreover, the best of the past can be preserved. The values of our society are worthy of respect. A future criminal justice manager will be responsible for upholding and preserving our constitutional protections and the political values that are associated with them.

We began this book by stating the job of the criminal justice manager may be summed up by the mnemonic "LODESTAR." In fact, though, this is not enough. The criminal justice manager has other important tasks and responsibilities. Maintaining high standards of ethics is an important aspect of criminal justice for managers, for individual criminal justice employees, and for each criminal justice organization. Maintaining good community relations also is important. Acting in a manner to reduce the level of ethnic, racial, class, and social strife will benefit the entire society as well as the criminal justice agencies serving it. Achieving community harmony and public consensus is a goal that can be attained through effective criminal justice performance and a sensitivity to public needs and concerns. Good media relations are important as well. It is via our public information media that the public learns of the activities of our criminal justice agencies, decides how well they are doing their jobs, and either supports or turns against them. An ethical, educated, community-oriented, well-trained, and wisely supervised workforce can be a very powerful tool in the kit of an effective criminal justice manager. It is, therefore, the additional task of the criminal justice manager to create such a workforce, to build for a better future.

Learning Objectives

Upon finishing this chapter you should be able to do the following:

1. Name and describe three patterns for change.

2. Identify the seven most common patterns of ethical failures occurring across the criminal justice system.

3. Discuss the 12 principles for dealing with the mass communications media that a criminal justice manager should consider.

4. Discuss what future challenges you predict for criminal justice.

IMPORTANT TERMS AND NAMES

- change agents
- cyclic change
- excessive force
- futurists
- futuristics

- futurologists
- oscillating change pattern
- rise-plateau-crash change
- straight-line change

References and Supplemental Sources

Bell, Wendell (2000). "Futures Studies and the Problem of Evil," *Future Studies*, 5(2) (November).

Bell, Wendell (1996; 1997). *Foundations of Futures Studies*, 2 volumes. Edison, NJ: Transaction.

Bennett, Georgette (1989). *Crimewarps: The Future of Crime in America*, revised edition. New York: Anchor Books.

Blumstein, Al (1995). *Youth Violence, Guns, and the Illicit-Drug Industry*. Available at http://www.drugtext.org/library/articles/blumstein.htm

Blumstein, Al, and Richard Rosenfeld (1998). "Exploring Recent Trends in U.S. Homicide Rates," *Journal of Criminal Law and Criminology*, 88(4): 1175–1216.

Blumstein, Al, and Joel Wallman, eds. (2000). *The Crime Drop in America*. New York: Cambridge University Press.

Blumstein, Al, and Joel Wallman, eds. (2006). *The Crime Drop in America*, 2nd ed. New York: Cambridge University Press.

Garner, Gerald (1987). *"Chief, the Reporters Are Here."* Springfield, IL: Charles C Thomas.

Inayatullah, Sohail (1990). "Deconstructing and Reconstructing the Future: Predictive, Cultural and Critical Methodologies," *Futures* (March 1990).

Inayatullah, Sohail (1992). "Linking the Future with the Present in Judicial Bureaucracies: Learning From the Hawaii Judiciary Case, " in Proceedings of the XI World Futures Studies Federation Conference, edited by Mika Mannermaa. Turku, Finland: World Futures Studies Federation and Hungarian Academy of Sciences.

Inayatullah, Sohail, and James Monma (1989). "A Decade of Forecasting: Some Perspectives on Futures Research in the Hawaii Judiciary," *Futures Research Quarterly* (Spring 1989).

International Association of Chiefs of Police (IACP) (1981). "A Balance of Forces: A Study of Justifiable Homicide by the Police" *IACP Newsletter*. Gaithersburg, MD: IACP.

Jones, Ronald B. (1987). "The Press at the Emergency Scene: Issues and Answers," pages 159-167 in *Police and the Media: Bridging Troubled Waters*, edited by Patricia A. Kelly. Springfield, IL: Charles C Thomas.

Kania, Richard R.E., and Ardie Dial (2008). "Prosecutor Misconduct," pages 165-182 in *Justice, Crime and Ethics*, 6th ed., edited by Michael C. Braswell, Belinda R. McCarthy, and Bernard J. McCarthy. Newark, NJ: LexisNexis Matthew Bender.

Lewin, Kurt (1989). "Group Decision and Social Change," pages 543-548 in *Classic Readings in Organizational Behavior*, edited by J. Steven Ott. Pacific Grove, CA: Brooks/Cole.

Mannion, Marea (1993). "Handling the Fallout When the "Big One" Arrives," *The Justice Professional*, 8(1): 123-145.

Marsh, Harry L. (1991). "A Comparative Analysis of Crime Coverage in Newspapers in the United States and Other Countries from 1960-1989: A Review of the Literature," *Journal of Criminal Justice*, 19(1): 67-79.

Mozee, David M. (1987). "Police/Media Conflict," pp. 141-145 in *Police and the Media: Bridging Troubled Waters*, edited by Patricia A. Kelly. Springfield, IL: Charles C Thomas.

Muraskin, Roslyn, and Albert Roberts, eds. (2009). *Visions for Change: Crime and Justice in the Twenty-First Century*, 5th ed. Upper Saddle River, NJ: Pearson/Prentice Hall.

Sherizen, Sanford (1978). "Social Creation of Crime News: All the News Fitted to Print," pp. 203-222 in *Deviance and Mass Media*, edited by Charles Winick, Beverly Hills, CA: Sage.

Skolnick, Jerome H., and Candace McCoy (1985). "Police Accountability and the Media," pp. 102-135 in *Police Leadership in America*, edited by William A. Geller. New York: Praeger.

Souryal, Sam S. (1995). *Police Organization and Administration*, 2nd ed. Cincinnati: Anderson.

Stephens, Gene (2005). "Policing the Future: Law Enforcement's New Challenges," *The Futurist* (March-April 2005).

Tafoya, William (1998). "How CyberCops Fight Terrorism," 7 August 1998 Online Chat with William Tafoya, for *The Washington Post*. Available at http://www.washingtonpost.com/wp-srv/zforum/national/tafoya080798.htm

Wambaugh, Joseph (1989). *The Blooding*. New York: William Morrow.

Wilson, Jerry V., and Paul Q. Fuqua (1975). *The Police and the Media*. Boston: Little, Brown.

About the Author

Michael Perdomo

Richard R.E. Kania joined Jacksonville State University of Alabama in December 2005 to be the department head of Criminal Justice. Prior to that, he had been at The University of North Carolina at Pembroke since 1999, leading their Department of Sociology and Criminal Justice. From 1982 to 1999, he was at Guilford College in Greensboro, NC, having risen to full professor to head the Department of Justice and Policy Studies there. He also has taught at UNC-Charlotte and for the Southern Police Institute of the University of Louisville. Kania was a Senior Fulbright Professor for the Central European University in Warsaw, Poland, while on sabbatical. In 2004-2005, he was awarded his second Fulbright to teach at the Belarusian State University in Minsk, in the Republic of Belarus.

Kania originally majored in anthropology at Florida State University, where he earned his BA with Honors in 1968. He continued his studies of anthropology at the University of Virginia, earning an MA there in 1974, and wrote his MA thesis on conflict resolution and the law ways of the Hopi of Arizona. In between the BA and the MA degrees, he served in the Army in Berlin and in Vietnam. He also was a city police officer in Virginia, and that experience led him to "change his major" midway into his doctoral studies and redirected him into a teaching career in criminal justice.

He is extensively published, with articles in more than 20 scholarly journals and a number of book chapters. He has authored one previous book, co-edited another, and has edited one journal special issue and several major government and research reports. His articles have been published in Poland, Belarus, Russia, and Romania. He is the recipient of several awards and grants and has held various offices in professional and public service organizations.

Kania has had managerial experience in the U.S. Army, working in operations, personnel, intelligence, contracting, facilities, and logistics assignments. He commanded an army engineer company in combat in Vietnam and served on the Army Staff in the Pentagon, rising to the rank of lieutenant colonel in the Army Reserve. His civilian managerial experience was as a criminal justice and public safety regional planner and as academic department head for three colleges.

Index